CASENOTE® Legal Briefs®

PROPERTY

Keyed to Courses Using

Dukeminier, Krier, Alexander, Strahilevitz, and Schleicher's Property, Concise Fourth Edition

Authored by: Publisher's Editorial Staff

ASPEN PUBLISHING

To contact Customer Service, e-mail customer.service@aspenpublishing.com, call 1-800-950-5259, or mail correspondence to:

Aspen Publishing
Attn: Order Department
1 Wall Street
Burlington, MA 01803

Printed in the United States of America.

1 2 3 4 5 6 7 8 9 0

ISBN 979-8-8941-0433-1

SUSTAINABLE FORESTRY INITIATIVE Certified Sourcing
www.forests.org
SFI-00756

ABOUT ASPEN PUBLISHING

Aspen Publishing is a leading provider of legal education content and digital learning solutions in the United States and globally. Our innovative products and platforms—designed based on best practices in learning science—engage students and enhance outcomes. From textbooks and audiobooks authored by renowned experts to digital platforms and products like LEAF, Connected eBooks, Connected Quizzing, PracticePerfect, and JD-Next, we empower the next generation of legal professionals with innovative, trusted, and accessible resources.

The Aspen Casebook Series, affectionately known as the "red and black" casebooks among law faculty and students, includes hundreds of highly regarded textbooks across more than 80 disciplines. These range from foundational courses like Torts and Contracts to emerging electives such as Sustainability and the Law of Policing. Our study aids, including the popular *Examples & Explanations* series, help law students master complex topics with clarity and confidence.

Aspen's expertise extends to undergraduate education with our Paralegal, Criminal Justice, and Business Law series, offering the same hallmark quality to a broader audience. JD-Next, our groundbreaking online law school prep course and admissions test, provides a realistic preview of law school, equips students with essential skills for academic success, and evaluates their readiness for legal studies.

Aspen Publishing Is Proud to Be a UWorld Company

Since 2003, UWorld has been a global leader in developing high-quality learning tools for students preparing for high-stakes exams. With a commitment to excellence, UWorld has helped millions of students in undergraduate, graduate, and professional programs in fields such as medicine, nursing, finance, and law achieve their academic and career goals.

Founded by Chandra S. Pemmasani, M.D., during his medical residency, UWorld began focusing on medical education and has since expanded into various academic fields, including law. In 2020, UWorld launched its Legal vertical, starting with its comprehensive Multistate Bar Exam (MBE®) Question Bank, followed by the acquisition of Themis Bar Review, which integrated resources to provide a complete bar exam preparation experience. In 2024, UWorld expanded its offerings by acquiring Aspen Publishing, enhancing its suite of legal education products.

Today, UWorld offers an unparalleled range of study materials that blend active learning methods with expert content, ensuring students and educators can access the most effective resources. From bar preparation to law school success, UWorld is committed to supporting the next generation of legal professionals. Learn more at uworld.com.

Format for the Casenote® Legal Brief

Nature of Case: This section identifies the form of action (e.g., breach of contract, negligence, battery), the type of proceeding (e.g., demurrer, appeal from trial court's jury instructions) or the relief sought (e.g., damages, injunction, criminal sanctions).

Fact Summary: This is included to refresh your memory and can be used as a quick reminder of the facts.

Rule of Law: Summarizes the general principle of law that the case illustrates. It may be used for instant recall of the court's holding and for classroom discussion or home review.

Facts: This section contains all relevant facts of the case, including the contentions of the parties and the lower court holdings. It is written in a logical order to give you a clear understanding of the case. The plaintiff and defendant are identified by their proper names throughout and are always labeled with a (P) or (D).

Issue: The issue is a concise question that brings out the essence of the opinion as it relates to the section of the casebook in which the case appears. Both substantive and procedural issues are included if relevant to the decision.

Palsgraf v. Long Island R.R. Co.

Injured bystander (P) v. Railroad company (D)

N.Y. Ct. App., 248 N.Y. 339, 162 N.E. 99 (1928).

NATURE OF CASE: Appeal from judgment affirming verdict for plaintiff seeking damages for personal injury.

FACT SUMMARY: Helen Palsgraf (P) was injured on R.R.'s (D) train platform when R.R.'s (D) guard helped a passenger aboard a moving train, causing his package to fall on the tracks. The package contained fireworks which exploded, creating a shock that tipped a scale onto Palsgraf (P).

RULE OF LAW
The risk reasonably to be perceived defines the duty to be obeyed.

FACTS: Helen Palsgraf (P) purchased a ticket to Rockaway Beach from R.R. (D) and was waiting on the train platform. As she waited, two men ran to catch a train that was pulling out from the platform. The first man jumped aboard, but the second man, who appeared as if he might fall, was helped aboard by the guard on the train who had kept the door open so they could jump aboard. A guard on the platform also helped by pushing him onto the train. The man was carrying a package wrapped in newspaper. In the process, the man dropped his package, which fell on the tracks. The package contained fireworks and exploded. The shock of the explosion was apparently of great enough strength to tip over some scales at the other end of the platform, which fell on Palsgraf (P) and injured her. A jury awarded her damages, and R.R. (D) appealed.

ISSUE: Does the risk reasonably to be perceived define the duty to be obeyed?

HOLDING AND DECISION: (Cardozo, C.J.) Yes. The risk reasonably to be perceived defines the duty to be obeyed. If there is no foreseeable hazard to the injured party as the result of a seemingly innocent act, the act does not become a tort because it happened to be a wrong as to another. If the wrong was not willful, the plaintiff must show that the act as to her had such great and apparent possibilities of danger as to entitle her to protection. Negligence in the abstract is not enough upon which to base liability. Negligence is a relative concept, evolving out of the common law doctrine of trespass on the case. To establish liability, the defendant must owe a legal duty of reasonable care to the injured party. A cause of action in tort will lie where harm, though unintended, could have been averted or avoided by observance of such a duty. The scope of the duty is limited by the range of danger that a reasonable person could foresee. In this case, there was nothing to suggest from the appearance of the parcel or otherwise that the parcel contained fireworks. The guard could not reasonably have had any warning of a threat to Palsgraf (P), and R.R. (D) therefore cannot be held liable. Judgment is reversed in favor of R.R. (D).

DISSENT: (Andrews, J.) The concept that there is no negligence unless R.R. (D) owes a legal duty to take care as to Palsgraf (P) herself is too narrow. Everyone owes to the world at large the duty of refraining from those acts that may unreasonably threaten the safety of others. If the guard's action was negligent as to those nearby, it was also negligent as to those outside what might be termed the "danger zone." For Palsgraf (P) to recover, R.R.'s (D) negligence must have been the proximate cause of her injury, a question of fact for the jury.

ANALYSIS

The majority defined the limit of the defendant's liability in terms of the danger that a reasonable person in defendant's situation would have perceived. The dissent argued that the limitation should not be placed on liability, but rather on damages. Judge Andrews suggested that only injuries that would not have happened but for R.R.'s (D) negligence should be compensable. Both the majority and dissent recognized the policy-driven need to limit liability for negligent acts, seeking, in the words of Judge Andrews, to define a framework "that will be practical and in keeping with the general understanding of mankind." The Restatement (Second) of Torts has accepted Judge Cardozo's view.

Quicknotes

FORESEEABILITY A reasonable expectation that change is the probable result of certain acts or omissions.

NEGLIGENCE Conduct falling below the standard of care that a reasonable person would demonstrate under similar conditions.

PROXIMATE CAUSE The natural sequence of events without which an injury would not have been sustained.

Party ID: Quick identification of the relationship between the parties.

Concurrence/Dissent: All concurrences and dissents are briefed whenever they are included by the casebook author.

Analysis: This last paragraph gives you a broad understanding of where the case "fits in" with other cases in the section of the book and with the entire course. It is a hornbook-style discussion indicating whether the case is a majority or minority opinion and comparing the principal case with other cases in the casebook. It may also provide analysis from restatements, uniform codes, and law review articles.

Holding and Decision: This section offers a clear and in-depth discussion of the rule of the case and the court's rationale. It is written in easy-to-understand language and answers the issue presented by applying the law to the facts of the case. When relevant, it includes a thorough discussion of the exceptions to the case as listed by the court, any major cites to the other cases on point, and the names of the judges who wrote the decisions.

Quicknotes: Conveniently defines legal terms found in the case.

Note to Students

Aspen Publishing is proud to offer *Casenote® Legal Briefs*—continuing thirty years of publishing America's best-selling legal briefs.

Casenote® Legal Briefs are designed to help you save time when briefing assigned cases. Organized under convenient headings, they show you how to abstract the basic facts and holdings from the text of the actual opinions handed down by the courts. Used as part of a rigorous study regimen, they can help you spend more time analyzing and critiquing points of law than on copying bits and pieces of judicial opinions into your notebook or outline.

Casenote® Legal Briefs should never be used as a substitute for assigned casebook readings. They work best when read as a follow-up to reviewing the underlying opinions themselves. Students who try to avoid reading and digesting the judicial opinions in their casebooks or online sources will end up shortchanging themselves in the long run. The ability to absorb, critique, and restate the dynamic and complex elements of case law decisions is crucial to your success in law school and beyond. It cannot be developed vicariously.

In addition to *Casenote® Legal Briefs*, Aspen Publishing offers the following study aids:

- *Casenote® Legal Briefs*
- *Emanuel® Law Outlines*
- Emanuel® *Law in a Flash Flash Cards*
- Emanuel® *CrunchTime® Series*

Each of these series is designed to provide you with easy-to-understand explanations of complex points of law. Each volume offers guidance on the principles of legal analysis and, consulted regularly, will hone your ability to spot relevant issues. We have titles that will help you prepare for class, prepare for your exams, and enhance your general comprehension of the law along the way.

To find out more about our law school tools for success, visit us at *www.AspenPublishing.com* or e-mail us at *customer.service@aspenpublishing.com*. We'll be happy to assist you.

How to Brief a Case

A. Decide on a Format and Stick to It

Structure is essential to a good brief. It enables you to arrange systematically the related parts that are scattered throughout most cases, thus making manageable and understandable what might otherwise seem to be an endless and unfathomable sea of information. There are, of course, an unlimited number of formats that can be utilized. However, it is best to find one that suits your needs and stick to it. Consistency breeds both efficiency and the security that when called upon you will know where to look in your brief for the information you are asked to give.

Any format, as long as it presents the essential elements of a case in an organized fashion, can be used. Experience, however, has led *Casenote® Legal Briefs* to develop and utilize the following format because of its logical flow and universal applicability.

NATURE OF CASE: This is a brief statement of the legal character and procedural status of the case (e.g., "Appeal of a burglary conviction").

There are many different alternatives open to a litigant dissatisfied with a court ruling. The key to determining which one has been used is to discover *who is asking this court for what.*

This first entry in the brief should be kept as *short as possible.* Use the court's terminology if you understand it. But since jurisdictions vary as to the titles of pleadings, the best entry is the one that addresses who wants what in this proceeding, not the one that sounds most like the court's language.

RULE OF LAW: A statement of the general principle of law that the case illustrates (e.g., "An acceptance that varies any term of the offer is considered a rejection and counteroffer").

Determining the rule of law of a case is a procedure similar to determining the issue of the case. Avoid being fooled by red herrings; there may be a few rules of law mentioned in the case excerpt, but usually only one is *the* rule with which the casebook editor is concerned. The techniques used to locate the issue, described below, may also be utilized to find the rule of law. Generally, your best guide is simply the chapter heading. It is a clue to the point the casebook editor seeks to make and should be kept in mind when reading every case in the respective section.

FACTS: A synopsis of only the essential facts of the case, i.e., those bearing upon or leading up to the issue.

The facts entry should be a short statement of the events and transactions that led one party to initiate legal proceedings against another in the first place. While some cases conveniently state the salient facts at the beginning of the decision, in other instances they will have to be culled from hiding places throughout the text, even from concurring and dissenting opinions. Some of the "facts" will often be in dispute and should be so noted. Conflicting evidence may be briefly pointed up. "Hard" facts must be included. Both must be *relevant* in order to be listed in the facts entry. It is impossible to tell what is relevant until the entire case is read, as the ultimate determination of the rights and liabilities of the parties may turn on something buried deep in the opinion.

Generally, the facts entry should not be longer than three to five *short* sentences.

It is often helpful to identify the role played by a party in a given context. For example, in a construction contract case the identification of a party as the "contractor" or "builder" alleviates the need to tell that that party was the one who was supposed to have built the house.

It is always helpful, and a good general practice, to identify the "plaintiff" and the "defendant." This may seem elementary and uncomplicated, but, especially in view of the creative editing practiced by some casebook editors, it is sometimes a difficult or even impossible task. Bear in mind that the *party presently* seeking something from this court may not be the plaintiff, and that sometimes only the cross-claim of a defendant is treated in the excerpt. Confusing or misaligning the parties can ruin your analysis and understanding of the case.

ISSUE: A statement of the general legal question answered by or illustrated in the case. For clarity, the issue is best put in the form of a question capable of a "yes" or "no" answer. In reality, the issue is simply the Rule of Law put in the form of a question (e.g., "May an offer be accepted by performance?").

The major problem presented in discerning what is *the* issue in the case is that an opinion usually purports to raise and answer several questions. However, except for rare cases, only one such question is really the issue in the case. Collateral issues not necessary to the resolution of the matter in controversy are handled by the court by language known as *"obiter dictum"* or merely *"dictum."* While dicta may be included later in the brief, they have no place under the issue heading.

To find the issue, ask *who wants what* and then go on to ask *why did that party succeed or fail in getting it.* Once this is determined, the "why" should be turned into a question.

The complexity of the issues in the cases will vary, but in all cases a single-sentence question should sum up the issue. *In a few cases,* there will be two, or even more rarely, three issues of equal importance to the resolution of the case. Each should be expressed in a single-sentence question.

Since many issues are resolved by a court in coming to a final disposition of a case, the casebook editor will reproduce the portion of the opinion containing the issue or issues most relevant to the area of law under scrutiny. A noted law professor gave this advice: "Close the book; look at the title on the cover." Chances are, if it is Property, you need not concern yourself with whether, for example, the federal government's treatment of the plaintiff's land really raises a federal question sufficient to support jurisdiction on this ground in federal court.

The same rule applies to chapter headings designating sub-areas within the subjects. They tip you off as to what the text is designed to teach. The cases are arranged in a casebook to show a progression or development of the law, so that the preceding cases may also help.

It is also most important to remember to *read the notes and questions* at the end of a case to determine what the editors wanted you to have gleaned from it.

HOLDING AND DECISION: This section should succinctly explain the rationale of the court in arriving at its decision. In capsulizing the "reasoning" of the court, it should always include an application of the general rule or rules of law to the specific facts of the case. Hidden justifications come to light in this entry: the reasons for the state of the law, the public policies, the biases and prejudices, those considerations that influence the justices' thinking and, ultimately, the outcome of the case. At the end, there should be a short indication of the disposition or procedural resolution of the case (e.g., "Decision of the trial court for Mr. Smith (P) reversed").The foregoing format is designed to help you "digest" the reams of case material with which you will be faced in your law school career. Once mastered by practice, it will place at your fingertips the information the authors of your casebooks have sought to impart to you in case-by-case illustration and analysis.

B. Be as Economical as Possible in Briefing Cases

Once armed with a format that encourages succinctness, it is as important to be economical with regard to the time spent on the actual reading of the case as it is to be economical in the writing of the brief itself. This does not mean "skimming" a case. Rather, it means reading the case with an "eye" trained to recognize into which "section" of your brief a particular passage or line fits and having a system for quickly and precisely marking the case so that the passages fitting any one particular part of the brief can be easily identified and brought together in a concise and accurate manner when the brief is actually written.

It is of no use to simply repeat everything in the opinion of the court; record only enough information to trigger your recollection of what the court said. Nevertheless, an accurate statement of the "law of the case," i.e., the legal principle applied to the facts, is absolutely essential to class preparation and to learning the law under the case method.

To that end, it is important to develop a "shorthand" that you can use to make marginal notations. These notations will tell you at a glance in which section of the brief you will be placing that particular passage or portion of the opinion.

Some students prefer to underline all the salient portions of the opinion (with a pencil or colored underliner marker), making marginal notations as they go along. Others prefer the color-coded method of underlining, utilizing different colors of markers to underline the salient portions of the case, each separate color being used to represent a different section of the brief. For example, blue underlining could be used for passages relating to the rule of law, yellow for those relating to the issue, and green for those relating to the holding and decision, etc. While it has its advocates, the color-coded method can be confusing and time-consuming (all that time spent on changing colored markers). Furthermore, it can interfere with the continuity and concentration many students deem essential to the reading of a case for maximum comprehension. In the end, however, it is a matter of personal preference and style. Just remember, whatever method you use, underlining must be used sparingly or its value is lost.

If you take the marginal notation route, an efficient and easy method is to go along underlining the key portions of the case and placing in the margin alongside them the following "markers" to indicate where a particular passage or line "belongs" in the brief you will write:

N	(NATURE OF CASE)
RL	(RULE OF LAW)
I	(ISSUE)
HL	(HOLDING AND DECISION, relates to the RULE OF LAW behind the decision)
HR	(HOLDING AND DECISION, gives the RATIONALE or reasoning behind the decision)
HA	(HOLDING AND DECISION, applies the general principle(s) of law to the facts of the case to arrive at the decision)

Remember that a particular passage may well contain information necessary to more than one part of your brief, in which case you simply note that in the margin. If you are using the color-coded underlining method instead of marginal notation, simply make asterisks or checks in the margin next to the passage in question in the colors that indicate the additional sections of the brief where it might be utilized.

The economy of utilizing "shorthand" in marking cases for briefing can be maintained in the actual brief writing process itself by utilizing "law student shorthand" within the brief. There are many commonly used words and phrases for which abbreviations can be substituted in your briefs (and in your class notes also). You can develop abbreviations that are personal to you and which will save you a lot of time. A reference list of briefing abbreviations can be found on page x of this book.

C. Use Both the Briefing Process and the Brief as a Learning Tool

Now that you have a format and the tools for briefing cases efficiently, the most important thing is to make the time spent in briefing profitable to you and to make the most advantageous use of the briefs you create. Of course, the briefs are invaluable for classroom reference when you are called upon to explain or analyze a particular case. However, they are also useful in reviewing for exams. A quick glance at the fact summary should bring the case to mind, and a rereading of the rule of law should enable you to go over the underlying legal concept in your mind, how it was applied in that particular case, and how it might apply in other factual settings.

As to the value to be derived from engaging in the briefing process itself, there is an immediate benefit that arises from being forced to sift through the essential facts and reasoning from the court's opinion and to succinctly express them in your own words in your brief. The process ensures that you understand the case and the point that it illustrates, and that means you will be ready to absorb further analysis and information brought forth in class. It also ensures you will have something to say when called upon in class. The briefing process helps develop a mental agility for getting to the *gist* of a case and for identifying, expounding on, and applying the legal concepts and issues found there. The briefing process is the mental process on which you must rely in taking law school examinations; it is also the mental process upon which lawyers rely in serving their clients and in making a living.

Abbreviations for Briefs

acceptance	acp
affirmed	aff
answer	ans
assumption of risk	a/r
attorney	atty
beyond a reasonable doubt	b/r/d
bona fide purchaser	BFP
breach of contract	br/k
cause of action	c/a
common law	c/l
Constitution	Con
constitutional	con
contract	K
contributory negligence	c/n
cross	x
cross-complaint	x/c
cross-examination	x/ex
cruel and unusual punishment	c/u/p
defendant	D
dismissed	dis
double jeopardy	d/j
due process	d/p
equal protection	e/p
equity	eq
evidence	ev
exclude	exc
exclusionary rule	exc/r
felony	f/n
freedom of speech	f/s
good faith	g/f
habeas corpus	h/c
hearsay	hr
husband	H
injunction	inj
in loco parentis	ILP
inter vivos	I/v
joint tenancy	j/t
judgment	judgt
jurisdiction	jur
last clear chance	LCC
long-arm statute	LAS
majority view	maj
meeting of minds	MOM
minority view	min
Miranda rule	Mir/r
Miranda warnings	Mir/w
negligence	neg
notice	ntc
nuisance	nus
obligation	ob
obscene	obs
offer	O
offeree	OE
offeror	OR
ordinance	ord
pain and suffering	p/s
parol evidence	p/e
plaintiff	P
prima facie	p/f
probable cause	p/c
proximate cause	px/c
real property	r/p
reasonable doubt	r/d
reasonable man	r/m
rebuttable presumption	rb/p
remanded	rem
res ipsa loquitur	RIL
respondeat superior	r/s
Restatement	RS
reversed	rev
Rule Against Perpetuities	RAP
search and seizure	s/s
search warrant	s/w
self-defense	s/d
specific performance	s/p
statute	S
statute of frauds	S/F
statute of limitations	S/L
summary judgment	s/j
tenancy at will	t/w
tenancy in common	t/c
tenant	t
third party	TP
third party beneficiary	TPB
transferred intent	TI
unconscionable	uncon
unconstitutional	unconst
undue influence	u/e
Uniform Commercial Code	UCC
unilateral	uni
vendee	VE
vendor	VR
versus	v
void for vagueness	VFV
weight of authority	w/a
weight of the evidence	w/e
wife	W
with	w/
within	w/i
without	w/o
without prejudice	w/o/p
wrongful death	wr/d

Table of Cases

CHAPTER 1

First Possession: Acquisition of Property by Discovery (or Conquest), Capture, and Creation

Quick Reference Rules of Law

Johnson v. M'Intosh

Holder of title granted by Native Americans (P) v. Subsequent purchaser (D)

21 U.S. (8 Wheat.) 543 (1823)

NATURE OF CASE: Appeal in an action to determine title to land.

FACT SUMMARY: Johnson (P) claimed valid title to land granted him by the chiefs of certain Native American tribes.

RULE OF LAW

The discovery of the Native American–occupied lands of this nation vested absolute title in the discoverers and rendered the Native American inhabitants themselves incapable of transferring absolute title to others.

FACTS: Johnson (P) claimed valid title to land by reason of two grants, purportedly made, in 1773 and 1775 respectively, by the chiefs of certain Native American tribes. The proofs showed that the chiefs executing the conveyances had the authority to do so, and that the tribes were in rightful possession of the lands they sold. Nevertheless, the trial court denied the power of the Native Americans to convey such lands since, although they had retained title to the land's occupancy, they nevertheless remained incapable of transferring absolute title to others. Johnson (P) appealed.

ISSUE: Do the Native American tribes have the power of conveying absolute title of their lands to others?

HOLDING AND DECISION: (Marshall, C.J.) No. The discovery of the Native American–occupied lands of this nation vested absolute title in the discoverers; and while the Native American inhabitants retained title of occupancy, they were nevertheless incapable of transferring absolute title to others. As the result, this title claimed by Johnson (P) cannot be recognized by the U.S. courts. The very history of America, from its discovery to the present, demonstrates this principle. For example, when the English discoverers first acquired territory on this continent, they assumed title to the lands despite their admitted possession by the natives. While still under Native American occupation, these lands and waters were conveyed to others by the English monarch. These extensive grants cannot be regarded as nullities. That this principle has been ever recognized is seen in the history of wars, negotiations, and treaties. In fact, all the nations of Europe who have acquired territory on this continent have recognized the principle. The validity of these titles has never been questioned by the courts. Finally, an absolute title cannot exist at the same time in different governments over the same land. It would be incompatible to vest absolute title in the Native Americans as a distinct nation and country. Therefore, they are regarded as merely occupants, to be protected while at peace but to be deemed incapable of transferring absolute title to others. Affirmed, with costs.

ANALYSIS

As reflected in the case of *Tee-Hit-Ton Indians v. United States*, 348 U.S. 272 (1955), the courts have generally followed the principal case and denied Native American land titles. However, Congress has followed a fairly consistent policy of making voluntary payments to the Native Americans. See Cohen, "Original Indian Title," 32 *Minn. L. Rev.* 28 (1947). In his conclusion, Mr. Cohen said, "The notion that America was stolen from the Indians is one of the myths by which we Americans are prone to hide our real virtues and make our idealism look as hard-boiled as possible." The story, nevertheless, is not pleasant.

Quicknotes

ABSOLUTE TITLE Exclusive title to land.

RIGHT OF DOMINION Possessing both title and ownership of property and having total power over its distribution.

Pierson v. Post

Fox killer (D) v. Fox hunter (P)

N.Y. Sup. Ct., 3 Cai. R. 175, 2 Am. Dec. 264 (1805)

NATURE OF CASE: Action of trespass on the case.

FACT SUMMARY: Post (P) was hunting a fox. Pierson (D), knowing this, killed the fox and carried it off.

RULE OF LAW

Property in wild animals is acquired only by occupancy, and pursuit alone does not constitute occupancy or vest any right in the pursuer.

FACTS: Post (P) found a fox upon certain wild, uninhabited, unpossessed waste land. He and his dogs began hunting and pursuing the fox. Knowing that the fox was being hunted by Post (P) and within Post's (P) view, Pierson (D) killed the fox and carried it off.

ISSUE: Has a person in pursuit of a wild animal acquired such a right to or property in the wild animal as to sustain an action against a person who kills and carries away the animal, knowing of the former's pursuit?

HOLDING AND DECISION: (Tompkins, J.) No. Property in wild animals is acquired by occupancy only. Mere pursuit vests no right in the pursuer. One authority holds that actual bodily seizure is not always necessary to constitute possession of wild animals. The mortal wounding of an animal or the trapping or intercepting of animals so to deprive them of their natural liberty will constitute occupancy. However, here, Post (P) only shows pursuit. Hence there was no occupancy or legal right vested in Post (P) and the fox became Pierson's (D) property when he killed and carried it off. The purpose of this rule is that if the pursuit of animals without wounding them or restricting their liberty were held to constitute a basis for an action against others for intercepting and killing the animals, "it would prove a fertile source of quarrels and litigation." Reversed.

DISSENT: (Livingston, J.) A new rule should be adopted: that property in wild animals may be acquired without bodily touch, provided the pursuer be in reach or have a reasonable prospect of taking the animals.

ANALYSIS

The ownership of wild animals is in the state for the benefit of all the state's people. A private person cannot acquire exclusive rights to a wild animal except by taking and reducing it to actual possession in a lawful manner or by a grant from the government. After the animal has been lawfully subjected to control, the ownership becomes absolute as long as the restraint lasts. Mere ownership of the land that an animal happens to be on does not constitute such a reduction of possession as to give the landowner a property right in the animal, except as against a mere trespasser who goes on such land for the purpose of taking the animal.

Quicknotes

SEIZURE The removal of property from one's possession due to unlawful activity or in satisfaction of a judgment entered by the court.

TRESPASS ON THE CASE Action at common law in early England granting a remedy to a person who sustains injury to their person or property as a result of the defendant's conduct.

Keeble v. Hickeringill

Duck pond owner (P) v. Duck frightener (D)

Queen's Bench, 11 East 574, 103 Eng. Rep. 1127 (1707)

NATURE OF CASE: Action for interference with lawful use of land.

FACT SUMMARY: Keeble (P) contended Hickeringill (D) scared ducks away from his pond resulting in damage.

RULE OF LAW

Damages may be recovered for the intentional frightening of game off another's land.

FACTS: Keeble (P) owned land containing a duck pond. He loaded the pond with decoys to seduce game to come to the pond so that he could hunt. Hickeringill (D) discharged a shotgun near the pond, which induced the game to stay away. Keeble (P) sued and was granted recovery. Hickeringill (D) appealed, contending Keeble (P) had no title to the game, and thus no cause of action existed.

ISSUE: May recovery of damages be had for the frightening of wild game off one's property?

HOLDING AND DECISION: (Holt, C.J.) Yes. Damages may be recovered for the intentional frightening of wild game off another's land. Although no title to the game existed, Keeble (P) was using his land in a lawful manner. Thus Hickeringill (D) interfered with this lawful use and is liable in damages.

ANALYSIS

Capture or control, in conjunction with being first in time, guides legal analysis of the ownership of wild animals. The present case represents somewhat of a departure from these rules, yet it is viewed as a natural and logical extension of them.

Quicknotes

INTERFERENCE WITH USE OF LAND An action to recover damages resulting from the wrongful interference with a party's property; otherwise, this is referred to as a trespass.

VIVARY A place where wild animals are kept.

Popov v. Hayashi

Baseball fan (P) v. Baseball fan (D)

Cal. Super. Ct., 2002 WL31833731 (2002)

NATURE OF CASE: Action for conversion, trespass to chattels, injunctive relief, and constructive trust.

FACT SUMMARY: Both Popov (P) and Hayashi (D) intended to establish and maintain control over a baseball that gave Barry Bonds his 73rd home run in 2001, but just as Popov (P) was getting it in his glove, a crowd engulfed him, and brought him to the ground. Hayashi (D), who was near Popov (P) and who also was brought to the ground by the crowd, found the ball and pocketed it. Popov (P) claimed he had established sufficient possession of the ball to gain title to it and brought suit to compel Hayashi (D) to return the ball to him.

RULE OF LAW

Where an actor undertakes significant but incomplete steps to achieve possession of a piece of abandoned personal property and the effort is interrupted by the unlawful acts of others, the actor has a legally cognizable pre-possessory interest in the property sufficient to support a claim of conversion.

FACTS: Barry Bonds, a professional baseball player, hit a record-setting 73rd home run on October 7, 2001. On that day, Popov (P) and Hayashi (D) and many others had positioned themselves in an area of the stadium where Bonds hit the greatest number of home runs in the hopes of catching a record-setting ball (so they brought their baseball gloves with them). The ball hit by Bonds initially landed in Popov's (P) glove, but it was not clear whether the ball was secure there, as Popov (P) may have lost his balance while reaching for the ball. However, even as the ball was going into his glove, a crowd engulfed him and he was tackled and brought to the ground, with people hitting and grabbing him. Hayashi (D), who had been near Popov (P), was also forced to the ground by the crowd, where he saw the ball. He pocketed it and revealed it only when a camera was trained on him, presumably because he wanted proof that he was the owner of the ball. Popov (P), seeing the ball, grabbed for it, believing it to be his, but Hayashi (D) refused to give it to him. Popov (P) then brought suit for conversion, trespass to chattels, injunctive relief, and constructive trust.

ISSUE: Where an actor undertakes significant but incomplete steps to achieve possession of a piece of abandoned personal property and the effort is interrupted by the unlawful acts of others, does the actor have a legally cognizable pre-possessory interest in the property sufficient to support a claim of conversion?

HOLDING AND DECISION: (McCarthy, J.) Yes. Where an actor undertakes significant but incomplete steps to achieve possession of a piece of abandoned personal property and the effort is interrupted by the unlawful acts of others, the actor has a legally cognizable pre-possessory interest in the property sufficient to support a claim of conversion. As an initial matter, there was no trespass to chattels—which requires injury to the chattel—because the ball itself was not damaged and because Popov (P) did not claim that Hayashi (D) interfered with his use and enjoyment of the ball. If there was a wrong at all, it was conversion, which is the wrongful exercise of dominion over the personal property of another. One, who has neither title nor possession nor any right to possession, may not assert a conversion claim. The key issue, therefore, is whether Popov (P) achieved possession or the right to it. "Possession," however, does not have one meaning; the meaning varies depending on the context in which it is used. Some guidelines, however, do exist, e.g., that possession requires both physical control over an item and intent to control it and exclude others from it. Here, Popov (P) clearly had the requisite intent, so the issue is whether he had exclusive dominion and control over the ball. Possession in this context is based on custom and what is physically possible. Here, "not only is it physically possible for a person to acquire unequivocal dominion and control of an abandoned baseball, but fans generally expect a claimant to have accomplished as much." Because Popov (P) did not establish by preponderance of the evidence that he would have retained control of the ball after all momentum ceased and after any incidental contact with other people or objects, he did not achieve full possession. This conclusion does not resolve the case, however, because Popov (P) was attacked illegally by the crowd, and because, therefore, it is unknown whether he would have retained control over the ball absent the crowd's actions. Because Popov (P) has a legally protected pre-possessory interest in the ball, he may advance a legitimate claim to the ball. Hayashi (D), too, was a victim of the crowd's illegal activity, but he was able to extricate himself from the crowd. Although Hayashi (D) exercised complete dominion and control over the ball, the ball was encumbered by the qualified pre-possessory interest of Popov (P). Thus, awarding the ball to either of the two parties is unfair to the other. Both have a superior claim to the ball against all the world, but not against each

Continued on next page.

other; they are equally entitled to the ball. Because the court sits in equity, it may devise an equitable solution to this problem. Here, that solution is equitable division, whereby both Popov (P) and Hayashi (D) have an equal and undivided interest in the ball. Accordingly, Popov's (P) conversion claim is sustained only as to his equal and undivided interest.

ANALYSIS

The parties agreed that before Bonds hit the ball, it belonged to Major League Baseball, but that at the time it was hit, it became intentionally abandoned property. Also, to effectuate its decision, the court ordered the sale of the ball, with the proceeds being equally split between the two men. The ball ultimately sold for $450,000—Hayashi (D) estimated that his share would cover only his legal fees.

Quicknotes

CONSTRUCTIVE TRUST A trust that arises by operation of law whereby the court imposes a trust upon property lawfully held by one party for the benefit of another, as result of some wrongdoing by the party in possession so as to avoid unjust enrichment.

CONVERSION The act of depriving an owner of their property without permission or justification.

INJUNCTIVE RELIEF A court order issued as a remedy, requiring a person to do, or prohibiting that person from doing, a specific act.

POSSESSORY INTEREST The right to possess particular real property to the exclusion of others.

TRESPASS TO CHATTELS Action for damages sustained as a result of defendant's unlawful interference with plaintiff's personal property.

Jacque v. Steenberg Homes, Inc.

Property owner (P) v. Company (D)

Wis. Sup. Ct., 563 N.W.2d 154 (1997)

NATURE OF CASE: Suit for intentional trespass to land.

FACT SUMMARY: The Jacques (P) brought suit against Steenberg Homes, Inc. (Steenberg) (D) claiming intentional trespass to their land when Steenberg (D) plowed a path across their field, over their protests, in order to deliver a mobile home.

RULE OF LAW

When nominal damages are awarded for an intentional trespass to land, punitive damages may also be awarded at the jury's discretion.

FACTS: Steenberg Homes (Steenberg) (D) was delivering a mobile home. It found the easiest route of delivery was through the Jacques' (P) land. Despite the Jacques' (P) protests, Steenberg (D) plowed a path through the Jacques' (P) field. The Jacques (P) sued Steenberg (D) for intentional trespass. At trial, Steenberg (D) conceded intentional trespass but argued that punitive damages could not be awarded since no compensatory damages had been awarded. Though the jury awarded $1 in nominal damages and $100,000 in punitive damages, the circuit court set aside the punitive damages award. The court of appeals affirmed, and the Jacques (P) appealed.

ISSUE: When nominal damages are awarded for an intentional trespass to land, may punitive damages also be awarded at the jury's discretion?

HOLDING AND DECISION: (Bablitch, J.) Yes. When nominal damages are awarded for an intentional trespass to land, punitive damages may also be awarded at the jury's discretion. Steenberg (D) argued that punitive damages could not be awarded by the jury without an award of compensatory damages as a matter of law. The Jacques (P) argued that the rationale supporting the compensatory damage award requirement is not applicable when the wrongful act is an intentional trespass to land. This court agrees. The rationale for the requirement is that if the individual cannot show actual harm, society has little interest in having the unlawful but harmless conduct deterred and punitive damages are inappropriate. The issue of whether nominal damages can support a punitive damage award in intentional trespass to land cases is one of first impression. This court has recognized that in certain circumstances of trespass the actual harm is not the damage to the land, but the loss of the individual's right to exclude others from his property, and the court has implied that the loss of this right may be punished by a large damage award despite the lack of measurable harm. Thus, the compensatory damages requirement should not apply when the tort supporting the award is intentional trespass to land. Next, we consider whether the $100,000 damage award was excessive. The court must consider three factors in determining whether a punitive damage award violates the Due Process Clause: (1) the degree of reprehensibility of the conduct; (2) the disparity between the harm suffered and the award; and (3) the difference between this remedy and the penalties authorized or imposed in comparable cases. Here the $100,000 award was not excessive. Steenberg's (D) intentional trespass demonstrated an indifference and reckless disregard for the law and for the rights of others. Moreover, such an award is necessary to deter similar conduct in the future. Reversed.

ANALYSIS

The Supreme Court has recognized the interest of a landowner in the right to exclude others from their land as one of the essential property rights. The law recognizes that harm occurs in every trespass to land by the nominal damage award, whether or not actual damages are sustained. The potential harm resulting from intentional trespass to land, which if repeated might ripen into prescription or adverse possession, may result in the owner's loss of property rights. Moreover, society's interest in deterring wrongdoing supports the conclusion in this case as well.

Quicknotes

COMPENSATORY DAMAGES Measure of damages necessary to compensate victim for actual injuries suffered.

PUNITIVE DAMAGES Damages exceeding the actual injury suffered for the purposes of punishment of the defendant, deterrence of the wrongful behavior, or comfort to the plaintiff.

TRESPASS TO LAND Physical invasion of the plaintiff's property that is intended and caused by the defendant's conduct.

Commonwealth v. Magadini

State (P) v. Convicted trespasser (D)

Mass. Sup. Jud. Ct., 52 N.E.3d 1041 (2016)

NATURE OF CASE: Appeal from conviction on seven counts of trespassing at three separate private properties.

FACT SUMMARY: Magadini (D), an unhoused man, was convicted of seven counts of trespassing in private buildings following seven separate incidents. For six of the incidents, Magadini (D) was seeking shelter from the cold. For the seventh incident, Magadini (D) refused to leave an ice cream shop after being asked to leave.

RULE OF LAW

An unhoused individual is still entitled to the necessity defense in a trial for trespass, even if the individual has not exhausted all conceivable lawful alternatives.

FACTS: Magadini (D) was unhoused and had been living in an outdoor gazebo. During the spring of 2014, Magadini (D) was found inside of two separate, private, mixed-use buildings on six separate days that were described as "cool," "cold," or "very cold." Magadini (D) had previously received a no trespass order for each of the buildings where he was found. Because of a prior incident, Magadini (D) was not permitted to stay at the city's unhoused shelter. Magadini's (D) remaining count was for using the restroom at an ice cream shop for 10 to 15 minutes after ignoring the shop clerk's requests for him to leave the premises. Magadini (D) did not dispute that he violated each of the trespass orders; his case was instead focused on the trial judge's denial of his ability to use the necessity defense.

ISSUE: May an unhoused individual be entitled to the necessity defense in a trial for trespass on private property, even if the individual has not exhausted all conceivable lawful alternatives?

HOLDING AND DECISION: (Hines, J.) Yes. An unhoused individual is still entitled to the necessity defense, even if the individual has not exhausted all conceivable lawful alternatives. Under Massachusetts law, the necessity defense requires a defendant to present some evidence of each of the following four conditions: (1) a clear and imminent danger, not one which is debatable or speculative; (2) a reasonable expectation that his or her action will be effective as a direct cause of abating the danger; (3) there exists no legal alternative which will be effective in abating the danger; and (4) the Legislature has not acted to preclude the defense by a clear and deliberate choice regarding the values at issue. On the first six counts of trespassing, where Magadini (D) was seeking shelter from the cold, the trial judge erred in determining that because Magadini (D) could have stayed in a hotel, motel, or at the police station, he failed to satisfy the third element of the necessity defense. A defendant is not required to show that he or she has exhausted or shown to be futile *all* conceivable alternatives; rather, he or she needs only to demonstrate that a jury could reasonably find that no alternatives were available. The six convictions for trespassing to seek shelter from the cold are remanded for a new trial with a jury instruction on the defense of necessity. However, Magadini (D) was not entitled to the necessity defense for the seventh count of trespassing, because he was not seeking shelter from the cold and therefore, did not meet the first element of a clear and imminent danger. Accordingly, the seventh conviction is affirmed and the other six are vacated.

ANALYSIS

The court in *Magadini* explicitly stated that Massachusetts law does not permit unhoused individuals to be punished simply for being unhoused. Similarly, in 2019, the United States Supreme Court let stand the Ninth Circuit Court of Appeal's ruling in *Martin v. Boise*, 920 F.3d 584 (9th Cir. 2019), in which the court determined that it was unconstitutional for the City of Boise to fine or jail unhoused people who stayed outside or in a public place when a bed in an emergency shelter was unavailable.

Quicknotes

NECESSITY DEFENSE A defense to liability for unlawful activity where the conduct is unavoidable and is justified by preventing the occurrence of a more serious harm.

TRESPASS Unlawful interference with, or damage to, the real or personal property of another.

Andrus v. Allard

Government official (D) v. Trader of Native American artifacts (P)

444 U.S. 51 (1979)

NATURE OF CASE: Appeal from declaratory judgment that regulations implementing the Eagle Protection Act and Migratory Bird Treaty Act were unconstitutional insofar as they prohibited commercial transactions in parts of birds legally killed before the birds came within the Acts' protections.

FACT SUMMARY: After they were prosecuted for violating regulations implementing the Eagle Protection Act and Migratory Bird Treaty Act (the Acts), traders (P) in Native American artifacts that contained bird feathers from birds killed before the Acts became effective brought suit asserting that the Acts did not apply to bird parts obtained prior to the Acts' effective dates, and that if the Acts did apply to such parts, the Acts and regulations were unconstitutional under the Fifth Amendment insofar as they prohibited commercial transactions in parts of birds legally killed before the birds came within the Acts' protection. The Government (D) appealed a judgment in favor of the traders (P).

RULE OF LAW

(1) The Eagle Protection Act and Migratory Bird Treaty Act contemplate regulatory prohibition of commerce in the parts of protected birds, without regard to when those birds were originally taken.

(2) The mere prohibition of the sale of lawfully acquired property does not effect a taking in violation of the Fifth Amendment.

FACTS: The Eagle Protection Act and Migratory Bird Treaty Act (the Acts) are conservation statutes designed to prevent the destruction of certain species of birds. The Government (D) promulgated regulations that prohibited commercial transactions in parts of birds legally killed before the birds came under the protection of the statutes. After traders (P) in Native American artifacts, who had sold "pre-existing" Native American artifacts partly composed of feathers of currently protected birds, were prosecuted for violations of both Acts, the traders brought suit in district court for declaratory and injunctive relief, alleging that the Acts did not forbid the sale of artifacts insofar as the constituent bird parts were obtained prior to the effective dates of the Acts, and that if the Acts and regulations did apply to such property, they violated the Fifth Amendment. The district court granted the relief sought, holding that the Acts were to be interpreted as not applicable to pre-existing, legally obtained bird parts, and that therefore the regulations were void as unauthorized extensions of the Acts and violated the traders' (P) Fifth Amendment property rights. The United States Supreme Court granted certiorari.

ISSUE:

(1) Do the Eagle Protection Act and Migratory Bird Treaty Act contemplate regulatory prohibition of commerce in the parts of protected birds, without regard to when those birds were originally taken?

(2) Does the mere prohibition of the sale of lawfully acquired property effect a taking in violation of the Fifth Amendment?

HOLDING AND DECISION: (Brennan, J.)

(1) Yes. The Eagle Protection Act and Migratory Bird Treaty Act (the Acts) contemplate regulatory prohibition of commerce in the parts of protected birds, without regard to when those birds were originally taken. With respect to pre-existing artifacts, Congress specifically declined to exempt any activities other than possession and transportation from the general ban. The legislative history shows that this precise use of terminology was intentional, and that the prohibition against the sale of bird parts lawfully taken before the effective date of federal protection is fully consonant with the Acts' purpose of preventing evasion of the statutory prohibitions for commercial gain. It was reasonable for Congress to conclude that the possibility of commercial gain presented a special threat to the preservation of the protected birds because that prospect created a powerful incentive both to evade statutory prohibitions against taking birds and to take a large volume of birds. Congress might well have viewed evasion as a serious danger because there is no sure means by which to determine the age of bird feathers; feathers recently taken can easily be passed off as having been obtained long ago. Reversed as to this issue.

(2) No. The mere prohibition of the sale of lawfully acquired property does not effect a taking in violation of the Fifth Amendment. The challenged regulations do not compel the surrender of the artifacts in question, and there is no physical invasion or restraint upon them. The denial of one traditional property right does not always amount to a taking. Nor is the fact that the regulations prevent the most profitable use of the traders' (P) property dispositive, since a reduction in the value of property is not necessarily equated with a taking. Government (D) regulation—by definition—involves the adjustment of rights for

Continued on next page.

the public good, and often this adjustment curtails some potential for the use or economic exploitation of private property. To require compensation in all such circumstances would effectively compel the Government (D) to regulate by purchase. Instead, the Fifth Amendment preserves governmental power to regulate, subject only to the dictates of "justice and fairness." Here, the traders (P) retain the rights to possess and transport their property, and to donate or devise the protected birds, so the Acts and regulations have not deprived them of all their property rights in the artifacts, and they may be able to derive some economic benefit from those rights. For example, they could display the artifacts for an admissions charge. In any event, loss of future profits that is unaccompanied by any physical property restriction does not readily support a takings claim, since the prediction of profitability is essentially a matter of reasoned speculation that courts are not especially competent to perform. Further, perhaps because of its very uncertainty, the interest in anticipated gains has traditionally been viewed as less compelling than other property-related interests. For these reasons, the Acts and regulations do not effect a taking of property in violation of the Fifth Amendment's Takings Clause. Reversed as to this issue.

ANALYSIS

In reaching its conclusion that the statutes and regulations did not effect a "taking" that would require just compensation under the Fifth Amendment, the United States Supreme Court relied on a "bundle of rights" conception of property ownership. That view is that where an owner possesses a full "bundle" of property rights, the destruction of one "strand" of the bundle is not a taking, because the aggregate must be viewed in its entirety. Here, under this view, the only "strand" of property rights that was destroyed was the traders' (P) right to sell the artifacts, with the rest of the bundle left intact. The "strands" with which the traders (P) were left were the rights of possession, display, use, gifting, bequeathing, etc.

Quicknotes

TAKING A governmental action that substantially deprives an owner of the use and enjoyment of their property, requiring compensation.

TAKINGS CLAUSE Provision of the Fifth Amendment to the United States Constitution prohibiting the government from taking private property for public use without providing just compensation therefor.

Eyerman v. Mercantile Trust Co.

Adjoining property owners (P) v. Executor of will (D)

Mo. Ct. App., 524 S.W.2d 210 (1975)

NATURE OF CASE: Appeal from lower court decision denying property owners' petition to prevent demolition of testator's home as directed by the testator in her will.

FACT SUMMARY: The will of Louise Johnson directed that after her death, the executor of her will should raze her home in St. Louis and sell the land. Adjoining property owners (P) filed suit to prevent the destruction of the home on the grounds the vacant lot would decrease the value of their properties.

RULE OF LAW

Because the taking of property by inheritance is not a natural right but one created by the state, the state may modify, add conditions, or prohibit testamentary orders or bequests if they are found to be against public policy.

FACTS: The will of Louise Johnson directed that after her death, the executor of her will should raze her home in St. Louis and sell the land. At the time of her death in 1973, the uncontradicted testimony at trial revealed the house and land together were valued at $40,000. If the house was razed, the land would only be worth $5,000. The adjoining property owners (P) alleged the value of their property would decrease due to the presence of the vacant lot. They also alleged the lot could become a public nuisance by attracting unwanted elements into the neighborhood. The home was also part of a subdivision, called Kingsbury Place, which required homeowners to maintain their homes at a certain level. The adjoining property owners (P) filed suit to prevent the destruction of the home. The lower court found that Johnson had the right to order the destruction of the home via her will and denied adjoining property owners' motion for an injunction. The adjoining property owners (P) appealed.

ISSUE: Because the taking of property by inheritance is not a natural right but one created by the state, may the state modify, add conditions, or prohibit testamentary orders or bequests if they are found to be against public policy?

HOLDING AND DECISION: (Rendlen, J.) Yes. Because the taking of property by inheritance is not a natural right but one created by the state, the state may modify, add conditions, or prohibit testamentary orders or bequests if they are found to be against public policy. Although a person may deal capriciously with his own property during his or her lifetime, that person's own self-interest will usually restrain them from doing so. However, there are no such restraints after death. Where a testator creates an order or bequest that is capricious and serves no valid purpose to the detriment of the public, the state has the authority to prohibit such testamentary provisions. The phrase "against public policy" typically means actions that conflict with the morals of the time and goes against societal interests. Public policy is identified by examining the federal and state constitutions, state statutes, and judicial decisions. This court's review of judicial decisions from other jurisdictions supports the conclusion that this type of senseless destruction of property is generally disfavored. No individual or group of individuals benefits from the destruction of Ms. Johnston's home. Instead, the beneficiaries of the will and the adjoining property owners will be financially harmed due to the capriciousness of the deceased testator. The executor has presented no reason, valid or otherwise, to raze the property. Accordingly, because the provision is against public policy, the provision is held invalid and the property owners' petition to prohibit the razing of the house is granted. Reversed and remanded.

DISSENT: (Clemens, J.) The majority improperly grants a benefit to the beneficiaries of the will who were not even a party to this case. In addition, while the majority's opinion rests on the nebulous public policy doctrine, the plaintiffs submitted no evidence that the vacant lot would create a nuisance. There was no requisite showing of probable harm to the plaintiffs. The plaintiffs' entire case was based on conjecture rather than actual evidence. Turning to public policy, courts are on very fragile ground when they only rely upon other judicial decisions as support for the existence of the alleged public policy. The proper role of the judiciary is not to create public policy. Rather, courts may only determine what the public policy is by reviewing the legislative acts of the state or national legislatures. Because the plaintiffs offered no evidence of actual harm, the will of the testator should have been given effect.

ANALYSIS

The crux of the dissent's position is that the court's decision was not based on evidence. While this portion of the decision did not delve into the elements of a preliminary injunction, typically the moving must show: (1) a likelihood of irreparable harm; (2) the balance of harms favors the moving party; (3) a likelihood of success on the merits of the case; and (4) the public interest favors

Continued on next page.

the injunction. Here, the portion of the majority's decision in the casebook focused on the public interest element, while the dissent focused on the irreparable harm element.

Quicknotes

PRELIMINARY INJUNCTION A judicial mandate issued to require or restrain a party from certain conduct; used to preserve a trial's subject matter or to prevent threatened injury.

TESTAMENTARY DISPOSITION A disposition of property that is effective upon the death of the grantor.

Matthews v. Bay Head Improvement Association

Resident (P) v. Beach association (D)

N.J. Sup. Ct., 471 A.2d 355 (1984)

NATURE OF CASE: Appeal from judgment in favor of the defendant in a case alleging violation of public access rights to shoreline areas.

FACT SUMMARY: Matthews (P) alleged that her right to use the beach was violated when Bay Head residents (D) formed an association denying her access to land held as a public trust.

RULE OF LAW

The public must be given access to and use of privately owned land as reasonably necessary for the enjoyment of adjacent public lands.

FACTS: The Bay Head Improvement Association (BHIS) (D) was formed as a privately owned nonprofit corporation in order to own and operate bathing beaches along the ocean. Membership was generally limited to residents of Bay Head, who paid for badges to wear in order to gain access to the beach. Matthews (P), a Point Pleasant inhabitant, sued the Borough of Bay Head and BHIS (D) because they prevented her from gaining access to the Atlantic Ocean and the public beachfront in Bay Head. The Public Advocate later intervened as a plaintiff and asserted that BHIS (D) had denied the general public its right of access to public trust lands along the beaches and its right to use private property fronting on the ocean incidental to the public's right under the public trust doctrine. The trial court held that the Association (D) was not an arm of the Borough of Bay Head, that the Association (D) was not a municipal agency, and that nothing in the record justified a finding that public privileges could attach to the private properties owned or leased by the Association (D). A divided appellate division affirmed. Matthews (P) appealed.

ISSUE: Must the public be given access to and use of privately owned land as reasonably necessary for the enjoyment of adjacent public lands?

HOLDING AND DECISION: (Schreiber, J.) Yes. The public must be given access to and use of privately owned land as reasonably necessary for the enjoyment of adjacent public lands. Where a municipal beach is dedicated to public use, the public use doctrine dictates that the beach and the ocean waters must be open to all on equal terms and without preference. Where use of dry sand is essential or reasonably necessary for enjoyment of the ocean, the public trust doctrine warrants the public's use of the upland dry sand area subject to an accommodation of the interests of the owner. The Bay Head residents (D) may not frustrate the public's right to enjoy the foreshore. By limiting membership only to residents and foreclosing the public, the Association (D) was acting in conflict with the public good and contrary to the strong public policy in favor of encouraging and expanding public access to and use of shoreline areas. Membership in the Association (D) must be open to the public at large and fees charged must be reasonable and may not discriminate between residents and nonresidents. Reversed in part and affirmed in part.

ANALYSIS

The public trust doctrine acknowledges that the ownership, domination, and sovereignty over land flowed by tidal waters is vested in the state in trust for the people. In order to exercise those rights guaranteed by the public trust doctrine, the public must have access to municipally owned dry sand areas as well as the foreshore. Municipal ordinances requiring nonresidents to pay a higher fee than residents for the use of the beach have also been struck down in New Jersey.

Quicknotes

PUBLIC TRUST DOCTRINE The government holds lands that are submerged beneath the water, or that are capable of being submerged, in trust for the public's benefit.

PUBLIC USE Basis for governmental taking of property pursuant to its power of eminent domain so that property taken may be utilized for the benefit of the public at large.

SOVEREIGNTY The absolute power conferred to the state to govern and regulate all persons located and activities conducted therein.

International News Service v. Associated Press

Wire service (D) v. Wire service (P)

248 U.S. 215 (1918)

NATURE OF CASE: Appeal from denial of injunctive relief.

FACT SUMMARY: Associated Press (AP) (P) sued to enjoin International News Service (D) from publishing as its own news stories obtained from early editions of AP (P) publications.

RULE OF LAW

Publication for profit of news obtained from other news-gathering enterprises is a misappropriation of a property right.

FACTS: Associated Press (AP) (P) sued International News Service (INS) (D) for the latter's admitted use of AP (P) news stories in INS (D) publications. INS (D) would obtain advance publication of AP (P) news and would then use such in its newspapers. AP (P) contended it had a proprietary right to all news it gathered through the efforts of its contributors. INS (D) contended any such right terminated upon its first publication. The court of appeals issued AP (P) an injunction, and the United States Supreme Court granted a hearing.

ISSUE: Is the publication for profit of news obtained from other news-gathering enterprises a misappropriation of a property-right?

HOLDING AND DECISION: (Pitney, J.) Yes. Publication for profit of news obtained from other news-gathering enterprises is a misappropriation of a property right. News itself is a collection of observable facts that obviously cannot be owned vis-á-vis by the public at large. The nonprofit communication of news, regardless of source, is endemic in a free society and involves no property right. However, when two competing news organizations are involved, each gaining their livelihood from beating the other's deadline, the use of such news, for profit, is a misappropriation of the other's product. As a result, injunctive relief is properly issued. Affirmed.

ANALYSIS

Some commentators suggest this case as a prime example of the "first in time, first in right" principle of ownership. Some go so far as to argue it provides authority for the proposition that all things created, tangible or intangible, belong to the creator. This expands the reach of this case beyond news gathering and into any area wherein exclusivity of design or idea is important. This would include everything from clothing design to computer programming.

Quicknotes

COPYRIGHT A form of intellectual property that grants to the "author" (i.e., creator) of a literary, musical, dramatic, or artistic work exclusive rights pursuant to Article I, § 8, cl. 8 of the U.S. Constitution over the reproduction, display, performance, distribution, and adaptation of that author's work for a period prescribed by statute.

MISAPPROPRIATION The unlawful use of another's property or funds.

White v. Samsung Electronics America, Inc.

Celebrity (P) v. Corporation (D)

971 F.2d 1395 (9th Cir. 1992)

NATURE OF CASE: Appeal from summary judgment in favor of defendants in an action brought for the violation of the common-law right of publicity and of state and federal statutes.

FACT SUMMARY: When Vanna White's (P) "identity" was used in an advertisement without her consent, she sued Samsung Electronics (D) for allegedly attempting to capitalize on her fame to enhance their fortune.

RULE OF LAW

The right of publicity protects a celebrity's property interest in his or her identity from commercial exploitation, regardless of the method by which it is appropriated.

FACTS: Samsung Electronics (D) ran advertisements in several publications featuring a robot dressed to resemble Vanna White (P), the hostess of the popular game show "Wheel of Fortune." Since White (P) had neither consented to the ads nor was paid for them, she sued, alleging infringement of various intellectual property rights. The district court granted Samsung's (D) motion for summary judgment on White's (P) claims under California Civil Code § 3344, the California common-law right of publicity, and the Lanham Act. White (P) appealed, claiming that her California common-law right of publicity had been violated because Samsung (D) had appropriated part of her identity for its own profit in selling its product.

ISSUE: Does the right of publicity protect a celebrity's property interest in his or her identity from commercial exploitation, regardless of the method by which it is appropriated?

HOLDING AND DECISION: (Goodwin, J.) Yes. The right of publicity protects a celebrity's property interest in his or her identity from commercial exploitation, regardless of the method by which it is appropriated. Prior case law has established that the California common-law right of publicity cause of action may be pleaded by alleging the defendant's use of the plaintiff's identity; the appropriation of plaintiff's name or likeness to defendant's advantage, commercially or otherwise; lack of consent; and resulting injury. The district court erred in reasoning that Samsung (D) had not appropriated White's (P) "name or likeness" with their robot ad and in finding that White's (P) claim failed to satisfy the second prong. The right of publicity does not require that appropriations of identity be accomplished through particular means to be actionable. A celebrity's identity can be valuable in the promotion of products, and the celebrity has an interest that may be protected from the unauthorized commercial exploitation of that identity. The identities of the most popular celebrities are not only the most attractive for advertisers, but also the easiest to evoke without resorting to obvious means such as name, likeness, or voice. Considering the robot's physical attributes, its dress, and its position on the "Wheel of Fortune" game show set, there is little doubt about which celebrity the ad is meant to depict. Because White (P) has alleged facts showing that Samsung (D) appropriated her identity, the district court erred by rejecting, on summary judgment, White's (P) common-law right of publicity claim. Affirmed in part, reversed in part.

CONCURRENCE AND DISSENT: (Alarcon, J.) All the California cases that my research has disclosed hold that a cause of action for appropriation of the right to publicity requires proof of the appropriation of a name or likeness. In each of the federal cases relied upon by the majority, the advertisement affirmatively represented that the person depicted therein was the plaintiff. In this case, it is clear a metal robot and not the plaintiff, Vanna White (P), is depicted in the commercial advertisement. The record does not show an appropriation of Vanna White's (P) identity. In reaching its conclusion, the majority confuses Vanna White (P), the person, with the role she has assumed as the current hostess on the "Wheel of Fortune" television game show. Those things White (P) claims identify her are not unique to her. They are, instead, attributes of the role she plays. The representation of those attributes, therefore, does not constitute a representation of Vanna White (P). I would affirm the district court's judgment in all respects.

ANALYSIS

This case was decided by a three-judge panel. Samsung (P) petitioned for a rehearing of the case before all the judges of the Ninth Circuit. The petition was denied.

Quicknotes

APPROPRIATION The act of making something one's own or making use of something to serve one's own interest.

Continued on next page.

COMMON LAW A body of law developed through the judicial decisions of the courts as opposed to the legislative process.

SUMMARY JUDGMENT Judgment rendered by a court inresponse to a motion made by one of the parties, claiming that the lack of a question of material fact in respect to an issue warrants disposition of the issue without consideration by the jury.

Moore v. Regents of the University of California

Leukemia patient (P) v. Medical center owners (D)

Cal. Sup. Ct., 793 P.2d 479 (1990)

NATURE OF CASE: Review of order reversing dismissal of action seeking damages for conversion, fraud, and breach of fiduciary duty.

FACT SUMMARY: Researchers at the University of California, Los Angeles, unbeknownst to Moore (P), used specimens of his tissue to produce a potentially lucrative cell line.

RULE OF LAW

A person whose tissue is used for profitable research and development without his knowledge may not maintain a conversion action therefor.

FACTS: In 1976 Moore (P) began treatment at University of California, Los Angeles (UCLA), for a life-threatening form of leukemia. Doctors there realized that his tissue had certain unique properties that showed promise of profitable development. While undergoing treatment, Moore (P) often had tissue removed, such as blood samples, as well as his spleen. While he consented to all these procedures, he was unaware of the nontreatment research being performed on his tissues. Eventually a cell line was developed, which showed promise of benefit in immunology. A patent on the cell line was issued. When he became aware of the use to which his tissue had been put, Moore (P) filed an action seeking damages for conversion, fraud, and breach of fiduciary duty. The trial court dismissed for failure to state a cause of action. The court of appeal reversed, holding that Moore (P) had stated a cause of action for conversion and breach of fiduciary duty. The California Supreme Court granted review.

ISSUE: May a person whose tissue is used for profitable research and development without his knowledge maintain a conversion action therefor?

HOLDING AND DECISION: (Panelli, J.) No. A person whose tissue is used for profitable research and development without his knowledge may not maintain a conversion action therefor. [The court first held that Moore (P) could maintain a breach of fiduciary duty cause of action based on nondisclosure and then discussed the conversion cause of action.] This court is of the opinion that existing law would not permit such an action. To maintain such an action, a plaintiff must prove interference with ownership or right of possession. A plaintiff in a position such as Moore (P) clearly had no right of possession, so a conversion action would necessitate interference with a proprietary interest. It cannot be said, however, that a person's tissue is "property." Such a notion is at odds with common views on ethics. Beyond that, Health and Safety Code § 7054.4 severs the interest of a person and his removed body parts. Since existing law does not create a conversion action under the circumstances here, an extension of existing law would be required to allow Moore (P) to proceed. This court declines to do so. First, if so held would stifle beneficial research. Conversion is a strict liability tort, and the specter of a conversion suit might dissuade researchers from undertaking important investigations. Second, fiduciary duty principles protect a patient, so a conversion cause of action is not necessary. Finally, the present area is one better left to the legislature. For these reasons, this court concludes that Moore (P) has not stated a conversion cause of action. Affirmed in part; reversed in part.

CONCURRENCE: (Arabian, J.) Human tissue should never be viewed as property, even by the person whose tissue is at issue.

DISSENT: (Mosk, J.) Current conversion law should be applied to a person's tissue, as a person should have at the least the right to do with his own tissue what any other person can do with it. Assuming that current conversion law doesn't extend to body tissue, it should be extended. To allow a person to economically benefit from the nonconsensual use of another's tissue can be considered a modern version of slavery or indentured servitude.

ANALYSIS

Probably more than any other area of law, property law carries the weight of tradition in its classifications. Modern technology often creates situations that are difficult to apply to traditional legal categories. The present case represents a prime example. The tort of conversion was created in a time when what was and was not capable of being called "property" was pretty clear; things are not so simple today.

Quicknotes

CONVERSION The act of depriving an owner of their property without permission or justification.

FIDUCIARY DUTY A legal obligation to act for the benefit of another, including subordinating one's personal interests to that of the other person.

FRAUD A false representation of facts with the intent that another will rely on the misrepresentation to their detriment.

Diamond v. Chakrabarty

Acting commissioner of patents and trademarks (P) v. Microbiologist (D)

447 U.S. 303 (1980)

NATURE OF CASE: Certiorari review of patentability of living organisms.

FACT SUMMARY: Chakrabarty (D) discovered a bacterium that can break down multiple components of crude oil. He filed a patent claim on the bacterium itself. The patent examiner rejected his claim. Chakrabarty (D) appealed the decision to the Patent Office Board of Appeals, and the Board affirmed the examiner's decision. The Court of Customs and Patent Appeals reversed that decision, and the Acting Commissioner of Patents and Trademarks (P) filed a petition for certiorari and the writ was granted.

RULE OF LAW

A microorganism that is not naturally occurring and is the product of manufacture is patentable subject matter.

FACTS: Chakrabarty (D) discovered a method of developing a bacterium that could break down multiple components of crude oil. Chakrabarty (D) filed a patent claim for the process of developing the bacterium, for an inoculum comprised of a carrier material and the bacterium, and for the bacterium itself. The patent examiner allowed the first two claims but rejected the patent claim for the bacterium itself. The basis for the rejection of the claim for the bacterium was that it was a living organism and, therefore, not patentable subject matter. Chakrabarty (D) appealed the examiner's decision to the Patent Office Board of Appeals. The decision was upheld but reversed by the Court of Customs and Patent Appeals. The Acting Commissioner of Patents and Trademarks (P) petitioned for certiorari review to resolve the issue. The writ was granted.

ISSUE: Does a microorganism constitute a "manufacture" or "composition of matter" such that it can be the subject matter of a patent?

HOLDING AND DECISION: (Burger, C.J.) Yes. Congress intends a broad interpretation of the term "manufacture" in the context of the statute governing patentable subject matter (35 U.S.C. Section 101). The term is interpreted as having the same meaning it is given in the dictionary: "The production of articles for use from raw or prepared materials by giving to these materials new forms, qualities, properties, or combinations, whether by hand-labor or machinery." This allows for very broad reading of the statute. Notwithstanding this broad construction, laws of nature and physical phenomena are not considered patentable subject matter. The petitioner (P) argues that the microorganism in question is not patentable subject matter because it is a living organism precluded from patenting by the 1930 Plant Patent Act. The Court rejected this argument because the relevant distinction made by Congress, in passing the Plant Patent Acts, was not between living and inanimate things but between products of nature and products of human ingenuity. In this case, Chakrabarty (D) applied for a patent for a product of his own ingenuity. The microorganism in question does not occur naturally. Petitioner's (P) final argument is that microorganisms are not patentable until Congress expressly authorizes patent protection for such organisms. Petitioner (P) contends that Congress could not have foreseen this type of technology when it enacted the statute at issue. The Court disagreed, believing that a finding that unforeseen inventions are not protected frustrates the purpose of patent law, which is to promote progress and ingenuity. The Court therefore rejected petitioner's (P) arguments and found that the microorganism in question is patentable subject matter. Affirmed.

DISSENT: (Brennan, J.) The dissenting opinion held that the majority misread the applicable legislation, finding that the case did not deal simply with the problem of "unanticipated inventions" but with the question of whether bacteria, a living organism, is patentable subject matter. The Plant Patent Acts clearly indicate that Congress did not intend living organisms to be patentable. Congress's purpose in passing the Plant Patent Acts was to address the problem of scientists attempting to patent living organisms. In addition, the 1970 Act specifically excludes bacteria from patent protection.

ANALYSIS

Naturally occurring organisms and plants are not patentable subject matter. As this case illustrates, however, when an organism is created through human ingenuity, it becomes patentable subject matter. The public policy behind intellectual property law is to promote human productivity and progress. This case underscores the fact that patent laws are designed to protect human ingenuity and scientific advances.

Continued on next page.

Quicknotes

CERTIORARI A discretionary writ issued by a superior court to an inferior court in order to review the lower court's decisions; the United States Supreme Court's writ ordering such review.

INTELLECTUAL PROPERTY A body of law pertaining to the ownership of rights in intangible products of the human intellect.

PATENT A limited monopoly conferred on the invention or discovery of any new or useful machine or process that is novel and non-obvious.

Feist Publications, Inc. v. Rural Telephone Service Co.

Publishing company (D) v. Phone book publisher (P)

499 U.S. 340 (1991)

NATURE OF CASE: Appeal from grant of summary judgment to plaintiff in suit for copyright infringement.

FACT SUMMARY: After Feist Publications, Inc. (Feist) (D) took 1,309 listings from Rural Telephone Service Co.'s (Rural's) (P) white pages when compiling Feist's (D) own white pages, Rural (P) filed suit for copyright infringement.

RULE OF LAW

To be copyrightable, a work must be original and possess at least some minimal degree of creativity.

FACTS: As a certified telephone service provided in northwest Kansas, Rural Telephone Service Co. (Rural) (P) published a typical telephone directory as a condition of its monopoly franchise. The white pages alphabetically listed the names, towns, and telephone numbers of Rural's (P) subscribers. Feist Publications, Inc. (Feist) (D) was a publishing company specializing in area-wide telephone directories. The Feist (D) directory that was the subject of this litigation contained 46,878 white pages' listings, compared to Rural's (P) approximately 7,700 listings. Feist (D) approached the 11 northwest Kansas telephone companies and offered to pay for the right to use their respective white pages' listings. When only Rural (P) refused to license its listings, Feist (D) used them without Rural's (P) consent. A typical Feist (D) listing included each individual's street address, while most of Rural's (P) did not. Of the 46,878 listings in Feist's (D) 1983 directory, 1,309 of those listings were identical to listings in Rural's (P) white pages. Rural (P) sued for copyright infringement. The district court granted summary judgment to Rural (P), and the court of appeals affirmed. Feist (D) appealed.

ISSUE: To be copyrightable, must a work be original and possess at least some minimal degree of creativity?

HOLDING AND DECISION: (O'Connor, J.) Yes. To be copyrightable, a work must be original and possess at least some minimal degree of creativity. This case concerns the interaction of two well-established propositions. The first is that facts are not copyrightable; the other, that compilations of facts generally are. There is an undeniable tension between these two propositions. The key to resolving the tension lies in understanding why facts are not copyrightable. No one may claim originality as to facts because facts do not owe their origin to an act of authorship. Factual compilations, on the other hand, may possess the requisite originality. Compilations were expressly mentioned in the Copyright Acts of 1909 and 1976. Even in a directory that contains absolutely no protectable written expression, only facts, meets the constitutional minimum for copyright protection if it features an original selection or arrangement. If the selection and arrangement are original, these elements of the work are eligible for copyright protection. No matter how original the format, though, the facts themselves do not become original through association. There is no doubt that Feist (D) took from the white pages of Rural's (P) directory a substantial amount of factual information. The question that remains is whether Rural (P) selected, coordinated, or arranged these uncopyrightable facts in an original way. It did not. Rural (P) simply took the data provided by its subscribers and listed it alphabetically by surname. There is nothing remotely creative about arranging names alphabetically in a white-pages directory. Rural (P) expended sufficient effort to make the white-pages directory useful, but insufficient creativity to make it original. Thus, because Rural's (P) white pages lack the requisite originality, Feist's (D) use of the listings cannot constitute infringement. Copyright rewards originality, not effort. Reversed.

ANALYSIS

In the words of the Court, copyright ensures authors the right to their original expression, but encourages others to build freely upon the ideas and information conveyed by a work. This principle, known as the idea/expression or fact/expression dichotomy, applies to all works of authorship. As applied to a factual compilation, assuming the absence of original written expression, only the compiler's selection and arrangement may be protected; the raw facts may be copied at will. This is the means, by which copyright advances the progress of science and art by encouraging creativity with the reward of exclusive rights for the original creation.

Quicknotes

COPYRIGHT A form of intellectual property that grants to the "author" (i.e., creator) of a literary, musical, dramatic, or artistic work exclusive rights pursuant to Article I, § 8, cl. 8 of the U.S. Constitution over the reproduction,

Continued on next page.

display, performance, distribution, and adaptation of that author's work for a period prescribed by statute.

COPYRIGHT INFRINGEMENT A violation of one of the exclusive rights granted pursuant to Article I, § 8, cl. 8 of the U.S. Constitution to an "author" (i.e., creator) of a literary, musical, dramatic, or artistic work over the reproduction, display, performance, distribution, and adaptation of that author's work for a period prescribed by statute.

SUMMARY JUDGMENT Judgment rendered by a court in response to a motion made by one of the parties, claiming that the lack of a question of material fact in respect to an issue warrants disposition of the issue without consideration by the jury.

United States Patent and Trademark Office v. Booking.com B.V.

Federal agency (P) v. Company seeking trademark registration (D)

2020 WL 3518365 (U.S. 2020)

NATURE OF CASE: Appeal from denial of trademark.

FACT SUMMARY: Booking.com (D), a digital travel company, sought to register four trademarks in connection with its services, each of which contained the name "Booking.com." The United States Patent and Trademark Office (PTO) (P) determined that the name was too generic to be granted a trademark under the Lanham Act.

RULE OF LAW

Terms that are styled as "generic.com" are not ineligible for federal trademark registration.

FACTS: Booking.com (D) filed applications to register four trademarks in connection with its services, each containing the term "Booking.com." The United States Patent and Trademark Office's (PTO's) (P) examining attorney and the PTO's (P) Trademark Trial and Appeal Board both concluded that the term "Booking.com" could not be registered because it was generic for the services at issue. The District Court for the Eastern District of Virginia reversed, ruling that "Booking.com" could be trademarked because it had acquired a secondary meaning. The Fourth Circuit Court of Appeals affirmed the district court's reversal. The United States Supreme Court granted certiorari.

ISSUE: Is a term styled as "generic.com" ineligible for federal trademark registration?

HOLDING AND DECISION: (Ginsburg, J.) No. Terms styled as "generic.com" are not ineligible for federal trademark registration. The PTO's (P) nearly *per se* rule that "generic.com" terms are ineligible is not an appropriate application of trademark law or policy. The Lanham Act, which governs the system of federal trademark registration, states that marks must be adequately distinct; generic terms are generally ineligible for trademark protection when consumers are unable to distinguish one producer's goods from another's. Though the term "booking" is generic, the PTO (P) argued that adding ".com" to the end of a generic name conveys no additional meaning, in the same way that adding "Company" to the name "Generic Company" conveys no additional meaning. However, this argument fails to acknowledge that ".com" conveys the source-identifying characteristic of association with a particular website. In its appeal before the District Court for the Eastern District of Virginia, Booking.com (D) submitted additional evidence demonstrating that the public regards "Booking.com" as descriptive of the services offered by Booking.com (D), instead of viewing it as a generic term. Consumers do not perceive "Booking.com" as a generic name that describes a class of online hotel-reservation services, but rather, as a name associated with a specific service. Therefore, the term "Booking.com" has acquired a secondary meaning and is entitled to trademark protection. Affirmed.

DISSENT: (Breyer, J.) The company's name, Booking.com (D), informs the consumer of the basic nature of the business, and is therefore a generic term that is not protected by trademark law. The Lanham Act did not repudiate *Goodyear's India Rubber Glove Mfg. Co. v. Goodyear Rubber Co.*, 128 U.S. 598 (1888), which held that appending the word "Company" to a generic name for a class of goods was insufficient for trademark protection. Though the majority argues that only one company can hold contractual rights to a specific domain name at any given time, the functional exclusivity of a domain name does not negate *Goodyear*'s applicability. Affording trademark protection to the owners of short, generic domain names is anti-competitive: it creates the impression that the owner is the most authoritative and trustworthy source of a particular good or service and requires the owner to expend less effort and expense in educating consumers than owners of less-generic domain names. These anti-competitive advantages stand in opposition to the goals of basic economic law in the United States.

ANALYSIS

The United States Supreme Court's decision in *USPTO v. Booking.com* marked the Court's first case regarding generic trademarks since its decision in *Kellogg Company v. National Biscuit Company* in 1938. In *Kellogg*, the Court established the Primary-Significance test, which requires an owner seeking to an establish a tradename to show that "the primary significance of the term in the minds of the consuming public is not the product but the producer." *Kellogg Co. v. Nat. Biscuit Co.*, 305 U.S. 111 (1938).

Quicknotes

GENERIC NAME A term that describes something generally without referencing the source or maker.

Continued on next page.

SECONDARY MEANING A word or mark that becomes associated with a particular merchant or product as its source of origin.

TRADEMARK Any word, name, symbol, device or combination thereof that is either currently utilized, or which a person has a bona fide intent to utilize, in commerce in order to distinguish their goods from those of another.

TRADENAME The name under which a business operates.

CHAPTER 2

Subsequent Possession: Acquisition of Property by Find, Adverse Possession, and Gift

Quick Reference Rules of Law

		PAGE
1.	*Armory v. Delamirie.* A finder of lost chattel has title superior to all but the rightful owner.	*26*
2.	*Hannah v. Peel.* The finder of a lost article is entitled to it as against all persons except the real owner.	*27*
3.	*Chaplin v. Sanders.* (1) The hostility/claim of right element of adverse possession requires only that the claimant treat the land as his own as against the world throughout the statutory period. (2) The open and notorious element of adverse possession is satisfied if the title holder has actual notice of the adverse use throughout the statutory period.	*28*
4.	*Howard v. Kunto.* Where several successive purchasers received record title to tract *A* under the mistaken belief that they were acquiring tract *B*, immediately contiguous thereto, and where possession of tract *B* is transferred and occupied in a continuous manner for more than 10 years by successive occupants, there is sufficient privity of estate to permit tacking and thus establish adverse possession as a matter of law.	*30*
5.	*O'Keeffe v. Snyder.* The discovery rule controls in actions involving the adverse possession of chattels.	*31*
6.	*Newman v. Bost.* A constructive delivery of a gift *causa mortis* will be effective where it plainly appears that it was the intention of the donor to make the gift, and where the things intended to be given are not present, or, where present, are incapable of manual delivery from their size or weight.	*32*
7.	*Gruen v. Gruen.* A valid *inter vivos* gift of chattel may be made where the donor reserves a life estate and the donee never has physical possession until after the donor's death.	*33*

Armory v. Delamirie

Jewel finder (P) v. Goldsmith (D)

King's Bench, 1 Strange 505 (1722)

NATURE OF CASE: Action in trover to recover the value of personal property.

FACT SUMMARY: Armory (P) found a jewel. He took it to Delamirie (D), a goldsmith, for appraisal, but Delamirie's (D) apprentice removed the stones, which Delamirie (D) refused to return.

RULE OF LAW

A finder of lost chattel has title superior to all but the rightful owner.

FACTS: Armory (P), a chimney sweeper's boy, found a jewel. He took the jewel to Delamirie's (D) goldsmith shop to learn what it was. Delamirie's (D) apprentice, under the pretense of weighing the jewel, removed the stones from the setting and told his master the value. Delamirie (D) offered Armory (P) three halfpence for the stones, but he refused, wanting the jewel back. Delamirie (D) returned the setting without the stones. Armory (P) sued in trover for money damages for the value of the intact jewel, with the stones.

ISSUE: Does a finder of lost chattel have title superior to all but the rightful owner?

HOLDING AND DECISION: (Pratt, C.J.) Yes. A finder of lost chattel has title superior to all but the rightful owner. Such title is a sufficient property interest in the finder upon which he may maintain an action against anyone (except the rightful owner) who violates that interest. Additionally, Delamirie (D) was liable, as he was responsible for the actions of his apprentice. As for the measure of damages, if Delamirie (D) did not show the stones were not of the finest value, their value would be so determined.

ANALYSIS

As to ownership, the finder is in a position similar to that of a bailee. The finder does not obtain absolute ownership but does have the right of ownership against everybody except the true owner. Here, the chattel, the jewel, was subsequently converted against the finder. Yet the finder, if they should subsequently lose the chattel, may reclaim it from a subsequent finder. The finder has a choice of remedies. They may recover the chattel in specie if it is still in the converter's possession, or they may recover full value from the wrongdoer. Notice that an action in trover, which is an action at law, is to recover the value of the chattel. If it is desired to have the item returned, an action in replevin must be brought in equity.

Quicknotes

BAILEE Person holding property in trust for another party.

REPLEVIN An action to recover personal property wrongfully taken.

TROVER An action for damages resulting from the unlawful conversion of, or to recover possession of, personal property.

Hannah v. Peel

Brooch finder (P) v. Homeowner (D)

King's Bench Div., K.B. 509 (1945)

NATURE OF CASE: Action to recover personal property.

FACT SUMMARY: Hannah (P) found a brooch at Peel's (D) home during World War II and sought to recover it after police handed it over to Peel (D).

RULE OF LAW

The finder of a lost article is entitled to it as against all persons except the real owner.

FACTS: During the Second World War, Peel's (D) home was requisitioned for use by the military. In August 1940, lance corporal Hannah (P) found a brooch in a crevice in a bedroom of the house. Hannah (P) gave the brooch to his commanding officer a month later, and in August 1942, the police handed the brooch to Peel (D), who subsequently sold it. There was no evidence that Peel (D) had any knowledge of the existence of the brooch before it was found by Hannah (P). Hannah (P) refused a reward offer from Peel (D), and maintained his right to possession of the brooch as against all persons other than the owner, who was unknown. On October 21, 1943, Hannah (P) filed suit to recover the brooch or its value and damages for its detention.

ISSUE: Is the finder of a lost article entitled to it as against all persons except the real owner?

HOLDING AND DECISION: (Birkett, J.) Yes. The general rule is that the finder of a lost article is entitled to it as against all persons except the real owner. This is because an occupier of land does not in all cases possess an unattached thing on his land even though the true owner has lost possession. Although a man possesses everything that is attached to or under his land, a man does not necessarily possess a thing that is lying unattached on the surface of his land even though the thing is not possessed by someone else. Here, the brooch was lost in the ordinary meaning of that term, and it had been lost for a very considerable time. Peel (D) was never physically in possession of the premises at any time. It is clear the brooch was never his, in the ordinary meaning of the term, in that he did not have the prior possession. Peel (D) had no knowledge of it, until it was brought to his attention by Hannah (P). Accordingly, judgment is rendered for Hannah (P).

ANALYSIS

The issue of finder's rights presented many problems for the English commentators. "The reason why these writers did not have better success in their efforts at definition was that they tried to state the essentials of all the possession cases in too simple a form; they tried, characteristically emphasizing human will, to reduce the essentials of possession to the form of a unilateral act. For them the [archetypical] case was the act of taking-occupation." Shartel, "Meanings of Possession," 16 *Minn. L. Rev.* 611, 615, 619 (1932).

Quicknotes

POSSESSION The holding of property with the right of disposition.

Chaplin v. Sanders

Title holder (P) v. Adverse possessors (D)

Wash. Sup. Ct., 676 P.2d 431 (1984)

NATURE OF CASE: Appeal of judgment against adverse possessors.

FACT SUMMARY: The Chaplins (P), title owners of a piece of land, and their neighbors, the Sanders (D), fight over a strip of land between the two properties.

RULE OF LAW

(1) The hostility/claim of right element of adverse possession requires only that the claimant treat the land as his own as against the world throughout the statutory period.

(2) The open and notorious element of adverse possession is satisfied if the title holder has actual notice of the adverse use throughout the statutory period.

FACTS: Peter and Patricia Sanders (D) owned property that adjoined property to the east owned by Kent and Barbara Chaplin (P) and Kenneth and Hazel Chaplin (P). The lawsuit concerned a strip of land owned on record by the Chaplins (P) that fell between the two properties. In 1957 or 1958, the Hibbards built the trailer park occupying the western parcel, now owned by Sanders (D), and when they did, they were not sure of the boundary on the east, and so included the strip of land now at issue in their development. It was now the location of a road into the trailer park, and a narrow strip of landscaped land to a drainage ditch between the road's east side and the Chaplin (P) property. The Chaplins' (P) predecessor, McMurray, had a survey conducted in 1960, and at that time discovered the true boundary and informed the Hibbards that their driveway encroached upon his land. When the Hibbards sold the property in 1962, they included in the sale contract a provision indicating that the driveway encroached on the adjoining property by approximately 20 feet. The western parcel changed hands several times after, and to the Sanders (D) in 1976, and none of the subsequent owners were told that the road encroached on the eastern parcel. The Chaplins (P) purchased the eastern parcel, which was still undeveloped, in 1978. They had a survey conducted in order to develop commercial buildings on the site. They brought this action to quiet title to the disputed portion and sought damages for increased construction costs. The trial court found that 1967 was the appropriate time from which to compute the 10-year period necessary to establish adverse possession and then found that the Sanders (D) satisfied each element of adverse possession with regard to the road, but not with regard to the property between the road and the ditch. The appeals court found that because the Sanders (D) had actual notice of the encroachment, the requirement of hostility had not been satisfied for either parcel, and reversed the trial court's holding with respect to the road, and also directed the lower court to quiet title in the Chaplins (P).

ISSUE:

(1) Does the hostility/claim of right element of adverse possession require only that the claimant treat the land as his own as against the world throughout the statutory period?

(2) Is the open and notorious element of adverse possession satisfied if the title holder has actual notice of the adverse use throughout the statutory period?

HOLDING AND DECISION: (Utter, J.)

(1) Yes. The hostility/claim of right element of adverse possession requires only that the claimant treat the land as his own as against the world throughout the statutory period. The purpose of the doctrine of adverse possession is to assure maximum utilization of land, encouraging the rejection of stale claims and quieting titles. Adverse possession requires that possession be (1) exclusive, (2) actual and uninterrupted, (3) open and notorious, and (4) hostile and under a claim of right made in good faith. The dual requirement that the claimant take possession in good faith and not recognize another's superior interest do not serve the purpose of adverse possession, and cases that support that dual requirement are overruled. The possessor's subjective belief whether the land possessed is or is not his own and his intent to dispossess or not dispossess another are irrelevant to a finding of hostility. In this case, the contract provision is not relevant, but the objective character of Hibbard's possession and that of his successors in interest is. The Sanders (D) and their predecessors used and maintained the property as though it was their own for at least 10 years, and that satisfies the element of hostility.

(2) Yes. The open and notorious element of adverse possession is satisfied if the title holder has actual notice of the adverse use throughout the statutory period. McMurray was aware of the Hibbards' use of the strip abutting the roadway, as is shown by the disparate condition of McMurray's undeveloped, overgrown

Continued on next page.

property and the cleared, mowed, and maintained strip of land separating the roadway and McMurray's land. Reversed and remanded.

ANALYSIS

The issue of intent to possess the property will likely arise as an issue on your exam. Keep in mind that intent is irrelevant to finding hostility—the possessor need not intend to claim property that they know is not theirs. Even if the possessor never gives the matter any thought, and simply assumes the property is his or hers, most states can still find adverse possession.

Quicknotes

ADVERSE POSSESSION A means of acquiring title to real property by remaining in actual, open, continuous, exclusive possession of the property for the statutory period.

CLAIM OF RIGHT Made by a person claiming a right in property, who is in possession and intends to claim ownership of that property without regard to the record title owner.

QUIET TITLE Equitable action to resolve conflicting claims to an interest in real property.

STATUTE OF LIMITATIONS A law prescribing the period in which a legal action may be commenced.

Howard v. Kunto

Record title owner (P) v. Adverse possessor (D)

Wash. Ct. App., 477 P.2d 210 (1970)

NATURE OF CASE: Action to quiet title.

FACT SUMMARY: The land occupied by Kunto (D) was not that to which he had record title, but he appealed a judgment quieting title in Howard (P) who did have record title.

RULE OF LAW

Where several successive purchasers received record title to tract *A* under the mistaken belief that they were acquiring tract *B*, immediately contiguous thereto, and where possession of tract *B* is transferred and occupied in a continuous manner for more than 10 years by successive occupants, there is sufficient privity of estate to permit tacking and thus establish adverse possession as a matter of law.

FACTS: The Kuntos (D) took possession of a summer home under a deed that unbeknownst to them described the adjoining property. After discovering the mistake, Howard (P) obtained a conveyance of the deed that described the property occupied by the Kuntos (D), then sought and obtained a judgment quieting title in himself. Several successive purchasers, over a period of over ten years, had taken possession of the disputed tract under the same mistaken deed. The Kuntos (D) appealed.

ISSUE: Where several successive purchasers received record title to tract *A* under the mistaken belief that they were acquiring tract *B*, immediately contiguous thereto, and where possession of tract *B* is transferred and occupied in a continuous manner for more than 10 years by successive occupants, is there sufficient privity of estate to permit tacking and thus establish adverse possession as a matter of law?

HOLDING AND DECISION: (Pearson, J.) Yes. Where several successive purchasers received record title to tract *A* under the mistaken belief that they were acquiring tract *B*, immediately contiguous thereto, and where possession of tract *B* is transferred and occupied in a continuous manner for more than ten years by successive occupants, there is sufficient privity of estate to permit tacking and thus establish adverse possession as a matter of law. The deed running between parties purporting to transfer land traditionally furnishes the privity of estate that connects the possession of successive occupants. The technical requirement of "privity" should not be used to upset the long periods of occupancy of those who in good faith received an erroneous deed description. The use of a summer cottage only in summer is uninterrupted possession sufficient to establish adverse possession. There is a public interest favoring early certainty as to the location of land ownership. Reversed with directions.

ANALYSIS

The *Howard* case provides a good example of how the sometimes seemingly unjust doctrine of adverse possession can produce a just result.

Quicknotes

PRIVITY OF ESTATE Common or successive relation to the same right in property.

QUIET TITLE Equitable action to resolve conflicting claims to an interest in real property.

RECORD TITLE Title to real property that is recorded in the public land records.

TACKING The attachment of periods of adverse possession by different adverse possessors in order to fulfill the requirement of continuous possession for the period prescribed by statute.

O'Keeffe v. Snyder

Artist (P) v. Adverse possessor (D)

N.J. Sup. Ct., 416 A.2d 862 (1980)

NATURE OF CASE: Appeal from reversal of award of replevin.

FACT SUMMARY: Snyder (D) contended that he had acquired three of O'Keeffe's (P) paintings by adverse possession.

RULE OF LAW

The discovery rule controls in actions involving the adverse possession of chattels.

FACTS: The painter Georgia O'Keeffe (P) brought an action against Snyder (D) for replevin or return of three small pictures painted by O'Keeffe (P). In her complaint, filed in March 1976, O'Keeffe (P) alleged that she was the owner of the paintings, and that they had been stolen from a New York art gallery in 1946. Snyder (D) asserted that he was a purchaser for value of the paintings, that he had acquired title by adverse possession, and that O'Keeffe's (P) action was barred by the expiration of the six-year period of limitations pertaining to an action in replevin. The appellate court, in reversing the trial court, concluded that the paintings were stolen, the defenses of expiration of the statute of limitations and title by adverse possession were identical, and that Snyder (D) had not proved the elements of adverse possession.

ISSUE: Does the discovery rule control in actions involving the adverse possession of chattels?

HOLDING AND DECISION: (Pollock, J.) Yes. The discovery rule provides that, in an appropriate case, a cause of action will not accrue until the injured party discovers, or by exercise of reasonable diligence and intelligence should have discovered, facts that form the basis of a cause of action. Here, O'Keeffe's (P) cause of action accrued when she first knew, or reasonably should have known through the exercise of due diligence, of the cause of action, including the identity of the possessor of the paintings. The focus of the inquiry will no longer be whether the possessor has met the tests of adverse possession, but whether the owner has acted with due diligence in pursuing his or her personal property. Under the discovery rule, if an artist diligently seeks the recovery of a lost or stolen painting but cannot find it or discover the identity of the possessor, the statute of limitations will not begin to run. Under the discovery rule, the burden is on the owner as the one seeking the benefit of the rule to establish facts that would justify deferring the beginning of the period of limitations. However, if the period of limitations does begin to run, the expiration of the six-year statutory limitation period should vest title as effectively under the discovery rule as under the doctrine of adverse possession. Reversed and remanded for further proceedings.

ANALYSIS

Prior to the ruling in this case, the discovery rule had been applied primarily in tort actions where the injuries allegedly suffered by the plaintiff were difficult to discover. The court in this case, after reviewing the difficulty of applying principles of adverse possession to cases involving artwork, ruled that the application of the discovery rule would mitigate the unjust results that would flow from strict adherence to the rules of adverse possession.

Quicknotes

ADVERSE POSSESSION A means of acquiring title to real property by remaining in actual, open, continuous, exclusive possession of property for the statutory period.

CHATTEL An article of personal property, as distinguished from real property; a thing personal and moveable.

DUE DILIGENCE The standard of care as would be taken by a reasonable person in accordance with the attendant facts and circumstances.

REPLEVIN An action to recover personal property wrongfully taken.

Newman v. Bost

Donee (P) v. Estate administrator (D)

N.C. Sup. Ct., 29 S.E. 848 (1898)

NATURE OF CASE: Appeal from a finding of a valid gift *causa mortis.*

FACT SUMMARY: Newman (P) sought to recover the value of certain gifts *causa mortis* sold by the decedent's administrator (D) who did not believe any valid gifts were made to Newman (P).

RULE OF LAW

A constructive delivery of a gift *causa mortis* will be effective where it plainly appears that it was the intention of the donor to make the gift, and where the things intended to be given are not present, or, where present, are incapable of manual delivery from their size or weight.

FACTS: The decedent was stricken with paralysis and died within a month. While so stricken, he directed his nurse, Houston, to call Newman (P), his housekeeper, into his bedroom. The decedent handed to Newman (P) his private keys and told her to take them and keep them, that he desired her to have them and everything in the house. He then pointed out certain articles of furniture, including a bureau, and repeated that everything was hers. One of the keys unlocked a bureau drawer in which was decedent's life insurance policy, payable to his estate, and a few notes. Newman (P) brought suit against Bost (D), the decedent's administrator, to recover $3,000, the proceeds of the life insurance policy; $300, the value of a piano which decedent allegedly gave Newman (P) and which was destroyed by fire; $200.94, the value of household property sold by Bost (D); and $45, the value of the bedroom furniture sold by Bost (D). The court found that decedent made a valid gift *causa mortis*, and Bost (D) appealed.

ISSUE: Will a constructive delivery of a gift *causa mortis* be effective where it plainly appears that it was the intention of the donor to make the gift, and where the things intended to be given are not present, or where present, are incapable of manual delivery from their size and weight?

HOLDING AND DECISION: (Furches, J.) Yes. A constructive delivery of a gift *causa mortis* will be effective where it plainly appears that it was the intention of the donor to make the gift, and where the things intended to be given are not present, or, where present, are incapable of manual delivery from their size or weight; but where the articles are present, and are capable of manual delivery, manual delivery must be made. Here, as for the life insurance policy, it could have been removed from the drawer and easily handed to Newman (P). The failure to do so prevented the policy from passing to her. However, the bureau and any other furniture that the keys would fit did pass to her because actual delivery would have been unreasonable because of their size and weight. The keys were thus an effective constructive delivery of those items. All other furniture, except that in Newman's own bedroom in the house, remained in the estate. The furniture in Newman's (P) bedroom passed to her, rather, as a gift *inter vivos* for she had use and control of it before decedent contemplated his death. As for the piano, it was not ever within her dominion and control and there was never any delivery, and so it did not pass to her. Remanded for a new trial.

ANALYSIS

The court above took a fairly restrictive view of the concept of delivery and believed that the concept of gifts *causa mortis* should be strictly construed. The court expressed the fear that to allow symbolic delivery would be to open the door to all sorts of fraud. Where one is holding the donor's property as a bailee, and the donor wishes to give to the bailee that property already in the possession of the bailee, it is not necessarily for the intended donee-bailee to return the property to the donor so that delivery of the gift can be made. To so require, it has been held, would be a senseless formality. *Matter of Mill's Estate*, 158 N.Y.S. 1100 (App. Div. 1916).

Quicknotes

CONSTRUCTIVE DELIVERY The transfer of title or possession of property by means other than actual delivery indicative of the parties' intent to effect a transfer.

GIFT *CAUSA MORTIS* A gift made contingent on the donor's anticipated death.

GIFT *INTER VIVOS* A gift that is made, and is to take effect, while the parties are living.

STATUTE OF WILLS An English law stating the requirements for a valid testamentary disposition.

SYMBOLIC DELIVERY A method of constructive delivery whereby the transfer of title or possession of property is effectuated by delivering an article symbolic of the property.

Gruen v. Gruen

Son/donee (P) v. Stepmother (D)

N.Y. Ct. App., 496 N.E.2d 869 (1986)

NATURE OF CASE: Appeal from an enforcement of an *inter vivos* gift.

FACT SUMMARY: Mrs. Gruen (D) contended her husband could not make a valid *inter vivos* gift to his son (P) and still retain present exclusive possession of the property for his life.

RULE OF LAW

A valid *inter vivos* gift of chattel may be made where the donor reserves a life estate and the donee never has physical possession until after the donor's death.

FACTS: Michael Gruen (P) received a letter from his father indicating the latter wished to make a gift of a painting, but that he wished to use it for his life. Gruen (P) never took possession of the painting. After his father's death, he requested the painting from his stepmother, Mrs. Gruen (D), who refused. Gruen (P) sued, contending a valid *inter vivos* gift had been made. His stepmother defended, contending no valid gift could be made if the donor retained a life estate and no physical delivery was made during life. The trial court held against Gruen (P), while the appellate court reversed. Mrs. Gruen (D) appealed.

ISSUE: May a valid *inter vivos* gift of chattel be made where the donor reserves a life estate and the donee does not take physical possession?

HOLDING AND DECISION: (Simons, J.) Yes. A valid *inter vivos* gift of chattel may be made where the donor reserves a life estate and the donee never takes physical possession until after the donor's death. In this case, donative intent was established constructively through the document of transfer, the letter. Acceptance is implied because the painting had value. Thus, a valid gift was made. Affirmed.

ANALYSIS

Various estates in chattel can be created just as various estates in land are. The property in this case happened to be personal rather than real, yet the creation of a remainder interest was valid. It is clear the elder Mr. Gruen intended to make a current transfer of such interest, while retaining a possessory interest.

Quicknotes

CHATTEL An article of personal property, as distinguished from real property; a thing personal and moveable.

DONATIVE INTENT Donor's intent to make a gift.

DONEE A person to whom a gift is made.

DONOR A person who gives real or personal property or value.

GIFT *INTER VIVOS* A gift that is made, and is to take effect, while the parties are living.

REMAINDER INTEREST An interest in land that remains after the termination of the immediately preceding estate.

CHAPTER 3

Possessory Estates

Quick Reference Rules of Law

White v. Brown

Beneficiary (P) v. Heir at law (D)

Tenn. Sup. Ct., 559 S.W.2d 938 (1977)

NATURE OF CASE: Appeal from a will interpretation.

FACT SUMMARY: The trial court held that Lide's will created a life estate in White (P) based on the fact the will specified the property was not to be sold.

RULE OF LAW

Unless the words and context of a will clearly evidence an intention to convey only a life estate, it will be interpreted as conveying a fee estate.

FACTS: Lide died leaving a will that provided, "I wish Evelyn White to have my home to live in and not be sold." Lide's niece, Brown (D), claimed the will created a life estate and she obtained a remainder interest. White (P) sued to quiet title, contending the will created a fee estate. The trial court found for Brown (D), and White (P) appealed.

ISSUE: Will a will be interpreted as conveying a fee estate unless the words and context clearly evidence an intention to convey a lesser estate?

HOLDING AND DECISION: (Brock, J.) Yes. Unless the words and context of a will clearly evidence an intention to convey only a life estate, it will be interpreted as conveying a fee estate. Interpreting the will language presented here as creating only a life estate would create a partial intestacy. There is a general policy against creating intestacy where a reasonable alternative interpretation exists. Taking these two policies together, the trial court should have construed the will as creating a fee estate in White (P). Reversed and remanded.

DISSENT: (Harbison, J.) The express language of the will indicated an insurmountable constraint on alienation, indicating a clear intent to create less than a fee estate.

ANALYSIS

This case illustrates two common rules of construction to which courts resort in interpreting conveyances. The intent of the testator is derived from the entire document, and extrinsic evidence is admissible only under limited circumstances. Because of this restraint on extrinsic evidence of intent, courts must resort to the rules of construction previously noted. Where the instrument is drafted by a layperson, such rules of construction are essential to provide uniformity in construction.

Quicknotes

ALIENATION Conveyance or transfer of property.

EXTRINSIC EVIDENCE Evidence that is not contained within the text of a document or contract, but which is derived from the parties' statements or the circumstances under which the agreement was made.

HOLOGRAPHIC WILL A will that is handwritten by the testator or testatrix.

INTESTACY To die without leaving a valid testamentary instrument.

LIFE ESTATE An interest in land measured by the life of the tenant or a third party.

QUITCLAIM A deed whereby the grantor conveys whatever interest they may have in the property without any warranties or covenants as to title.

TESTATRIX A woman who dies having drafted and executed a will or testament.

Mahrenholz v. County Board of School Trustees

Possibility-of-reverter holder (P) v. Grantee (D)

Ill. App. Ct., 417 N.E.2d 138 (1981)

NATURE OF CASE: Appeal from dismissal of action to quiet title.

FACT SUMMARY: Mahrenholz (P) contended he obtained a possessory interest in land when the School District (D) ceased using the property for classes, allegedly breaching a deed restriction.

RULE OF LAW

Only where the grantor creates a possibility of reverter will he or his successors become possessory owners of the property immediately upon the breaking of the condition.

FACTS: Mahrenholz (P) sued to quiet title to land deeded to the School District (D) "for school purposes." The land grant specifically stated that "this land to be used for school purpose only; otherwise to revert to Grantors herein." The heir of the grantors subsequently conveyed his interest in the land to Mahrenholz's (P) predecessor in interest. Mahrenholz (P) contended that the original conveyance created a fee simple determinable which gave rise to a possibility of reverter. This allowed him to become the possessory owner of the property by operation of law when the site ceased being used to hold classes. The trial court held that the conveyance created a fee simple subject to a condition subsequent and because the heir had not affirmatively enforced his right of reentry, he had no possessory interest to convey. Mahrenholz (P) appealed.

ISSUE: Will a grantor automatically obtain possessory ownership of the estate only where the grant created a possibility of reverter?

HOLDING AND DECISION: (Jones, J.) Yes. Only where the grantor creates a possibility of reverter will he or his successors become possessory owners immediately upon the breach of the deed restriction. A grant of use for an exclusive purpose followed by an express provision for reverter creates a fee simple determinable and a possibility of reverter. The deed in this case created such use and therefore the heir held a possibility of reverter. His conveyance to Mahrenholz's (P) predecessor conveyed this interest which became possessory, if at all, when the land was no longer used for classes. Therefore, the trial court erred in dismissing the action. Reversed and remanded.

ANALYSIS

This case illustrates the difference in theory between the possibility of reverter created by a fee simple determinable and the right of reentry created by a fee simple subject to a condition subsequent. In the former, the breach of condition precedent automatically terminates the possessory estate. In the latter, termination is merely a right that must be exercised by the holder. This is purely an academic distinction as any possessory interest will have to be formally terminated before the estate holder will abandon the estate.

Quicknotes

DETERMINABLE FEE An interest in property that may last forever or until the happening of a specified event.

FEE SIMPLE DEFEASIBLE ESTATE A fee simple interest in land that is subject to being terminated upon the happening of a future event.

FEE SIMPLE SUBJECT TO A CONDITION SUBSEQUENT An estate in land that represents total ownership, except that it is capable of being defeated upon the occurrence or nonoccurrence of a specified condition.

QUIET TITLE Equitable action to resolve conflicting claims to an interest in real property.

REVERSIONARY INTEREST An interest retained by a grantor of property in the land transferred, which is created when the owner conveys less of an interest than they own and which returns to the grantor upon the termination of the conveyed estate.

RIGHT OF REENTRY An interest in property reserved in the conveyance of a fee that gives the holder the right to resume possession of property upon the happening of a condition subsequent.

Note: There are no principal cases in Chapter 4 of the casebook.

CHAPTER 5

Co-Ownership and Marital Interests

Quick Reference Rules of Law

PAGE

1. *Delfino v. Vealencis.* Partition sales are employed only where partition in kind is unworkable. 40

2. *Spiller v. Mackereth.* Absent an owner physically barring a cotenant from entry upon the owned premises, that owner is not liable to the cotenant for rent. 41

3. *Parker v. Shecut.* A cotenant in common ousts their cotenant from their jointly-held property by changing the locks on the property, not providing the other cotenant a working key, and manifesting no intention to do so. 42

4. *Sawada v. Endo.* Tenancy-by-the-entirety property may not be reached by the separate creditors of either spouse. 44

Delfino v. Vealencis

Tenant in common (P) v. Cotenant (D)

Conn. Sup. Ct., 436 A.2d 27 (1980)

NATURE OF CASE: Appeal from judicially ordered partition sale.

FACT SUMMARY: The trial court held the rights of the parties would be best protected by a partition sale rather than a partition in kind.

RULE OF LAW

Partition sales are employed only where partition in kind is unworkable.

FACTS: The Delfinos (P) owned an undivided 99/144 interest in land, in which Vealencis (D) owned an undivided 45/144 interest. The property was held as a tenancy in common. Delfino (P) wanted to develop residential housing on the tract and sought a partition sale. Vealencis (D) defended, contending partition in kind. She used her portion of the property for the operation of a rubbish removal business. The court held the partition in kind was unavailable and a partition sale was necessary. Vealencis (D) appealed, contending the property, rectangular in shape and having only three cotenants, could easily be subjected to partition in kind.

ISSUE: Are partition sales employed only where partition in kind is unworkable?

HOLDING AND DECISION: (Healey, J.) Yes. Partition sales are employed only where partition in kind is unavailable. Partition sales should be employed only in extraordinary circumstances, as the forced sale of a party's interest should be avoided. In this case, the limited number of competing interests, and the relative ease of division makes partition in kind very workable. Reversed and remanded.

ANALYSIS

The court rejected the proposition that the property could not be used jointly. The trial court had found that the use for residential property was mutually exclusive with use as rubbish removal business. The shape of the property allowed for easy partition.

Quicknotes

PARTITION IN KIND A separation of undivided interests in land so that the parties may possess their interests separately.

PARTITION SALE A court-ordered sale of property held in joint tenancy, as a cotenant or in tenancy by the entirety, if the property is incapable of being divided; the income is distributed in proportion to the parties' interests in the sold property.

Spiller v. Mackereth

Cotenant in possession (D) v. Tenant in common (P)

Ala. Sup. Ct., 334 So. 2d 859 (1976)

NATURE OF CASE: Appeal from judgment awarding damages for back rent.

FACT SUMMARY: Spiller (D), cotenant of a warehouse with Mackereth (P), ignored her demand that he cease using the whole premises or pay her rent.

RULE OF LAW

Absent an owner physically barring a cotenant from entry upon the owned premises, that owner is not liable to the cotenant for rent.

FACTS: Spiller (D) and Mackereth (P) were tenants in common of a warehouse. When their tenant vacated, Spiller (D) began using the entire warehouse as a storage facility. Mackereth (P) demanded that Spiller (D) either vacate half the premises or pay rent. Spiller (D) ignored the demand. Mackereth (P) sued for rent. A trial court awarded $2,100 back rent. Spiller (D) appealed.

ISSUE: Absent an owner physically barring a cotenant from entry upon the owned premises, is that owner liable to the cotenant for rent?

HOLDING AND DECISION: (Jones, J.) No. Absent an owner physically barring a cotenant from entry upon the owned premises, the owner is not liable to the cotenant for rent. As a general rule a cotenant has the full right to use the premises and cannot be liable to cotenants for rent. The only exception to this occurs when there is an "ouster." For there to be an ouster, a cotenant must physically bar the other cotenant from entry. Merely ignoring an order to partially vacate does not constitute ouster. Here, there is no evidence that Spiller (D) physically barred Mackereth (P) from entry, so there was no ouster. Reversed.

ANALYSIS

Ouster can exist in different degrees. When it is not done under a claim of absolute ownership, it can support an action for back rent. When done under a claim of such ownership, it can give rise to adverse possession, if the other elements required therefor are present.

Quicknotes

ABSOLUTE OWNERSHIP Ownership of property that exists exclusively to one party.

ADVERSE POSSESSION A means of acquiring title to real property by remaining in actual, open, continuous, exclusive possession of property for the statutory period.

OUSTER The unlawful dispossession of a party lawfully entitled to possession of real property.

PER MY ET PER TOUT By half and by whole; refers to the holding of interests in a joint tenancy whereby a joint tenant is entitled to the whole property for purposes of survivorship and to their share for purposes of alienation.

Parker v. Shecut

Cotenant in common (P) v. Cotenant in common (D)

S.C. Sup. Ct., 562 S.E.2d 620 (2002)

NATURE OF CASE: Appeal from affirmance of judgment for defendant in action for ouster.

FACT SUMMARY: Anne Parker (P) alleged that her brother, Bo Shecut (D), with whom she was a tenant in common in a beach house, ousted her from their property, and she sought payment of rent by Bo (D) for the ouster period. Bo (D) denied that he had ousted Anne (P).

RULE OF LAW

A cotenant in common ousts their cotenant from their jointly-held property by changing the locks on the property, not providing the other cotenant a working key, and manifesting no intention to do so.

FACTS: In 1993, Anne Parker (P) and her brother, Bo Shecut (D), became tenants in common in, among other properties, a beach house. The siblings agreed orally to manage their properties together, and they each deposited an equal amount of money in a banking account under the name Shecut Investments. The beach house was maintained as rental property through 1995, and, despite problems with the property arrangement, they treated the property as equal joint owners. Then, in 1996, without consulting Anne (P), Bo (D) made the beach house his primary residence, and ceased renting the house. According to Anne (P), Bo (D) told her in March 1996 that she was not welcome to use the beach house. He also told her he had changed the locks. Prior to this time, Anne (P) had access to the beach house when it was not being rented. Anne (P) visited the beach house on one occasion in 1997 and discovered her keys no longer worked. Bo (D) had, in fact, changed the locks after the house had been vandalized on June 13, 1997, and he admitted that after that date Anne (P) no longer had a working key. In an action to sever their tenancy in common for all their jointly-held properties, Anne (P) claimed, inter alia, that Bo (D) had ousted her from the beach house when he changed the locks and failed to give her a working key. She sought payment of rent by Bo (D) for the alleged ouster period. The Master in Equity hearing the case determined that Bo (D) had not ousted Anne (P), and that, therefore, he did not owe Anne (P) anything for his exclusive use of the beach house after June 13, 1997. The state's appellate court affirmed, and the state's highest court granted review.

ISSUE: Does a cotenant in common oust their cotenant from their jointly-held property by changing the locks on the property, not providing the other cotenant a working key, and manifesting no intention to do so?

HOLDING AND DECISION: (Pelicones, J.) Yes. A cotenant in common ousts their cotenant from their jointly-held property by changing the locks on the property, not providing the other cotenant a working key, and manifesting no intention to do so. Ouster is the actual turning out or keeping excluded a party entitled to possession of any real property. Actual ouster does not mean a physical eviction, but a possession attended with such circumstances as to evince a claim of exclusive right and title and a denial of the right of the other tenants to participate in the profits. Where one cotenant has ousted the other cotenant, and kept them out by force, the ousting cotenant is liable as a trespasser for the rental value of the property beyond their ownership share. Here, contrary to the intermediate appellate court's conclusion, Anne (P) produced evidence of ouster or exclusion, as the preponderance of the evidence demonstrated ouster. Bo's (D) testimony established that on June 13, 1997, he changed the locks to the beach house, he had not given Anne (P) a working key, and that he had no intention of giving Anne (P) a key. Bo's (D) actions in changing the locks and refusing to provide Anne (P) with a key were so distinctly hostile to Anne's (P) rights that Bo's (D) intention to disseize were clear and unmistakable. Bo's (D) actions clearly evinced his claim of exclusive right and a denial of Anne's (P) right to use the property. Accordingly, Bo (D) ousted Anne (P) on June 13, 1997, and, therefore, may be liable to Anne (P) for damages, in the form of rent, from the date of ouster. Reversed and remanded.

ANALYSIS

The acts relied upon to establish an ouster must be of an unequivocal nature, and so distinctly hostile to the rights of the other cotenants that the intention to disseize is clear and unmistakable. Only in rare, extreme cases will the ouster by one cotenant of other cotenants be implied from exclusive possession and dealings with the property, such as collection of rents and improvement of the property.

Quicknotes

DISSEIZE To remove another, usually wrongfully or by ouster, from possession of real property.

Continued on next page.

OUSTER The unlawful dispossession of a party lawfully entitled to possession of real property.

TENANTS IN COMMON Two or more people holding an interest in property, each with equal right to its use and possession; interests may be partitioned, sold, conveyed, or devised.

Sawada v. Endo

Judgment creditors (P) v. Judgment debtor (D)

Haw. Sup. Ct., 561 P.2d 1291 (1977)

NATURE OF CASE: Action to set aside conveyance of real property.

FACT SUMMARY: Endo (D) and his wife conveyed tenancy-by-the-entirety property to their son after Endo (D) had been sued.

RULE OF LAW

Tenancy-by-the-entirety property may not be reached by the separate creditors of either spouse.

FACTS: Endo (D), who had no liability insurance, severely injured Helen (P) and Masako Sawada (P). Suits for personal injuries were filed against Endo (D). Endo's (D) only real asset was real property held as a tenant by the entirety with his wife. This was conveyed to their son, for no consideration, shortly after the Sawadas (P) had filed suit. Endo (D) and his wife continued to live on the land even though they had not reserved an estate in it. The Sawadas (P) each recovered a judgment against Endo (D) but they were unable to satisfy it. The Sawadas (P) subsequently brought an action to set aside the conveyance of Endo's (D) property to the son, alleging that it was fraudulent. Endo's (D) wife had died prior to the action. Endo (D) alleged that the conveyance could not be deemed fraudulent because the separate creditor of either spouse may not reach property held as tenants by the entirety.

ISSUE: May tenancy-by-the-entirety property be reached by the separate creditors of either spouse?

HOLDING AND DECISION: (Menor, J.) No. Tenancy-by-the-entirety property may not be reached by the separate creditors of either spouse. While this is a question of first impression, and there are four separate views, we hold that the separate creditors of either spouse cannot reach property held as a tenancy by the entirety. The other views are that: (1) the creditor may reach the entire property subject to the wife's contingent right of survivorship if the husband is the debtor; (2) the creditor may reach the property subject only to the other spouse's right of survivorship; and (3) the right of survivorship may be levied upon. Tenancy-by-the-entirety property is generally the family residence and public policy considerations of promoting family solidarity, as well as *stare decisis*, favor the result reached herein. Since the Sawadas (P) could not have reached the property, the conveyance to the son was not fraudulent. Affirmed.

DISSENT: (Kidwell, J.) Under the Married Women's Act there is equality between the spouses. On this basis, the court should choose to allow creditors of either spouse to reach their right of survivorship.

ANALYSIS

In *Hurd v. Hughes*, 12 Del. Ch. at 193, the court stated in support of its decision not to allow creditors of one spouse to reach tenancy-by-the-entirety property, "But creditors are not entitled to special consideration. If the debt arose prior to the creation of the estate, the property was not a basis of credit, and if the debt arose subsequently, the creditor presumably had notice of the characteristics of the estate which limited his right to reach the property."

Quicknotes

FRAUDULENT CONVEYANCE Conveyances made within one year of filing the bankruptcy petition with intent to defraud creditors and which may be voidable.

MARRIED WOMEN'S PROPERTY ACT Legislation that secured to women the separate and independent control of their property.

STARE DECISIS Doctrine whereby courts follow legal precedent unless there is good cause for departure.

TENANCY BY THE ENTIRETY The ownership of property by a husband and wife whereby they hold undivided interests in the property with right of survivorship.

CHAPTER 6

Tradition, Tension, and Change in Landlord-Tenant Law

Quick Reference Rules of Law

Wetzel v. Glen St. Andrew Living Community, LLC

Tenant (P) v. Landlord (D)

901 F.3d 856 (7th Cir. 2018)

NATURE OF CASE: Appeal from dismissal of action for violations of the Fair Housing Act (FHA), 42 U.S.C. §§ 3601–3619.

FACT SUMMARY: Wetzel (P), who was openly lesbian, brought suit under the Fair Housing Act (Act), 42 U.S.C. §§ 3601–3619, against Glen St. Andrew Living Community, LLC (St. Andrew) (D), a residential community, alleging that St. Andrew (D) failed to provide her with non-discriminatory housing and that it retaliated against her for complaining about the abuse she suffered from other tenants. St. Andrew (D) insisted that the Act afforded Wetzel (P) no recourse because it imposes liability only on those who act with discriminatory animus, an allegation she had not expressly made as to any defendant.

RULE OF LAW

(1) Under the Fair Housing Act, 42 U.S.C. §§ 3601–3619, post-acquisition discrimination based on sexual orientation that creates a hostile housing environment can be imputed to a landlord that has the means of curtailing such a hostile environment but fails to do so, even where the landlord does not itself have discriminatory animus.

(2) Under the Fair Housing Act's § 3604(b), a tenant-resident of a residential community states a claim for post-acquisition sexual orientation discrimination against the residential community's landlord-operator where the resident alleges that the landlord's failure to respond to such discrimination by other residents adversely affected the provision of services and facilities connected to the resident's rental.

(3) Discriminatory animus is not an element of a retaliation claim under the Fair Housing Act's § 3617.

FACTS: Wetzel (P), who was openly lesbian, moved into Glen St. Andrew Living Community, LLC (St. Andrew) (D), a residential community for older adults. Her tenancy was governed by a form Tenant's Agreement (Agreement) that governed all tenancies in the community. Beyond a private apartment, the Agreement guaranteed three meals daily served in a central location, access to a community room, and use of laundry facilities. It conditioned tenancy at St. Andrew (D) on refraining from activity that St. Andrew (D) determined unreasonably interfered with the peaceful use and enjoyment of the community by other tenants or that was a direct threat to the health and safety of other individuals. It also required compliance with a "Tenant Handbook," and authorized St. Andrew (D) to institute eviction proceedings against a tenant in breach. Wetzel (P) spoke openly to staff and other residents about her sexual orientation. Many residents openly and repeatedly berated her, and even physically abused her, by, for example, causing her to be ejected from her motorized scooter, and throwing objects at her head. She was bombarded with threats, slurs, derisive comments about her family, taunts about a deadly massacre, physical violence, and spit. Wetzel (P) routinely reported the verbal and physical abuse to St. Andrew's (D) management staff (D), and initially this resulted in Wetzel (P) getting a reprieve from the abuse, but overall, the management staff (D) told her not to worry about the harassment, dismissed the conduct as accidental, denied her accounts, and branded her a liar. Then, the management staff (D) took affirmative steps to retaliate against Wetzel (P) for all her complaining. They relegated her to a less desirable dining room location, barred her from the lobby except to get coffee, and halted her cleaning services. They falsely accused her of smoking in her room in violation of St. Andrew's (D) policy and even slapped her. This caused Wetzel (P) to withdraw to her room for meals, and to avoid the common areas. After around 15 months, she brought suit under the Fair Housing Act (FHA or Act), 42 U.S.C. §§ 3601–3619, alleging that the management staff (D) and St. Andrew (D) failed to provide her with non-discriminatory housing and that it retaliated against her for complaining about the abuse and sex-based harassment she suffered from other tenants. She also brought analogous state-law claims. All of the defendants moved for dismissal, contending that the FHA does not make a landlord accountable for failing to stop tenant-on-tenant harassment unless the landlord's inaction was animated by discriminatory animus. In the alternative, the defendants argued that Wetzel's (P) harassment claim had to be dismissed insofar as it relied on 42 U.S.C. § 3604(b) because that section does not cover post-acquisition harassment claims—in other words, harassment claims brought by a tenant already occupying her home. The defendants also asserted that Wetzel's (P) retaliation claim failed because it too lacked an allegation that the defendants were motivated by discriminatory animus. The district court agreed with each of the defendants' arguments and dismissed all Wetzel's (P) claims. The district court

Continued on next page.

also relinquished supplemental jurisdiction over Wetzel's (P) state-law claims. The Seventh Circuit Court of Appeals granted review.

ISSUE:

(1) Under the Fair Housing Act, 42 U.S.C. §§ 3601–3619, can post-acquisition discrimination based on sexual orientation that creates a hostile housing environment be imputed to a landlord that has the means of curtailing such a hostile environment but fails to do so, even where the landlord does not itself have discriminatory animus?

(2) Under the Fair Housing Act's § 3604(b), does a tenant-resident of a residential community state a claim for post-acquisition sexual orientation discrimination against the residential community's landlord-operator where the resident alleges that the landlord's failure to respond to such discrimination by other residents adversely affected the provision of services and facilities connected to the resident's rental?

(3) Is discriminatory animus an element of a retaliation claim under the Fair Housing Act's § 3617?

HOLDING AND DECISION: (Wood, C.J.)

(1) Yes. Under the Fair Housing Act (FHA or Act), 42 U.S.C. §§ 3601–3619, post-acquisition discrimination based on sexual orientation that creates a hostile housing environment can be imputed to a landlord that has the means of curtailing such a hostile environment but fails to do so, even where the landlord does not itself have discriminatory animus. The Act effectively prohibits a hostile housing environment that arises from discriminatory harassment that unreasonably interferes with the use and enjoyment of a home. A hostile-housing-environment claim requires a plaintiff to show that: (1) the plaintiff endured unwelcome harassment based on a protected characteristic; (2) the harassment was severe or pervasive enough to interfere with the terms, conditions, or privileges of the plaintiff's residency, or in the provision of services or facilities; and (3) that there is a basis for imputing liability to the defendant. Here, it is undisputed that discrimination based on sexual orientation qualifies as discrimination under the FHA, so the first element is satisfied. Moving to the second element, harassment is severe or pervasive if it objectively interferes with the enjoyment of the premises or inhibits the privileges of rental. That standard requires a court to consider the totality of the circumstances, including the frequency of the discriminatory conduct, its severity, and whether it is physically threatening or humiliating rather than merely offensive. While isolated minor affronts are not enough, either a small number of "severe episodes" or a "relentless pattern of lesser harassment" may suffice. Here, it seems that based on Wetzel's (P) allegations—which the court must take as true at this stage of the proceeding, and which could be rebutted at a trial—the harassment was both severe and pervasive, and not, as the defendants contend, mere squabbles and bickering between "crotchety senior residents." Thus, the second element is satisfied. That leads to the third element, which is a matter of first impression in this circuit. To determine whether there is a basis to impute the hostile housing environment to St. Andrew (D), the starting point is the FHA's text, which makes it unlawful "[t]o discriminate... because of... sex," and forbids a housing provider to "interfere with any person in the exercise or enjoyment of... any right granted or protected by section... 3604... of this title." The focus on the actor rather than the benefitted class, St. Andrew (D) deduces, limits who can be a defendant under these sections to one accused of having discriminatory animus. However, St. Andrew (D) relies on language defining the substantive contours of an FHA action to ascertain a landlord's potential liability for actionable abuse—in other words, it is looking at what is prohibited, not who is subject to those prohibitions. Because the FHA does not address who may be liable for discrimination it prohibits, analogous anti-discrimination statutes must serve as guidance. Title VII, which governs discrimination in employment, is one such statute. It is especially apt to look to that statute for guidance since Title VII and the FHA have been described as "functional equivalents." Under operative language in Title VII identical to that of the 42 U.S.C. § 3604(b), an employer may be liable under some circumstances when its own negligence is a cause of prohibited harassment. When Congress uses the same language in two statutes having similar purposes, particularly when one is enacted shortly after the other, it is appropriate to presume that Congress intended that text to have the same meaning in both statutes. The FHA followed Title VII by four years, and St. Andrew (D) provides no reason why the FHA requires in all instances that the defendant acted with discriminatory animus when an identically worded statute has not been read in such a manner. However, because there are important differences between an employer-employee relationship, in which one is the agent of the other, and the relationship between a landlord and a tenant, in which the tenant is largely independent of the landlord, other anti-discrimination statutes need to be considered. One such statute is Title IX of the Education Amendments of 1972, 20 U.S.C. §§ 1681–1688. Like the FHA and Title VII, Title IX aims to

Continued on next page.

eradicate sex-based discrimination from a sector of society—education. The Supreme Court has held that Title IX supports a private right of action on the part of a person who experiences sex discrimination in an education program or activity receiving federal financial aid. In *Davis v. Monroe County Board of Education,* 526 U.S. 629 (1999), the Court confronted the question whether a school district's failure to respond to student-on-student harassment in its schools can support a private suit for money damages, and concluded that the district could be held accountable for its own decision to remain idle in the face of known student-on-student harassment in its schools. In addition, the Court held that the district itself subjected Davis to discrimination by remaining deliberately indifferent to known acts of student-on-student sexual harassment when the harasser was under the school's disciplinary authority, since it exercised substantial control over both the harasser and the premises on which the misconduct took place. Much of what the Court said in *Davis* can be applied readily to the housing situation. Here, the management staff (D) had actual knowledge of the severe harassment Wetzel (P) was enduring and were deliberately indifferent to it. Thus, they subjected Wetzel (P) to conduct that the FHA forbids; the Supreme Court's interpretation of analogous anti-discrimination statutes confirms that her claim against St. Andrew (D) is covered by the Act. St. Andrew (D) responds that there is no agency or custodial relationship between a landlord and tenant, and from that it reasons that a landlord has no duty to protect its tenants from discriminatory harassment. However, that is not the announced rule, which is only that the duty not to discriminate in housing conditions encompasses the duty not to permit known harassment on protected grounds. The landlord does have responsibility over the common areas of the building, which is where the majority of Wetzel's (P) harassment took place, and the incidents within her apartment occurred precisely because the landlord was exercising a right to enter. More broadly, St. Andrew (D) has a statutory duty not to discriminate. Next, St. Andrew (D) argues that it would be unfair to hold it liable for actions that it was incapable of addressing, since it could only minimally affect the conduct of its tenants who expect to live free from a landlord's interference. Control in the absolute sense, however, is not required for liability. Liability attaches because a party has available to it incentives and sanctions that can be applied to affect conduct, but fails to use them. St. Andrew (D) had many tools for remedying harassment pursuant to the Agreement, which allowed St. Andrew (D) to evict any tenant who engaged in acts or omissions that constituted a direct threat to the health and safety of other individuals, or who engaged in any activity that St. Andrew (D) determined unreasonably interfered with the peaceful use and enjoyment of the community by other tenants. The mere reminder that eviction (along with liability for attorneys' fees) was a possibility might have deterred some of the discriminatory behavior. St. Andrew (D) also could have updated the Tenant Handbook to clarify the anti-harassment and anti-abuse provisions therein. With respect to the common areas, St. Andrew (D) could have suspended privileges for tenants who failed to abide by the anti-harassment policies, instead of taking a blame-the-victim approach. St. Andrew (D) asserts that if it can be held liable under these circumstances, landlords may renounce control of the premises completely. However, that is not a practical option for a landlord of premises with common areas, especially since property law requires that landlords provide tenants a residence that is free from interference with permissible uses, even where such interference is caused by a third party, if the interference is caused on the landlord's property and the landlord could legally control the conduct that caused the interference.

(2) Yes. Under the Fair Housing Act's § 3604(b), a tenant-resident of a residential community states a claim for post-acquisition sexual orientation discrimination against the residential community's landlord-operator where the resident alleges that the landlord's failure to respond to such discrimination by other residents adversely affected the provision of services and facilities connected to the resident's rental. St. Andrew (D) argues that Wetzel's (P) § 3604(b) claim falls outside the scope of post-acquisition actions available under that section of the Fair Housing Act. In doing so, it relies on precedent that ruled that such a claim could proceed when discriminatory conduct constructively evicts a resident, and when occupancy is governed by discriminatory terms. St. Andrew (D) contends that these comprise the exclusive set of claims that can proceed post-acquisition under § 3604(b). However, St. Andrew's (D) reading of that precedent is too narrow, since the precedent merely identified two possible situations that could give rise to post-acquisition liability under § 3604(b) that were specific to the case at bar. Moreover, St. Andrew's (D) argument also ignores that § 3604(b) protects not only against discrimination in the "terms, conditions, or privileges of sale or rental," but also discrimination "in the provision of services or facilities in connection therewith." The latter language most naturally encompasses

Continued on next page.

conduct that follows acquisition, as few "services or facilities" are provided prior to the point of sale or rental, and far more attach to a resident's occupancy. Here, Wetzel (P) alleged that while management staff (D) did nothing to mitigate the harassment that she brought to their attention, other residents' harassment confined her to her room for prolonged stretches. Regular harassment also impeded her from eating the meals she had paid for at the dining hall, visiting the lobby and other common spaces, and obtaining access to the laundry room. These were concrete violations of the Agreement, which guaranteed "three-well balanced meals per day to be served in a central location," a community room, and available laundry facilities. At a minimum then, Wetzel (P) has a cognizable post-acquisition claim because discrimination affected the provision of services and facilities connected to her rental.

(3) No. Discriminatory animus is not an element of a retaliation claim under the Fair Housing Act's § 3617. Wetzel (P) claimed that management staff (D) impermissibly retaliated against her after she complained about the discriminatory harassment she was subjected to by other residents. She alleged that they did so by restricting her access to facilities and common spaces, downgrading her dining seat, halting her cleaning services, and attempting to build a case for her eviction. St. Andrew (D) asserts that this claim must fail because Wetzel (P) did not allege discriminatory animus on the part of any of the defendants. To prove retaliation, a plaintiff must show that: (1) the plaintiff engaged in protected activity; (2) the plaintiff suffered an adverse action; and (3) there was a causal connection between the two. Discriminatory animus is not something a plaintiff must prove in order to prove retaliation, except when bringing an interference claim. In fact, if the Fair Housing Act's anti-retaliation provision were interpreted to require that a plaintiff allege discriminatory animus, it would be an anomaly. The Fair Housing Act's anti-retaliation provision makes it unlawful "to coerce, intimidate, threaten, or interfere with any person in the exercise or enjoyment of, or on account of his having exercised or enjoyed, . . . any right granted or protected by § 603, 3604, 3605, or 3606 of this title." 42 U.S.C. § 3617. Thus, like all anti-retaliation provisions, it provides protections not because of who people are, but because of what they do. Reversed and remanded. The district court is also instructed to reinstate the state-law claims it dismissed for want of jurisdiction.

ANALYSIS

Wetzel (P) not only had a cognizable post-acquisition claim under the Fair Housing Act because discrimination affected the provision of services and facilities connected to her rental, but, as a matter of property law, the discrimination she suffered diminished the privileges of her rental – and § 3604(b) protects against discrimination in the ". . . privileges of sale or rental." Although she had not been constructively evicted from her apartment, occupancy of the unit was not the only privilege of rental. Use of the totality of the rented premises was another, as was the covenant of quiet enjoyment. See Restatement (Second) of Property: Landlord & Tenant § 4.3.

Quicknotes

ANIMUS Intention, will.

CONSTRUCTIVE EVICTION An action whereby the landlord renders the property unsuitable for occupancy, either in whole or in part, so that the tenant is forced to leave the premises.

COVENANT OF QUIET ENJOYMENT A promise contained in a lease or a deed that the tenant or grantee will enjoy unimpaired use of the property.

DISCRIMINATION Unequal treatment of a class of persons.

HARASSMENT Conduct directed at a particular person with the intent to inflict emotional distress and with no justification therefor; a criminal prosecution commenced without a reasonable expectation of its resulting in a conviction.

RETALIATION The infliction of injury or penalty upon another in return for an injury or harm caused by that party.

Ernst v. Conditt

Lessor (P) v. Sublessees (D)

Tenn. Ct. App., 390 S.W.2d 703 (1964)

NATURE OF CASE: Appeal from award of damages for past due rent and removal of improvements constructed on leased real property.

FACT SUMMARY: After Ernst (P) leased property to Rogers, who assigned his lease to Conditt (D), Ernst (P) sought damages from Conditt (D) for past due rent and removal of improvements.

RULE OF LAW

An assignment arises when a lessee transfers his entire interest under a lease.

FACTS: On June 18, 1960, Ernst (P) leased a tract of land to Frank D. Rogers for a term of one year and seven days, beginning on June 23, 1960. On August 4, 1960, Rogers, having sold his business to Conditt (D), executed a document that extended the term of the lease to two years, and "sublet" the premises to Conditt (D). The document, which stated that Rogers remained personally liable under the terms of the amended lease, was signed by Rogers, Ernst (P), and Conditt (D). At the end of the lease term, Ernst (P) filed suit against Conditt (D), seeking past due rent and removal of improvements constructed on the property. The trial court, holding that the document constituted an assignment, rather than a sublease, held that Conditt (D), and not Rogers, was directly liable for the monies owed.

ISSUE: Does an assignment arise when a lessee transfers his entire interest under a lease?

HOLDING AND DECISION: (Chattin, J.) Yes. Under the common-law rule, if an instrument purports to transfer the lessee's interest for the entire remainder of the lease term, an assignment has occurred. However, if the instrument purports to transfer the lessee's interest for any length of time less than the remainder of the lease term, a sublease has been established. Under the modern rule, the intention of the parties governs in construing deeds, leases, and other written transfers of property interests. Here, under both the common law and modern rule, the agreement between Rogers and Conditt (D) is an assignment, rather than a sublease. Rogers did not retain any interest in the lease, and he also did not reserve a right of reentry in the event of a breach of any of the conditions or covenants of the lease by Conditt (D). The use of the word "sublet" is not conclusive, because it appears from all the facts and circumstances and the instrument itself that all of the parties intended an assignment rather than a sublease. Affirmed.

ANALYSIS

This case illustrates the two methods used to distinguish an assignment from a sublease. Under the common-law test, an assignment arises when a lessee transfers their right to possession for the entire term of the lease. Under the less commonly used modern rule, the intention of the parties governs, although the actual words used are often persuasive in the final determination.

Quicknotes

ASSIGNMENT A transaction in which a party conveys their entire interest in property to another.

RIGHT OF REENTRY An interest in property reserved in the conveyance of a fee that gives the holder the right to resume possession of property upon the happening of a condition subsequent.

SUBLEASE A transaction in which a tenant or lessee conveys an interest in the leased premises that is less than their own or retains a reversionary interest.

Kendall v. Ernest Pestana, Inc.

Tenant (P) v. Lessor (D)

Cal. Sup. Ct., 709 P.2d 837 (1985)

NATURE OF CASE: Appeal of denial of injunctive relief and damages.

FACT SUMMARY: Ernest Pestana, Inc. (D) arbitrarily withheld permission from Kendall (P), its tenant, to sublet its leasehold.

RULE OF LAW

Absent contractual language to the contrary, a lessor may not arbitrarily withhold consent to an assignment.

FACTS: Through a series of leases and assignments, Ernest Pestana, Inc. (D) became lessor of certain hangar space at a municipal airport, with Kendall (P) and other lessees. The lease contained a consent clause regarding subleases. At one point, Kendall (P) and other lessees approached management of Ernest Pestana, Inc. (D), requesting permission to sublet. Permission was denied for no apparent commercially reasonable reason. Kendall (P) and the others sued Ernest Pestana, Inc. (D) for injunctive and declaratory relief, as well as damages. The trial court sustained Ernest Pestana, Inc.'s (D) demurrer, and the appellate court affirmed. The state supreme court granted review.

ISSUE: Absent contractual language to the contrary, may a lessor arbitrarily withhold consent to an assignment?

HOLDING AND DECISION: (Broussard, J.) No. Absent contractual language to the contrary, a lessor may not arbitrarily withhold consent to an assignment. The basic social policy in this area is that interests in property, including those of a leasehold nature, should be freely alienable. Restrictions on alienability are to be strictly construed against the lessor. The lessor does have a reversionary interest in the property and therefore is entitled to assurance that a lessee will not sublet to an irresponsible individual who may commit waste. This is a commercially reasonable rationale for denying permission to sublet. There are no doubt others. Absent some sort of reasonable basis for denial of permission, however, it seems that public policy favoring free alienability should override whatever minor interest a lessor might have in arbitrarily denying permission to sublet. The major arguments in favor of retaining the right are unpersuasive. The lessor's common-law right to look to no one but the lessee for rent has been curtailed. The argument that the lessee could have bargained for free subletting rights does not stand up to scrutiny. What the parties contemplated is not always clear, and doubts should be resolved in favor of alienability. Finally, the argument based on *stare decisis* is also to be found wanting. When changed conditions warrant overruling precedent, a court may do so. Here, since the complaint alleged that Ernest Pestana, Inc. (D) had unreasonably withheld approval, a cause of action was stated. Reversed.

ANALYSIS

The rule of the present case could well prove to have a more limited application than one might gather at first glance. The opinion does give a lessor the option of contracting in the power to arbitrarily veto a sublease. Also, it only applies to commercial leases. How the court would rule in residential leases is a matter of speculation.

Quicknotes

ASSIGNMENT A transaction in which a party conveys their entire interest in property to another.

DEMURRER The assertion that the opposing party's pleadings are insufficient and that the demurring party should not be made to answer.

FREE ALIENABILITY Unrestricted transferability.

INJUNCTIVE RELIEF A court order issued as a remedy, requiring a person to do, or prohibiting that person from doing, a specific act.

STARE DECISIS Doctrine whereby courts follow legal precedent unless there is good cause for departure.

Berg v. Wiley

Locked-out tenant (P) v. Landlord (D)

Minn. Sup. Ct., 264 N.W.2d 145 (1978)

NATURE OF CASE: Appeal from award of damages for wrongful eviction.

FACT SUMMARY: Wiley (D), lessor of commercial property to Berg (P) for the purpose of operating a restaurant thereon, locked Berg (P) out of the premises when Berg (P) delayed making certain remodeling changes to meet health code requirements.

RULE OF LAW

A landlord may not remove breaching or defaulting tenant's possessions or bar such tenant's access to the leasehold without resorting to judicial remedies.

FACTS: Wiley (D) leased commercial property to Berg (P) for the purpose of operating an establishment called "A Family Affair Restaurant." Wiley (D) made a demand that Berg (P) make certain remodeling changes to alleviate alleged health code violations and notified Berg (P) of his intention to retake possession if the changes were not made within a two-week period. At the end of the period, Berg (P) closed the restaurant and put up a sign that said "Closed for Remodeling." Wiley (D) then entered the premises in Berg's (P) absence and changed the locks. Berg (P) brought this action to recover lost profits, damage to chattels, and emotional distress due to the wrongful eviction. The trial court awarded Berg (P) $31,000 for lost profits and $3,540 for loss of chattels, and the jury specially found that Berg (P) neither abandoned nor surrendered the premises. Wiley (D) appealed.

ISSUE: May a landlord remove breaching or defaulting tenant's possessions or bar such tenant's access to the leasehold without resorting to judicial remedies?

HOLDING AND DECISION: (Rogosheske, J.) No. The evidence amply supports the jury's finding that Berg (P) did not abandon or surrender the premises, and the lockout was thus not justified on the ground of abandonment and surrender. As to self-help procedures employed by landlords to remove defaulting tenants, the common-law rule was to permit such removal if accomplished peaceably. Wiley (D) contended that only actual or threatened violence constitutes a nonpeaceable entry. This is not correct. In response to a long-applied policy to discourage landlords from taking the law into their own hands, the modern trend in this area of the law has been to bar self-help to dispossess a breaching tenant, and this represents the rule that should be applied here. A landlord may not remove breaching or defaulting tenant's possessions or bar the tenant's access to the leasehold without resorting to judicial remedies. Wiley's (D) failure to resort to judicial remedies rendered the lockout wrongful as a matter of law. Affirmed.

ANALYSIS

In this respect, the trend of the law on leaseholds is moving toward the property law concept that the covenant to pay rent and the right to quiet possession are not interdependent. The notion of the sanctity of one's home and the emphasis in recent legal history on the right of privacy have doubtless swayed legislators, commentators, and courts in this area.

Quicknotes

SELF-HELP Acting without recourse to the legal system.

TENANT IN POSSESSION A party in possession of property by title or right.

WRONGFUL EVICTION The unlawful dispossession of a person from property.

Sommer v. Kridel

Landlord (P) v. Repudiating-lessee (D)

N.J. Sup. Ct., 378 A.2d 767 (1977)

NATURE OF CASE: Appeal from award of damages for past due rent.

FACT SUMMARY: Kridel (D), the lessee, vacated the apartment, which he leased from Sommer (P), before the end of the lease term.

RULE OF LAW

A landlord has a duty to mitigate damages when he seeks to recover rents due from a defaulting tenant.

FACTS: On March 10, 1972, Kridel (D), the lessee, entered into a lease with Sommer (P) for the rental of an apartment. The term of the lease was from May 1, 1972, to April 30, 1974. One week after signing the agreement, Kridel (D) paid Sommer (P) a sum of money to satisfy the first month's rent and the security deposit. On May 19, 1972, Kridel (D) repudiated the lease and acknowledged the forfeiture of the sum already paid to Sommer (P). Although a third party was subsequently interested in renting the same apartment, Sommer (P) did not re-let the apartment until September 1, 1973. Sommer (P) brought suit against Kridel (D) to recover the total amount due for the full two-year term of the lease. The trial court's ruling in favor of Kridel (D) was reversed at the appellate level, and Kridel (D) appealed.

ISSUE: Does a landlord have a duty to mitigate damages when he seeks to recover rents due from a defaulting tenant?

HOLDING AND DECISION: (Pashman, J.) Yes. A landlord does have an obligation to make a reasonable effort to mitigate damages when a tenant defaults on a lease. The landlord's duty to mitigate consists of making reasonable efforts to re-let the apartment. The burden of proof shall be upon the landlord to establish that he used reasonable diligence in attempting to re-let the premises. Among the factors to be considered in determining whether the landlord has exercised reasonable diligence are whether the landlord offered or showed the apartment to any prospective tenants, or whether the availability of the apartment was advertised in local newspapers. Here, despite the availability of a prospective tenant who was ready, willing, and able to rent the apartment, Sommer (P) allowed the apartment to lie empty in order to increase the amount of damages. Sommer (P) could have reasonably avoided the damages that accrued by virtue of the apartment lacking a tenant. Reversed.

ANALYSIS

This case illustrates the modern trend of analyzing landlord-tenant issues under contract, rather than real property law. Increasingly, the courts agree that the contract rule requiring mitigation of damages for residential leases best effectuates notions of basic fairness and equity. The contract rule also promotes efficiency considerations by giving landlords an incentive to make use of any available property.

Quicknotes

DEFAULT Failure to carry out a legal obligation.

FORFEITURE The loss of a right or interest as a penalty for failing to fulfill an obligation.

LEASE An agreement or contract that creates a relationship between a landlord and tenant (real property) or lessor and lessee (real or personal property).

LESSEE One who leases property from a landlord, receiving the right to immediate possession of the property but not legal title.

MITIGATION Reduction in penalty.

Village Commons, LLC v. Marion County Prosecutor's Office

Landlord (P) v. Tenant (D)

Ind. Ct. App., 882 N.E.2d 210 (2008)

NATURE OF CASE: Appeal from lower court decision finding that landlord actually and constructively evicted tenant from premises after a series of unremedied water leaks over the course of several years.

FACT SUMMARY: The Marion County Prosecutor's Office (MCPO) (D) rented a basement space from Village Commons, LLC (P). Over the course of two years, there were multiple water leaks from ceilings and pipes that were not repaired by Village Commons (P). MCPO (D) eventually left the space and ceased paying rent.

RULE OF LAW

If an act or omission by the landlord materially deprives the lessee from the beneficial use or enjoyment of the leased property, the lessee may abandon the property and avoid any further obligations under the lease.

FACTS: The Marion County Prosecutor's Office (D) (MCPO) rented a basement space from Village Commons, LLC (P) in Indiana. Over the course of two years, there were multiple water leaks from ceilings and pipes that were not repaired by Village Commons (P). The leaks occurred in office spaces, evidence rooms, and bathrooms. While Village Commons (P) attempted some repairs in October 2002, it eventually informed MCPO (D) that it should cease using the most damaged areas. MCPO (D) eventually left the space in January of 2003 and ceased paying rent. Three years remained on the lease at the time, including $380,477 in unpaid rental payments. Village Commons (P) brought suit alleging that MCPO (D) breached the lease by terminating it. According to the lease, MCPO (D) was not able to terminate the lease or set off rental payments due to any damage to the premises. After a bench trial, the trial court found that Village Commons (P) constructively and actually evicted MCPO (D). Village Commons (P) appealed.

ISSUE: If an act or omission by the landlord materially deprives the lessee from the beneficial use or enjoyment of the leased property, may the lessee abandon the property and avoid any further obligations under the lease?

HOLDING AND DECISION: (Riley, J.) Yes. If an act or omission by the landlord materially deprives the lessee from the beneficial use or enjoyment of the leased property, the lessee may abandon the property and avoid any further obligations under the lease. There was substantial evidence in the record that there were repeated and unremedied water leaks in the space over the course of two years. The trial court's findings in this regard were not clearly erroneous. The constructive eviction occurred in January of 2003, when MCPO (D) was forced to leave the premises due to the leaks that Village Commons (P) continuously failed to repair. It is clear the leaks were not transitory or fleeting as Village Commons (P) argues. In addition, Village Commons (P) informed MCPO (D) to cease using portions of the leased premises where the leaks were occurring. This is a form of actual eviction. Village Commons (P) is correct that MCPO (D) did not have the power under the lease to terminate it unilaterally. However, that is not what occurred here. Rather, it was the acts and omissions of Village Commons (P) that ended MCPO's (D) obligation to pay rent under the lease. Accordingly, the trial court's findings and rulings were correct. Affirmed.

ANALYSIS

Under constructive eviction, the tenant must leave within a reasonable time period after the tenant's beneficial use of the property has been disrupted. As always, the tenant must give proper notice to the landlord of any maintenance or repair issues. Most states allow the landlord time to repair the damages. In this case, the repeated water leaks and Village Commons' (P) failure to repair them over several years, all with notice, provided substantial evidence of a constructive eviction.

Quicknotes

CONSTRUCTIVE EVICTION An action whereby the landlord renders the property unsuitable for occupancy, either in whole or in part, so that the tenant is forced to leave the premises.

EVICTION The removal of a person from possession of property.

Hilder v. St. Peter

Lessee (P) v. Lessor (D)

Vt. Sup. Ct., 478 A.2d 202 (1984)

NATURE OF CASE: Action by tenant to recover rent.

FACT SUMMARY: Hilder (P) leased from St. Peter (D) a residential premise that had serious deficiencies.

RULE OF LAW

An implied warranty of habitability exists in residential leases.

FACTS: Hilder (P) leased an apartment from St. Peter (D). During the course of tenancy, various problems with the apartment manifested themselves, including sewage leaks, nonfunctioning toilets, water leaks, falling plaster, and broken locks. These were brought to St. Peter's (D) attention, but nothing was done. Hilder (P) paid the agreed rent, but after 14 months of renting the premises, she brought an action seeking recovery of the rental monies. The trial court awarded damages to Hilder (P), and St. Peter (D) appealed.

ISSUE: Does an implied warranty of habitability exist in residential leases?

HOLDING AND DECISION: (Billings, C.J.) Yes. An implied warranty of habitability exists in residential leases. The old view of leases was that the lessee took the property as he found it. This view was proper in an agrarian society, but in a modern urban setting is improper. The modern tenant bargains for viable habitation, and if he receives less, he is not getting that for which he contracts in a lease. For this reason, a rented dwelling which is not habitable amounts to a breach of contract by the lessor, and standard contract damages are available, as well as tort damages arising therefrom. Affirmed in part, reversed in part, and remanded.

ANALYSIS

The seminal case in this area was *Green v. Superior Ct.,* 10 Cal. 3d 616 (1974). The analysis of the court there was the same as the analysis here. Residential tenancies, the court determined, were no longer land conveyances but rather contracts with certain inherent expectations embodied in them.

Quicknotes

IMPLIED WARRANTY OF HABITABILITY A warranty implied by a landlord that the premises are suitable, and will remain suitable, for habitation.

CHAPTER 7

The Land Transaction

Quick Reference Rules of Law

Hickey v. Green

Would-be buyer (P) v. Breaching seller (D)

Mass. App. Ct., 442 N.E.2d 37 (1982), *rev. denied,* 445 N.E.2d 156 (1983)

NATURE OF CASE: Appeal from grant of specific performance of a real estate contract.

FACT SUMMARY: Green (D) contended that the real estate sales contract she orally entered with Hickey (P) was unenforceable based on the Statute of Frauds.

RULE OF LAW

An oral contract for the transfer of interest in land may be specifically enforced despite the Statute of Frauds if the party seeking performance changed his or her position in reasonable reliance on the contract and injustice can be avoided only through specific performance.

FACTS: Green (D) orally agreed to sell a parcel to Hickey (P) and accepted a check as a deposit. In reliance on the contract, Hickey (P) accepted a deposit on his home from a purchaser, intending to build a new home on the land he purchased from Green (D). Subsequently, Green (D), knowing Hickey (P) sold his house in reliance on the contract, refused to sell the land to Hickey (P). Hickey (P) sued for specific performance. Green (D) defended, contending the contract was unenforceable under the Statute of Frauds. The trial court granted specific performance, and Green (D) appealed.

ISSUE: Can an oral contract for the sale of real estate be specifically enforced if the party seeking enforcement changed his or her position in reasonable reliance upon the contract?

HOLDING AND DECISION: (Cutter, J.) Yes. An oral contract for the transfer of an interest in land may be specifically enforced, despite the Statute of Frauds requirement of writing, if the party seeking enforcement changed his or her position in reasonable reliance on the contract and injustice can be avoided only through specific performance. In this case, Hickey (P) clearly changed his position in reliance on the contract by selling his house in anticipation of occupying another on Green's (D) land. The reliance was reasonable, and Green (D) was fully aware of this change in position when she refused to honor the contract. As a result, it would be manifestly unjust to refuse specific performance in this case. Therefore, it must be ordered. Remanded.

ANALYSIS

This case could have been decided on different grounds. Some commentators, spurred by dicta in the opinion, contend that the check Hickey (P) gave Green (D) as a deposit on the land constituted an adequate memorandum to satisfy the requirements of the Statute of Frauds.

Quicknotes

RELIANCE Dependence on a fact that causes a party to act or refrain from acting.

SPECIFIC PERFORMANCE An equitable remedy whereby the court requires the parties to perform their obligations pursuant to a contract.

STATUTE OF FRAUDS A statute that requires specified types of contracts to be in writing in order to be binding.

Lohmeyer v. Bower

Property buyer (P) v. Seller (D)

Kan. Sup. Ct., 227 P.2d 102 (1951)

NATURE OF CASE: Specific performance of real estate contract.

FACT SUMMARY: Lohmeyer (P), claiming unmerchantable title, sued for rescission of real estate sales contract, which Bower (D) cross-complained for specific performance.

RULE OF LAW

A party cannot convey good merchantable title if violations of covenants or zoning ordinances exist on the subject property at the time it is to be sold.

FACTS: Lohmeyer (P) contracted to buy a specific parcel of property from Bower (D). The contract provided Bower (D) would convey, by warranty deed good merchantable title, free and clear of encumbrances, but subject to all recorded restrictions and easements applying to the property. The contract further stated that Bower (D) would be allowed sufficient time to correct any defects in the title. Upon examination of the title, Lohmeyer (P) learned that the subject property was in violation of both a city zoning ordinance and a restrictive covenant previously imposed on the lot. He then sued for rescission of the contract and return of his money. Bower (D) contested Lohmeyer's (P) right to rescind and cross-complained for specific performance. The trial court held for Bower (D) and ordered specific performance of the contract. Lohmeyer (P) appealed.

ISSUE: May property that is in violation of restrictive covenants or city zoning ordinances be conveyed under good merchantable title?

HOLDING AND DECISION: (Parker, J.) No. For a title to be merchantable, it must be free from reasonable doubt and must not expose the prospective purchaser to the hazard of potential litigation. A title to property that is in violation of city zoning ordinances or restrictive covenants clearly does not meet the requirement of merchantability. It is obvious that Lohmeyer (P) would be exposed to potential litigation upon purchase of the property in question. It must be stressed that it is the existence of the violation of the ordinance and covenant that makes the title unmerchantable, not the presence of the ordinance or covenant. Furthermore, the contract provision allowing Bower (D) to correct any defect in title is immaterial in the present case, since any action Bower (D) might take to correct the title defects would materially alter the subject property and effect a breach of contract. Accordingly, the trial court is reversed and Lohmeyer's (P) plea for rescission is granted.

ANALYSIS

As stated in the principal case, the existence of zoning laws generally does not make a title unmarketable. There are several exceptions to this general principle. First, if violations of the laws exist, as in *Lohmeyer*, title may be deemed unmarketable. This is due, however, to the risk of litigation, rather than the presence of the ordinances in and of themselves. Also, where zoning regulations are imposed after the contract is entered into and where they would materially frustrate the buyer's intended use of the property, many courts will not enforce the contract. This again is done for reasons other than unmarketable title. Finally, where the seller knows of relevant zoning laws that would interfere with the buyer's intended use of the property but informs the buyer such use would be permitted, the courts will refuse to enforce the contract.

Quicknotes

EARNEST MONEY A payment made by a buyer to a seller to evidence the intent to fulfill the obligations of a contract to purchase property.

EASEMENT The right to utilize a portion of another's real property for a specific use.

MERCHANTABLE TITLE Title, that although not perfect, would be acceptable to a reasonably well-informed buyer exercising ordinary business prudence.

RESCISSION The canceling of an agreement and the return of the parties to their positions prior to the formation of the contract.

RESTRICTIVE COVENANT A promise contained in a deed to limit the uses to which the property will be made.

SPECIFIC PERFORMANCE An equitable remedy whereby the court requires the parties to perform their obligations pursuant to a contract.

Stambovsky v. Ackley

Repudiating homebuyer (P) v. Haunted house owner (D)

N.Y. App. Div., 572 N.Y.S.2d 672 (1991)

NATURE OF CASE: Appeal from the dismissal action for rescission of contract of sale.

FACT SUMMARY: Stambovsky (P), purchaser, contended that he should be entitled to rescind the contract of sale and recover his down payment because Ackley (D), the owner of the house, did not disclose that the house was haunted.

RULE OF LAW

Where a condition that has been created by the seller materially impairs the value of the contract and is peculiarly within the knowledge of the seller or unlikely to be discovered by a prudent purchaser exercising due care with respect to the subject transaction, nondisclosure constitutes a basis for rescission as a matter of equity.

FACTS: Stambovsky (P) discovered that the house he had recently contracted to purchase was widely reputed to be possessed by poltergeists, reportedly seen by Ackley (D), the seller, and members of her family on numerous occasions over the previous nine years. Stambovsky (P) promptly sought rescission of the contract of sale. The New York Supreme Court dismissed the complaint, holding that Stambovsky (P) had no remedy at law within the jurisdiction. Stambovsky (P) appealed.

ISSUE: Does nondisclosure of a condition that has been created by the seller and is peculiarly within the knowledge of the seller or unlikely to be discovered by a prudent purchaser exercising due care with respect to the subject transaction constitute a basis for rescission as a matter of equity?

HOLDING AND DECISION: (Rubin, J.) Yes. Where a condition that has been created by the seller materially impairs the value of the contract and is peculiarly within the knowledge of the seller or unlikely to be discovered by a prudent purchaser exercising due care with respect to the subject transaction, nondisclosure constitutes a basis for rescission as a matter of equity. The unusual facts of this case clearly warrant a grant of equitable relief to Stambovsky (P), who did not have any familiarity with the folklore of the village of Nyack, where the house was located, and could not readily learn that the home he had contracted to buy was haunted. New York law fails to recognize any remedy for damages incurred as a result of the seller's mere silence, applying the doctrine of *caveat emptor*. However, Ackley (D) deliberately fostered the public belief that her home was possessed. Having undertaken to inform the public-at-large, to whom she has no legal relationship, about the supernatural occurrences on her property, she may be said to owe no less a duty to her contract vendee. Where, as here, Ackley (D) not only took unfair advantage of the buyer's (P) ignorance but created and perpetuated a condition about which he was unlikely even to inquire, enforcement of the contract would be offensive to the court's sense of equity. Application of the remedy of rescission, within the bounds of the narrow exception to the doctrine of *caveat emptor*, is entirely appropriate to relieve Stambovsky (P) from the consequences of a most unnatural bargain. Reversed.

DISSENT: (Smith, J.) This court should require something more substantial than a poltergeist before discarding the doctrine of *caveat emptor*.

ANALYSIS

The doctrine of *caveat emptor* requires that a buyer act prudently to assess the fitness and value of their purchase and operates to bar the purchaser who fails to exercise due care from seeking the equitable remedy of rescission. It was apparent from this case, however, that the most careful inspection would not reveal the presence of ghosts at the premises. Therefore, there was no sound policy reason to deny the buyer relief for failing to discover a state of affairs that the most prudent purchaser would not be expected even to contemplate.

Quicknotes

CAVEAT EMPTOR Let the buyer beware; doctrine that a buyer purchases something at their own risk.

EQUITY Fairness; justice; the determination of a matter consistent with principles of fairness and not in strict compliance with rules of law.

NONDISCLOSURE The failure to communicate certain facts to another person.

POLTERGEIST Noise; ghost responsible for making noises.

RESCISSION The canceling of an agreement and the return of the parties to their positions prior to the formation of the contract.

Jones v. Lee

Real estate sellers (P) v. Real estate buyers (D)

N.M. Ct. App., 971 P.2d 858 (1998)

NATURE OF CASE: Suit to recover damages for breach of a contract to purchase real estate.

FACT SUMMARY: The Lees (D) entered a written contract to buy real estate owned by the Joneses (P) for $610,000. Three months after the Lees (D) backed out of the deal, the Joneses (P) sold the property for $540,000.

RULE OF LAW

The non-defaulting party under a real estate contract is entitled to an award of damages following a breach of the contract.

FACTS: The parties entered a written agreement under which the Lees (D) would buy a home owned by the Joneses (P) for $610,000, with the Lees (D) paying $6,000 in earnest money to solidify the deal. Two months after entering the written contract, the Lees (D) informed the Joneses (P) that they could not go through with the purchase for financial reasons. The Joneses (P) rejected the Lees' (D) proposed termination agreement and sold the home three months after the breach for $540,000. The Joneses (P) sued the Lees (D) for breach of contract, requesting an award of damages. The trial court returned judgment for the Joneses (P) for the $70,000 difference between the contract price and the actual sale price, for special damages in the amount of $4,109, and for punitive damages, with a total judgment in the amount of $157,118.94. The Lees (D) appealed.

ISSUE: Is the non-defaulting party under a real estate contract entitled to an award of damages following a breach of the contract?

HOLDING AND DECISION: (Donnelly, J.) Yes. The non-defaulting party under a real estate contract is entitled to an award of damages following a breach of the contract. A seller generally can choose from three remedies when a buyer breaches an agreement to purchase real estate: (1) rescission of the contract, (2) specific performance, or (3) damages. In this case, by choosing to pursue damages, the Joneses (P) had the burden of proving the damages they sought. New Mexico analyzes such damages claims under the "loss of the bargain" rule, which requires a showing of the difference between the purchase price and the property's market value when the breach occurred. The parties here agreed that the market value was $610,000 when the breach occurred—which means that the Joneses (P) suffered no compensatory damages, the Lees (D) argued, because the market value and the contract price were identical when the breach occurred. Such an identity of value normally limits a seller's recovery to nominal damages or retention of the buyer's earnest money; the exception to this rule occurs when, as here, the sellers also have incurred special damages. The trial court in this case failed to enter the required findings of fact on the date of the breach and the property's market value on that date. The case therefore must be remanded on the issue of compensatory damages so that the trial court can enter the appropriate factual determinations. Further, the trial court correctly awarded the Joneses (P) special damages for $1,859 in expenses incurred because of the home's solar system and heating warranty. Such expenses are recoverable if they were reasonably foreseeable, and the purchase agreement rendered them reasonably foreseeable in this case. Special damages here also properly included $2,250 for half of the interest on mortgage payments made by the Joneses (P) after the breach. These damages, too, were reasonably foreseeable. Finally, the record also supports an award of punitive damages against the Lees (D). When they breached the contract, claiming "financial reasons" for terminating the transaction, their checking account held approximately $577,000, and their monthly income totaled more than $16,000. The record shows further that the Lees (D) intimidated the Joneses (P) to induce them to accept the termination agreement. Under the circumstances, the Lees (D) breached the contract in a wanton and utterly reckless manner, thereby justifying an award of punitive damages. Affirmed in part; vacated in part and remanded.

ANALYSIS

On remand, the trial judge in *Jones* must calculate compensatory damages by choosing between the parties' stipulated value for the property at the time of the breach—$610,000—and the eventual actual sale price of $540,000. Though the parties' purpose in stipulating to the property's value at the time of the breach was unclear, a stipulation on a fact-issue should receive special, deferential consideration when a trial court establishes a factual record. The Joneses' (P) compensatory damages on remand thus were likely limited to retention of the Lees' (D) earnest money because the market value and contract price at the time of the breach would have been identical.

Continued on next page.

Quicknotes

EARNEST MONEY A payment made by a buyer to a seller to evidence the intent to fulfill the obligations of a contract to purchase property.

MEASURE OF DAMAGES The quantum of damages, as determined in litigation, sustained or incurred by a party to the litigation.

PUNITIVE DAMAGES Damages exceeding the actual injury suffered for the purposes of punishment of the defendant, deterrence of the wrongful behavior or comfort to the plaintiff.

SPECIAL DAMAGES Damages caused by a specific act that are not the usual consequence of that act and which must be specifically pled and proven.

Brown v. Lober

Purchaser (P) v. Seller's executor (D)

Ill. Sup. Ct., 389 N.E.2d 1188 (1979)

NATURE OF CASE: Appeal from award of damages for breach of the covenant of quiet enjoyment.

FACT SUMMARY: Brown (P) acquired the subject property under a general warranty deed despite the fact a two-thirds interest in mineral rights had previously been reserved.

RULE OF LAW

The mere existence of a superior title does not constitute a breach of the covenant of quiet enjoyment.

FACTS: Brown (P) acquired a parcel of property from Bost under a general warranty deed containing no exceptions. Unknown to Brown (P), the property contained a reservation of a two-thirds interest in mineral rights by Bost's grantor. Seventeen years after purchasing the land, Brown (P) contracted to sell the mineral rights for $6,000, but was forced to lower the price to $2,000 when the parties learned of the prior reservation of rights. Because the 10-year statute of limitations prevented Brown (P) from suing for breach of warranty, he chose to sue Bost's executor, Lober (D), for breach of the covenant of quiet enjoyment of the premises. In effect, Brown (P) claimed that the existence of the rights reservation constituted a constructive eviction. The trial court held for Lober (D) and the appellate court reversed. The case was then appealed to the Illinois Supreme Court.

ISSUE: Does the mere existence of a paramount title in a third-party constitute a breach of the covenant of quiet enjoyment by the vender of property?

HOLDING AND DECISION: (Underwood, J.) No. Brown (P) was in no way hindered from the peaceable possession and enjoyment of his property by someone holding superior title. The mere fact that he had to renegotiate his contract for the assignment of mineral rights does not constitute an interference with quiet enjoyment. Thus, the suit was premature. The covenant of quiet enjoyment guarantees only possession and enjoyment of the premises, not a perfect title. Since there was no interference with the use of the property or assertion of an adverse title, there was no breach. The reservation of mineral rights was a matter of public record and Brown (P) could therefore have maintained an action for breach of warranty. However, he let the statute of limitations run and lost his opportunity. He may not now prevail on a premature claim of breach of quiet enjoyment. Reversed.

ANALYSIS

A general warranty deed typically contains the following five covenants: covenant of seisin, covenant of right to convey, covenant against encumbrances, covenant of quiet enjoyment, and covenant of warranty. Sometimes a sixth covenant, of further assurances, is included in the deed. This states that the covenantor will perform any reasonably necessary acts to perfect the purchaser's title. The general warranty deed covenants serve to warrant title against imperfections that occurred before the time which the grantor assumed their title, as well as during their time of title. The first three covenants (seisin, right to convey, and against encumbrances) are deemed present covenants. Thus, a breach occurs, if at all, at the time the covenant is made, and a cause of action arises at that time. In contrast, the last three covenants are future covenants and are not breached until the time the covenantee's possession is actually interfered with.

Quicknotes

COVENANT AGAINST ENCUMBRANCES A guarantee in a contract that the interest in property being conveyed is unencumbered.

COVENANT OF QUIET ENJOYMENT A promise contained in a lease or a deed that the tenant or grantee will enjoy unimpaired use of the property.

COVENANT OF SEISIN A promise that the conveyor of property has the lawful right to convey the interest they are attempting to transfer.

COVENANTEE A party for whom a promise is made pursuant to a written agreement.

FUTURE COVENANTS A written promise to do, or to refrain from doing, a particular activity in the future.

GENERAL WARRANTY DEED A deed that guarantees the conveyor possesses that title that they purport to convey.

PRESENT COVENANTS Covenant to do an act at the present moment.

RESERVATION OF RIGHTS A clause in a deed or other instrument reserving particular rights to the grantor of the property.

Murphy v. Financial Development Corp.

Defaulting mortgagor (P) v. Foreclosing mortgagee (D)

N.H. Sup. Ct., 495 A.2d 1245 (1985)

NATURE OF CASE: Appeal from order setting aside a foreclosure.

FACT SUMMARY: Murphy (P) contended that Financial Development Corp. (Financial) (D) failed to use due diligence in attempting to get a reasonable price for his property in a foreclosure sale.

RULE OF LAW

Mere compliance with statutory requirements may not discharge a mortgagee's duty to exercise good faith and due diligence in selling the property at foreclosure.

FACTS: Murphy (P) was the mortgagor of his residence, the mortgagee being Financial Development Corp. (Financial) (D). Murphy (P) defaulted on loan payments and attempted several times to renegotiate and refinance the debt. Financial (D) cooperated by postponing the foreclosure sale at least once, but subsequently held the sale after proper notice. No one other than Murphy (P) appeared at the sale, at which Financial (D) pledged its mortgage and obtained title to the property. Murphy (P) sued to set aside the sale on the basis that Financial (D) failed to use due diligence in obtaining a fair price for the property. A special master was appointed who held for Murphy (P) and awarded attorney fees. Financial (D) appealed.

ISSUE: Does compliance with foreclosure sale statutes fulfill the mortgagee's duties to the mortgagor?

HOLDING AND DECISION: (Douglas, J.) No. Mere compliance with statutory requirements may not discharge a mortgagee's duty to exercise good faith and due diligence in selling the property at foreclosure. A mortgagee has an affirmative duty to act as a fiduciary toward the mortgagor's equity in the home. In this case, $27,000 was pledged for property worth twice that. No other bids were affirmatively solicited. Thus the base notice requirements did not discharge the mortgagee's duties. However, no bad faith was present, and thus no attorney fees were recoverable. Affirmed in part, reversed in part, and remanded.

ANALYSIS

The property was sold soon after the foreclosure sale, but before any controversy had arisen. The buyer clearly was a bona fide purchaser; thus, title to the property was not at issue here. Damages were set at the difference between a fair price for the property and the price obtained at foreclosure. This differred from the master's ruling, which used the fair market value as a starting point.

Quicknotes

BONA FIDE PURCHASER A party who purchases property in good faith and for valuable consideration without notice of a defect in title.

DUE DILIGENCE The standard of care as would be taken by a reasonable person in accordance with the attendant facts and circumstances.

FAIR MARKET VALUE The price of particular property or goods a buyer would offer and a seller accept in the open market, following full disclosure.

FORECLOSURE An action to recover the amount due on a mortgage of real property where the owner has failed to meet their mortgage repayment obligations, terminating the owner's interest in the property, which must then be sold to satisfy the debt.

POWER OF SALE MORTGAGE A clause contained in a mortgage granting the mortgagee the authority to sell the property that is the subject of the mortgage upon default of the mortgage payments.

PROMISSORY NOTE A written promise to tender a stated amount of money at a designated time and to a designated person.

U.S. Bank National Association v. Ibanez

Purported mortgage holder (P) v. Home owner (D)

Mass. Sup. Jud. Ct., 941 N.E.2d 40 (2010)

NATURE OF CASE: Appeal from lower court decision finding that purported mortgage holders, attempting to foreclose on two properties, failed to demonstrate they actually held the mortgage on the properties at issue.

FACT SUMMARY: U.S. Bank National Association (U.S. Bank) (P) and Wells Fargo (P) foreclosed on two properties. The mortgages on each of the properties had been sold and assigned multiple times during their existence. After the foreclosure process, U.S. Bank (P) and Wells Fargo (P) brought actions in state court seeking a declaration that they were the owners in fee simple of the two properties.

RULE OF LAW

Any foreclosure proceeding initiated by a party that lacks the jurisdiction and authority to conduct the foreclosure shall be null and void.

FACTS: Antonio Ibanez (D) purchased a home in Springfield, Massachusetts, for $103,500 with a loan secured by a mortgage to the lender, Rose Mortgage, Inc. The mortgage was then assigned multiple times to different mortgage companies. In 2006, the latest holder of the mortgage pooled it with 1,200 other mortgages into a trust known as a mortgage-backed security. This process, known as a securitization, allowed these trusts to be bought and sold by investors. Eventually, U.S. Bank National Association (U.S. Bank) (P) purchased a mortgage-backed security that allegedly included Ibanez's (D) mortgage. That transaction occurred via a private placement memorandum. That document states the trust would include all mortgages placed into it and those mortgages would be reflected on an attached schedule of mortgages. A similar scenario played out with a mortgage taken out by Mark and Tammy LaRace (D). It was also pooled into a mortgage-backed security and eventually purchased by Wells Fargo (P). U.S. Bank (P) and Wells Fargo (P) foreclosed on the two properties in 2007, a process that does not require judicial approval. The foreclosure process included the properties being placed up for sale and then purchased by U.S. Bank (P) and Wells Fargo (P), respectively. (There is no dispute both homeowners defaulted on their loans.) After the foreclosure process, U.S. Bank (P) and Wells Fargo (P) brought actions in state court seeking a declaration that they were the owners in fee simple of the two properties. At the trial court level, the judge found both plaintiffs failed to prove they had the authority to foreclose on the properties. Specifically, using U.S. Bank (P) as an example, that entity did not provide the court with a schedule or any documentation that the Ibanez (D) mortgage was actually included in the mortgage-backed security that U.S. Bank (P) purchased in 2006. U.S. Bank (P) and Wells Fargo (P) appealed and the case was transferred to the Massachusetts Supreme Judicial Court.

ISSUE: Is any foreclosure proceeding initiated by a party that lacks the jurisdiction and authority to conduct the foreclosure null and void?

HOLDING AND DECISION: (Gants, J.) Yes. Any foreclosure proceeding initiated by a party that lacks the jurisdiction and authority to conduct the foreclosure shall be null and void. In these actions to quiet title to property, U.S. Bank (P) and Wells Fargo (P) have the burden of proving they were the fee simple owners of the properties. To do so, the plaintiffs need to demonstrate that they properly adhered to the statutory foreclosure process in Massachusetts. Massachusetts, like many states, does not require judicial approval before an entity forecloses on a property. The mortgagor/homeowner may petition a court to enjoin the foreclosure if he or she desires. Any mortgage includes a power of sale. However, one who sells under a power of sale must strictly follow the terms. Powers of sale have restrictions on who can actually foreclose on the property. The foreclosure can be exercised only by a mortgagee or its successors or assigns. U.S. Bank (P) claims that the private placement memorandum it received when it purchased the mortgage-backed security in 2006 made U.S. Bank (P) the holder of the Ibanez (D) mortgage. However, U.S. Bank (P) did not provide the lower court with a schedule or any documentation that the Ibanez (D) mortgage was actually included in the mortgage-backed security that U.S. Bank (P) purchased in 2006. Read closely, the private placement memorandum reveals an intent that certain mortgages would be included in the pool, but there simply was no evidence attached to that document stating which mortgages were included, if any. The last assignment on the record of Ibanez's (D) mortgage was to an entity called Option One. Accordingly, U.S. Bank (P) did not have the authority to foreclose on the mortgage. Wells Fargo (D) similarly could not demonstrate it actually held the mortgage on the LaRace (D) property. Affirmed.

CONCURRENCE: (Cordy, J.) Assignments of mortgages need not be recorded to be effective. However, the assignment or similar transaction must actually occur. In these complicated mortgage-backed security

Continued on next page.

transactions, the onus is on the mortgage holders to demonstrate that the assignment has passed to them before a foreclosure can proceed.

ANALYSIS

This litigation and others like it were spawned after the housing crisis began in 2008. With the rate of foreclosures skyrocketing around the country, courts began to examine more closely the complicated array of transactions that occur after a homeowner takes out a mortgage. This particular decision resulted in a large number of foreclosures being placed into legal limbo until the foreclosing parties could remedy the defects in the various transactions.

Quicknotes

FORECLOSURE An action to recover the amount due on a mortgage of real property where the owner has failed to meet the mortgage obligations, terminating the owner's interest in the property which must then be sold to satisfy the debt.

MORTGAGE An interest in land created by a written instrument providing security for the payment of a debt or the performance of a duty.

MORTGAGEE Party to whom an interest in property is given in order to secure a loan.

MORTGAGOR Party who grants an interest in property in order to secure a loan.

Horne v. Harbour Portfolio

Class of home buyers (P) v. Real estate company (D)

304 F. Supp. 3d 1332 (N.D. Ga. 2018)

NATURE OF CASE: Ruling on motion to dismiss for 12 claims brought against real estate company under the Fair Housing Act.

FACT SUMMARY: Harbour Portfolio VI, LP and Harbour Portfolio VII, LP (Harbour) (D), a real estate company and mortgage lender, sold foreclosed homes to African-American buyers in predominately African-American neighborhoods. Buyers who purchased homes from Harbour (D) received unfavorable mortgage rates and terms and were responsible for significant repairs and maintenance on homes that were in poor condition. Twelve of these buyers (P) sued Harbour (D) for discrimination under the Fair Housing Act, alleging that its lending policies had a disparate impact and that Harbour (D) engaged in intentional targeting.

RULE OF LAW

(1) Evidence that a lender's policy of purchasing homes only in predominately African-American neighborhoods and advertising its properties only through yard signs and word of mouth is an adequate basis for a prima facie case of disparate impact under the Fair Housing Act.

(2) Evidence that home buyers were targeted by a lender who advertised properties only through yard signs and word of mouth, plus evidence of the racial demographics in the relevant community, is an adequate basis for a prima facie case of intentional targeting under the Fair Housing Act.

FACTS: Harbour Portfolio VI, LP and Harbour Portfolio VII, LP (Harbour) (D), a real estate company and mortgage lender, purchased nearly all its properties from Fannie Mae's portfolio of "real estate owned" properties, which are homes that were foreclosed upon but not purchased by third parties. Harbour (D) did not make any repairs to the homes, which were often in poor or uninhabitable condition, before selling them for four to five times the purchase price. The homes were in predominately African-American neighborhoods. The buyers (P) purchased the homes under a Contract for Deed (CFD) agreement with a 9.9–10% interest rate over a 30-year term. Additionally, the buyers (P) assumed the burden of home repairs, maintenance, property taxes, and homeowner's insurance. In the event of default, the CFDs contained a forfeiture clause that would give Harbour (D) the right to cancel the contract, keep all amounts paid, and evict the buyer without compensation. Harbour (D) advertised by placing signs in front of properties and relying upon word of mouth; this marketing scheme was designed to attract African-American buyers. Twelve buyers (P) brought claims under the Fair Housing Act (FHA), with some of the buyers filing additional claims of discrimination under other applicable statutes. The buyers (P) alleged that Harbour (D) engaged in reverse redlining—a form of discrimination where plaintiffs are given credit on unfair terms because of their race and geographic area—because Harbour (D) drew African-American buyers to predominately African-American neighborhoods. Harbour (D) filed a motion to dismiss the 12 claims brought against it under the FHA.

ISSUE:

(1) Is evidence that a lender's policy of purchasing homes only in predominately African-American neighborhoods and advertising its properties only through yard signs and word of mouth an adequate basis for a prima facie case of disparate impact under the Fair Housing Act?

(2) Is evidence that home buyers were targeted by a lender who advertised properties only through yard signs and word of mouth, plus evidence of the racial demographics in the relevant community, an adequate basis for a prima facie case of intentional targeting under the Fair Housing Act?

HOLDING AND DECISION: (Story, J.)

(1) Yes. Evidence that a lender's policy of purchasing homes only in predominately African-American neighborhoods and advertising its properties only through yard signs and word of mouth is an adequate basis for a prima facie case of disparate impact under the Fair Housing Act (FHA). Harbour (D) argued that the buyers (P) failed to state an adequate claim for disparate impact under the FHA, because they did not meet the four-factor test established by *Texas Department of Housing & Community Affairs v. Inclusive Communities Project, Inc.*, 35 S. Ct. 2507 (2015). The Court in *Inclusive Communities* ruled that a plaintiff must (1) show statistically imbalanced lending patterns that adversely impact a minority group; (2) identify a facially neutral policy followed by the defendant during the same period of time; (3) show how that policy is artificial, arbitrary, and unnecessary; and (4) allege how that policy was a substantial cause of the adverse lending patterns. The buyers (P) have shown sufficient evidence of each factor. First, the buyers (P) alleged that Harbour

Continued on next page.

(D) purchased homes exclusively from Fannie Mae, whose sales in Fulton and DeKalb County, Georgia, were located in census tracks with a mean of 71.37% African-American residents. Meanwhile, non-Fannie Mae census tracts had only a mean of 48.37% African-American residents. Additionally, the buyers (P) alleged that Harbour's (D) policies were facially neutral, but because Fannie Mae properties constituted less than a quarter of the foreclosure properties available, a jury could reasonably infer that the policy of purchasing from Fannie Mae was arbitrary. The buyers (P) presented adequate evidence demonstrating that Harbour (D) intentionally targeted African-American home buyers by advertising properties via signs in front of each house for sale and by word of mouth, which were policies designed to reach the primarily African-American residents of communities where Harbour (D) had purchased properties.

(2) Yes. Evidence that home buyers were targeted by a lender who advertised properties only through yard signs and word of mouth, plus evidence of the racial demographics in the relevant community, is an adequate basis for a prima facie case of intentional targeting under the Fair Housing Act. In reverse redlining cases, if a plaintiff presents direct evidence that a lender intentionally targeted a plaintiff for an unfair loan on basis of his or her protected class, the plaintiff is not required to make an additional showing that the lender makes loans on more favorable terms to others. Accordingly, Harbour's (D) argument that the buyers (P) failed to show they were treated differently than similarly situated people outside of their protected class is without merit.

Motion to dismiss denied.

ANALYSIS

Reverse redlining is the subject of a significant amount of fair housing litigation. In 2019, the City of Philadelphia and Wells Fargo Bank settled a 2017 claim alleging that Wells Fargo targeted African-American and Latinx neighborhoods with predatory loans, including exorbitant fees and high interest rates. Wells Fargo paid $10 million to settle the claim, $8.5 million of which went to grants to assist home buyers with closing costs, while $1 million went to the city's foreclosure prevention program and $500,000 went towards a Philadelphia program to maintain and clean vacant land.

Quicknotes

PRIMA FACIE CASE An action where the plaintiff introduces sufficient evidence to submit the issue to the judge or jury for determination.

REDLINING Practice in which a loan provider or insurer designates neighborhoods as poor financial risks and refuses to provide loans or insurance on properties in the neighborhoods.

CHAPTER 8

Title Assurance

Quick Reference Rules of Law

Luthi v. Evans

Subsequent assignee of oil and gas leases (P) v. Prior assignee (D)

Kan. Sup. Ct., 576 P.2d 1064 (1978)

NATURE OF CASE: Appeal from award of lease interest.

FACT SUMMARY: Grace V. Owens assigned her interest in all her Coffey County leases "whether or not the same are specifically enumerated above . . ." to International Tours, Inc. (D); Owens subsequently assigned a lease, unenumerated in the first assignment, to J.R. Burris (P).

RULE OF LAW

An instrument that describes the property to be conveyed as "all of the grantor's property in a certain county," is not sufficiently specific as to be effective against subsequent purchasers and mortgagees, unless they have actual knowledge of the transfer.

FACTS: On February 1, 1971, Grace V. Owens assigned all her interests in seven oil and gas leases located in Coffey County, Kansas, to International Tours, Inc. (D). The instrument further assigned Owens's interest in all Coffey County oil and gas leases "whether or not the same are specifically enumerated above. . . ." (This is an example of a "Mother Hubbard" clause.) The assignment was recorded on February 16, 1971. On January 30, 1975, Owens assigned a Coffey County oil and gas lease that had not been specifically enumerated in the first instrument to J.R. Burris (P). Burris's (P) personal check of the records and his abstract of title did not reveal the prior assignment. The district court found the recording of the first assignment to be insufficient notice to a subsequent innocent purchaser of a lease not specifically enumerated therein. The court of appeals reversed, and this appeal followed.

ISSUE: Does the recording of an instrument that uses a "Mother Hubbard" clause to describe the property conveyed constitute constructive notice to a subsequent purchaser?

HOLDING AND DECISION: (Prager, J.) No. The purpose of statutes authorizing the recording of conveyances is to provide notice to subsequent purchasers of instruments affecting specific tracts of land. Thus, the land conveyed must be described with sufficient specificity, either in the instrument itself or by specific reference to other recorded conveyances. Instruments containing a "Mother Hubbard" clause, while valid as between parties, thereto, are not sufficient description of the land conveyed to be effective against subsequent purchasers and mortgagees, unless they have actual knowledge of the transfer. Here, the conveying instrument used a "Mother Hubbard" clause to describe the oil and gas lease in question. This was an insufficient description; further, Burris (P) had no actual knowledge of the transfer. Reversed.

ANALYSIS

Generally, the description in a recorded instrument must be sufficient to point out the property to one examining the record. If the property cannot be located and identified, as would be the case, for example, where the description is no more than "all other lands owned by the vendor in this state," then the sale is void as to third persons who deal upon the faith of the public records.

Quicknotes

ABSTRACT OF TITLE A summary of the history of title to a certain parcel of real property, including and transfers of, or liens against, such property.

CONVEYANCE The transfer of property, or title to property, from one party to another party.

RECORD AN INSTRUMENT The recording of a document in the public record.

Messersmith v. Smith

Prior grantee (P) v. Subsequent purchaser (D)

N.D. Sup. Ct., 60 N.W.2d 276 (1953)

NATURE OF CASE: Action to quiet title.

FACT SUMMARY: In a race-notice recording statute jurisdiction, subsequent bona fide purchasers failed to record their deeds properly before a prior purchaser properly recorded.

RULE OF LAW

An unacknowledged deed does not qualify for recordation and therefore the recording does not give constructive notice to subsequent purchasers.

FACTS: Caroline Messersmith and her nephew, Frederick Messersmith (P), each owned an undivided one-half interest in land. On April 23, 1951, Smith (D) negotiated an oil and gas lease with Caroline Messersmith, which was recorded on May 14, 1951. On May 7, 1951, Caroline Messersmith executed a mineral deed to the land, which was recorded on May 26, 1951. On its face, the deed indicated that it had been acknowledged, but Caroline Messersmith had not, in fact, acknowledged it. On May 7, 1946, Caroline Messersmith delivered a quit-claim deed to Frederick Messersmith (P) for the land, and the deed was recorded on July 9, 1951. On May 9, 1951, Smith (D) executed the mineral deed he had received from Caroline Messersmith to Seale, which was recorded on May 26, 1951. Seale asserted this deed which Smith (D) got from Caroline Messersmith and which was recorded on May 26, 1951, as cutting off Frederick Messersmith's (P) prior deed which was not recorded until July 9, 1951. The jurisdiction had a race-notice recording statute.

ISSUE: Does a deed that is unacknowledged, though recorded, impart constructive notice to the world so to prevent a subsequent purchaser from being a bona fide purchaser without notice?

HOLDING AND DECISION: (Morris, C.J.) No. The recording of an instrument affecting title that does not meet the statutory requirements of the recording laws affords no constructive notice. The deed from Caroline to Smith (D) contained a certificate of acknowledgment on its face, but that is not conclusive as to its actual acknowledgment. Here, the grantor, Caroline, did not appear before an officer to acknowledge the execution of the instrument. Caroline did not acknowledge the deed to Smith (D) and, therefore, the deed was not properly recorded by Smith (D), and Seale (D) could not be a subsequent purchaser in good faith. Seale (D) must rely wholly upon his position as an innocent purchaser in compliance with the recording statutes. Therefore, Frederick Messersmith's (P) title was not cut off by the conveyance to Smith (D) and Seale. Reversed. Rehearing denied.

ANALYSIS

An unacknowledged deed does not give constructive notice because it does not qualify for recordation. Therefore, Smith's (D) deed and Seale's deed were not properly recorded. They did not prevail over Messersmith (P) because the jurisdiction had a race-notice statute, which means that the first to record a deed without actual or constructive notice of a prior deed will prevail.

Quicknotes

ACTION TO QUIET TITLE Equitable action to resolve conflicting claims to an interest in real property.

BONA FIDE PURCHASER A party who purchases property in good faith and for valuable consideration without notice of a defect in title.

CONSTRUCTIVE NOTICE Knowledge of a fact that is imputed to an individual who was under a duty to inquire and who could have learned of the fact through the exercise of reasonable prudence.

RACE-NOTICE RECORDING STATUTE Statute determining priority of interests in real property whereby a person who records first has a preference over others receiving an interest in the property from the same source only if the party received no notice of the prior unrecorded conveyance.

Board of Education of Minneapolis v. Hughes

Subsequent purchaser (P) v. Prior grantee (D)

Minn. Sup. Ct., 136 N.W. 1095 (1912)

NATURE OF CASE: Action to determine adverse claims to certain real property.

FACT SUMMARY: Hughes (D) and Duryea & Wilson purchased the same lot from Hoerger. Hughes's (D) deed did not contain his name. Hughes (D) inserted it later. Duryea & Wilson sold to Board of Education of Minneapolis (P). Hughes's (D) deed was recorded before Duryea & Wilson's, but Board of Education of Minneapolis's (P) was recorded before either Hughes's (D) or Duryea & Wilson's.

RULE OF LAW

The recording of a deed from a grantee in an unrecorded deed to a third person is not notice of the prior unrecorded deed to a subsequent purchaser.

FACTS: On May 17, 1906, Hoerger executed and delivered a deed to convey certain land to Hughes (D). Hughes's (D) name was not inserted as grantee. Hughes (D) filled it in shortly before recording the deed on December 16, 1910. On April 27, 1909, Duryea & Wilson were delivered a deed by Hoerger for the same lot. This deed was recorded on December 21, 1910. On November 19, 1909, Duryea & Wilson delivered a deed to the Board of Education of Minneapolis (P) for the lot. This deed was recorded on January 27, 1910.

ISSUE: Where a grantor has made a prior deed that has not been recorded, does the recording of a deed from the grantee to a third person constitute notice of the unrecorded deed to a subsequent purchaser?

HOLDING AND DECISION: (Bunn, J.) No. There are two questions that must be decided here. The first is whether Hughes's (D) deed became operative since his name was not inserted. A deed that does not name a grantee is inoperative as a conveyance until the grantee's name is legally inserted. Such a deed becomes operative without a new execution or acknowledgment if the grantee, with express or implied authority from the grantor, inserts his name in the blank space for the grantee. The authority may be parole and implied from the circumstances. In this case Hughes's (D) had such authority, in the absence of evidence showing the lack of it. Hence, Hughes's (D) deed became operative when he inserted his name. The second question to be decided is whether Hughes (D) is a subsequent purchaser whose deed was duly recorded. Hughes's (D) conveyance dates from the time he filled in the blank space, which was after the deed from Hoerger to Duryea & Wilson. Hence, Hughes (D) was a subsequent purchaser. Record of a deed from a prior grantee is not notice to a subsequent purchaser of a prior unrecorded conveyance by the grantor to the prior grantee. In this case the recording of Duryea's deed to Board of Education (P) did not act as notice to Hughes (D). It was necessary that the deed to Board of Education (P) be recorded before the deed to Hughes (D); it was also necessary that the deed to Duryea & Wilson be recorded first. Order reversed and new trial granted.

ANALYSIS

As between the parties, at least, a blank paper signed, sealed, and delivered and which is subsequently filled in without authority from the grantor will not pass title to any property. However, although blank when signed and sealed, if the deed is written with the grantor's authority and so delivered, it will be operative as a deed.

Quicknotes

CONVEYANCE The transfer of property, or title to property, from one party to another party.

ESTOPPEL An equitable doctrine precluding a party from asserting a right to the detriment of another who justifiably relied on the conduct.

GRANTEE The party to whom property is conveyed.

GRANTOR Conveyor of property or settlor of a trust.

IMPLIED AUTHORITY Inferred power granted to an agent to act on behalf of the principal in order to effectuate the principal's objective.

NULLITY An act having no legal effect.

RECORDATION The recording of a document in the public record.

Guillette v. Daly Dry Wall, Inc.

v. Subsequent purchaser of unrestricted lot (D)

Mass. Sup. Jud. Ct., 325 N.E.2d 572 (1975)

NATURE OF CASE: Appeal from injunction in suit to enforce restrictive covenants.

FACT SUMMARY: Daly Dry Wall (Daly) (D), a grantee who took without knowledge of restrictions binding neighboring lots that had been deeded by a common grantor, proceeded to ignore the restrictions.

RULE OF LAW

A grantee is bound by restrictions in deeds to its neighbors from a common grantor, even if it takes without actual notice and his deed does not mention them, if the grantor has placed in writing the same restrictions on his remaining land.

FACTS: In 1967 and 1968, Guillette (P), the Walcotts (P), and the Paraskivas (P) bought individual lots in the same subdivision. Each of these three deeds either set out restrictions maintaining the subdivision as a residential area for single-family dwellings or incorporated such restrictions by reference. Additionally, the Guillette (P) deed provided that the lots retained by the seller were similarly restricted. Daly (D) purchased a lot in 1972 and the deed contained no restrictions; though the deed referred to the same recorded plan, this plan was also silent as to restrictions. After Daly (D) learned of the restrictions, it obtained a building permit for 36 apartment type units. Guillette (P) and the others sought to enjoin the construction. Daly (D) appealed the injunction and the case was transferred to this court.

ISSUE: Is a grantee bound by restrictions contained in deeds to its neighbors from a common grantor, even though he has no actual notice and his deed is silent as to restrictions, if the grantor has, in writing, placed the same restrictions on his remaining land?

HOLDING AND DECISION: (Braucher, J.) Yes. Although the Statute of Frauds prevents enforcement of restrictions against the grantor or subsequent purchasers of a lot not expressly restricted, where the common grantor has not bound his remaining land in writing, reciprocity of restriction between the grantor and grantee can be enforced. Therefore, if a grantor similarly restricts his remaining land by writing, a subsequent purchaser from the common grantor acquires title subject to the restrictions in the deed to the earlier purchaser. Further, each grantee within the scope of the common scheme may enforce the restrictions against other such grantees. Here, the Guillette (P) deed similarly restricted the grantor's remaining land. The deed was properly recorded. As a subsequent purchaser, Daly (D) took subject to these restrictions. Affirmed.

ANALYSIS

Cases are equally divided between the position illustrated by *Guillette v. Daly Dry Wall* and the position that restrictions on neighboring property deeded by a common grantor are not in the subsequent purchaser's chain of title.

Quicknotes

CHAIN OF TITLE Successive transfers of particular property.

COMMON GRANTOR Mutual conveyor of property.

GRANTEE The party to whom property is conveyed.

GRANTOR Conveyor of property or settlor of a trust.

RESTRICTIVE COVENANT A promise contained in a deed to limit the uses to which the property will be made.

STATUTE OF FRAUDS A statute that requires specified types of contracts to be in writing to be binding.

Waldorff Insurance and Bonding, Inc. v. Eglin National Bank

Condo owner (P) v. Foreclosing manager (D)

Fla. Dist. Ct. App., 453 So. 2d 1383 (1984)

NATURE OF CASE: Appeal from foreclosure judgment.

FACT SUMMARY: Eglin National Bank (Eglin) (D) contended it had no notice of Waldorff Insurance and Bonding, Inc.' s (Waldorff's) (P) ownership of the condominium unit, and thus it obtained good title upon foreclosure.

RULE OF LAW

Subsequent successors to legal title, after a contract to convey title has been executed, take title subject to all equitable interests of which they have notice.

FACTS: Choctaw Partnership (Chocktaw) mortgaged a condominium project to Eglin (D). It sold a single unit to Waldorff (P), which occupied the unit and paid all expenses and rent. Choctaw executed a second mortgage in favor of Eglin (D) on which it defaulted. Eglin (D) foreclosed on the project, including the unit occupied by Waldorff (P). Waldorff (P) sued, contending it had better title. The trial court held Eglin (D) had no notice of Waldorff's (P) ownership merely because of possession. Waldorff (P) appealed.

ISSUE: Do subsequent successors to legal title, after a contract to convey title has been executed, take title subject to all equitable interests of which they have notice?

HOLDING AND DECISION: (Shivers, J.) Yes. Subsequent successors to legal title, after a contract to convey title has been executed, take title subject to all equitable interests of which they have notice. A contract to convey legal title on payment of the purchase price creates an equitable interest in the purchaser. Beneficial ownership passes to the purchaser while the seller retains mere naked title. The occupancy of the unit placed Eglin (D) on notice of Waldorff's (P) interest. Thus Waldorff (P) retained greater title. Reversed and remanded.

ANALYSIS

Choctaw owed Waldorff (P) $35,000 in insurance premiums on the project. The parties agreed that Waldorff (P) would receive full title to the unit in return for a cancellation of the debt. The court rejected Eglin's (D) argument that because Waldorff (P) wrote the Choctaw debt off for tax purposes, no consideration supported the purchase. Choctaw's receipt of cancellation of a debt constituted sufficient consideration.

Quicknotes

BENEFICIAL OWNER A party holding equitable but not legal title to property that is held by a third party for their benefit.

CONSIDERATION Value given by one party in exchange for performance, or a promise to perform, by another party.

EQUITABLE INTEREST A beneficiary's interest in a trust.

Lick Mill Creek Apartments v. Chicago Title Insurance Co.

Developer (P) v. Title insurance company (D)

Cal. Ct. App., 283 Cal. Rptr. 231 (1991)

NATURE OF CASE: Appeal from dismissal of action for indemnification for hazardous waste cleanup costs.

FACT SUMMARY: After paying for removal and cleanup of hazardous substances existing but unknown at the time a title insurance policy was issued on its property, Lick Mill Creek Apartments (P) sued Chicago Title Insurance Co. (D) for reimbursement, contending that the presence of hazardous waste rendered the title unmarketable and constituted an encumbrance on title.

RULE OF LAW

A title insurance company is obligated to protect the insured against defects in title but not against loss arising from physical damage to property.

FACTS: While acquiring lots for development, Lick Mill Creek Apartments (Lick Mill) (P) purchased title insurance from Chicago Title Insurance Co. (Chicago Title) (D). Before issuing the policy, Chicago Title (D) commissioned a survey and inspection of the entire site. Unbeknownst to Chicago Title (D) or Lick Mill (P), the government had been keeping records documenting the presence of hazardous substances in the soil, subsoil, and groundwater of the property. After Lick Mill (P) purchased the property, it incurred costs for removal and cleanup of the hazardous materials. It then sought indemnity from Chicago Title (D) for the cost of the cleanup, arguing that the presence of hazardous substances rendered the title defective or unmarketable within the terms of the title insurance policy. Lick Mill (P) also contended that liability for the costs of the cleanup constituted an encumbrance on title. The trial court concluded that Chicago Title's (D) insurance policy did not cover the costs of removing hazardous substances. Lick Mill (P) appealed.

ISSUE: Is a title insurance company obligated to protect the insured against defects in title but not against loss arising from physical damage to property?

HOLDING AND DECISION: (Agliano, P.J.) Yes. A title insurance company is obligated to protect the insured against defects in title but not against loss arising from physical damage to property. Title insurance covers title marketability, which relates to defects affecting legally recognized rights and incidents of ownership. Title insurance does not cover market value. It is possible to hold perfectly marketable title to valueless, unmarketable land. Here, the presence of hazardous material may affect the market value of Lick Mill's (P) land, but it does not affect the title to the land. Chicago Title (D) was obligated, under its policy, to insure Lick Mill (P) against unmarketability of title. But since marketability of title and the market value of the land itself are separate and distinct, Lick Mill (P) could not claim coverage, under the policy, for the property's physical condition. Furthermore, it could not claim coverage for an encumbrance where no lien has been filed against the property. "Encumbrances" include only liens, easements, restrictive covenants, and other such interests in or rights to the land that are held by third persons. The mere possibility that the state may attach a lien in the future to secure payment of cleanup costs is not sufficient to create an encumbrance on title. Affirmed.

ANALYSIS

Title insurance reflects the faith of the insurer in the validity of title, not the physical condition of the property. Title insurance policies are contractual devices. Most courts will construe policies to insure only what they say they insure. This will be true even if the court subscribes to the presumption that policies are to be strictly construed in favor of the insured and against the title insurance company.

Quicknotes

ENCUMBRANCE An interest in property that operates as a claim or lien against its title making it potentially unmarketable.

INDEMNITY The duty of a party to compensate another for damages sustained.

LIEN A claim against the property of another in order to secure the payment of a debt.

TITLE INSURANCE A policy insuring against loss incurred as the result of a defective title.

TITLE MARKETABILITY Title, that although not perfect, would be acceptable to a reasonably well-informed buyer exercising ordinary business prudence.

CHAPTER 9

Judicial Land Use Controls: The Law of Nuisance

Quick Reference Rules of Law

Morgan v. High Penn Oil Co.

Property owners (P) v. Oil refinery owner/operator (D)

N.C. Sup. Ct., 77 S.E.2d 682 (1953)

NATURE OF CASE: Appeal from award of damages and injunction in action for temporary damages and abatement of private nuisance.

FACT SUMMARY: The Morgans (P) sought to enjoin High Penn Oil Co. (High Penn) (D) from emitting noxious nauseating and annoying gases and odors from its refinery, and to recover damages for past impairment of the use and enjoyment of their property resulting from such refinery emissions, asserting that High Penn's (D) use constituted a private nuisance. High Penn (D) contended that the evidence was insufficient to establish either an actionable or an abatable private nuisance.

RULE OF LAW

Where a person or entity intentionally and unreasonably engages in conduct that substantially interferes with another's interest in the use and enjoyment of their land, and the person or entity intends to continue engaging in such conduct, the person or entity has engaged in a private nuisance that is abatable and for which the person or entity may be held liable.

FACTS: The Morgans (P) had resided on their nine-acre property since August 1945 and had since established a trailer park and restaurant on the property, which improvements they rented to third parties, and they also supplemented their income by renting out part of their residence. High Penn Oil Co. (High Penn) (D) had operated an oil refinery, located approximately 1,000 feet from the Morgans' (P) dwelling, since October 1950. Claiming that High Penn's (D) gas and odor emissions constituted a private nuisance, the Morgans (P) brought suit for temporary damages and to enjoin High Penn (D) from emitting such gases and odors in the future. The Morgans (P) offered evidence to show that the refinery regularly emitted nauseating gases and odors in large quantities, which invaded not only their property, but also neighboring residential and commercial properties, and made people of ordinary sensitiveness uncomfortable and sick. The Morgans (P) also established that High Penn (D) was the only entity within over a mile radius of their property and neighboring properties that emitted gases or odors in annoying quantities into the air in the neighborhood. Further, they presented evidence that High Penn (D) disregarded their demand to abate the emissions. A jury found that High Penn's (D) oil refinery emissions constituted a nuisance and awarded damages. The trial also issued an injunction prohibiting High Penn (D) from continuing the nuisance. High Penn (D) appealed, and the state's highest court granted review.

ISSUE: Where a person or entity intentionally and unreasonably engages in conduct that substantially interferes with another's interest in the use and enjoyment of their land, and the person or entity intends to continue engaging in such conduct, has the person or entity engaged in a private nuisance that is abatable and for which the person or entity may be held liable?

HOLDING AND DECISION: (Ervin, J.) Yes. Where a person or entity intentionally and unreasonably engages in conduct that substantially interferes with another's interest in the use and enjoyment of their land, and the person or entity intends to continue engaging in such conduct, the person or entity has engaged in a private nuisance that is abatable and for which the person or entity may be held liable. The key principles of private nuisance are that private nuisance is a field of tort liability rather than a single type of tortious conduct, that the interest invaded by a private nuisance is the interest in the use and enjoyment of land, that any substantial non-trespassory invasion of another's interest in the private use and enjoyment of land by any type of liability forming conduct is a private nuisance, that the invasion that subjects a person to liability for private nuisance may be either intentional or unintentional, that a person is subject to liability for an intentional invasion when the person's conduct is unreasonable under the circumstances of the particular case, and that a person is subject to liability for an unintentional invasion when their conduct is negligent, reckless, or ultrahazardous. An invasion of another's interest in the use and enjoyment of land is intentional under the law of private nuisance when the person or entity whose conduct is in question as a basis for liability acts for the purpose of causing it, or knows that it is resulting from their conduct, or knows that it is substantially certain to result from their conduct. A private nuisance exists whenever one uses one's own property in a way that substantially interferes with another's interest in the private use and enjoyment of that other's land. Liability arises, if the conduct was unintentional, when the actions are negligent, reckless, or ultrahazardous. However, if the conduct is intentional, the person or entity intentionally creating or maintaining a private nuisance is liable for the resulting injury to others regardless of the degree of care or skill exercised by them to avoid such injury. Applying

Continued on next page.

these principles in this case, the evidence supports a finding that High Penn (D) intentionally and unreasonably caused noxious gas and odors to escape the refinery and substantially interfered with the Morgans' (P) use and enjoyment of their land, thus creating a private nuisance, and that High Penn (D) intended to use its refinery in this manner indefinitely, so that it would maintain the private nuisance it created. Accordingly, the Morgans (P) are entitled to temporary damages for the past interference with their use and enjoyment of their property, as well as a mandatory or prohibitory injunction requiring High Penn (D) to abate this private nuisance so it will not interfere with the Morgans' (P) property rights in the future. [The trial court's ruling is affirmed as to this issue.]

ANALYSIS

Private nuisances may be classified as nuisances per se or at law, and nuisances per accidens or in fact. A nuisance per se or at law is an act, occupation, or structure that is a nuisance at all times and under any circumstances, regardless of location or surroundings. Nuisances per accidens or in fact are those that become nuisances by reason of their location, or by reason of the manner in which they are constructed, maintained, or operated. Here, High Penn's (D) oil refinery was a lawful enterprise, and, for that reason, could not be a nuisance per se or at law. High Penn (D) took the position that an oil refinery cannot become a nuisance per accidens or in fact unless it is constructed or operated in a negligent manner. However, the court rejected this position, noting that a private nuisance per accidens or in fact may be created or maintained without negligence, and that most private nuisances per accidens or in fact are intentionally created or maintained, and are redressed by the courts without allegation or proof of negligence. As this case illustrates, a person or entity that intentionally creates or maintains a private nuisance is liable for the resulting injury to others regardless of the degree of care or skill exercised by them to avoid such injury.

Quicknotes

INJUNCTION An equitable remedy requiring a person, entity, or governmental unit to do, or prohibiting that person, entity, or governmental unit from doing, a specific act.

NUISANCE PER ACCIDENS Also known as a nuisance in fact, an action, occupation, or building that becomes a nuisance as the result of its location or method of operation.

NUISANCE PER SE Also known as a nuisance in law, an action, occupation, or building that is a nuisance at any time and under any condition.

PRIVATE NUISANCE An unlawful use of property interfering with the enjoyment of the private rights of an individual or a small number of persons.

Boomer v. Atlantic Cement Company

Landowners (P) v. Cement plant (D)

N.Y. Ct. App., 257 N.E.2d 870 (1970)

NATURE OF CASE: Action to enjoin maintenance of nuisance and for damages.

FACT SUMMARY: Trial court refused to issue injunction that would close down plant but awarded permanent damages instead.

RULE OF LAW

Although the rule in New York is that a nuisance will be enjoined even when there is a marked disparity shown in economic consequence between the effect of the injunction and the effect of the nuisance, an injunction should not be applied if the result is to close down a plant. Permanent damages may be awarded as an alternative.

FACTS: A group of landowners (P), complaining of injury to their property from dirt, smoke, and vibration emanating from a neighboring cement plant (D), brought an action to enjoin the continued operation of the plant and for damages. The trial court held that the plant constituted a nuisance, found substantial damage but, because an injunction would shut down the plant's operation, refused to issue one. Permanent damages of $185,000 were awarded the group of landowners (P) instead.

ISSUE: Where the issuance of an injunction to enjoin the maintenance of a business would shut down a business, may permanent damages be issued as an alternative?

HOLDING AND DECISION: (Bergan, J.) Yes. Damages may be awarded as an alternative to an injunction in nuisance cases. Another alternative would be to grant the injunction but postpone its effect to a specified future date to give opportunity for technical advances to permit the plant (D) to eliminate the nuisance. However, there is no assurance that any significant technical improvement would occur. Moreover, the problem is universal and can only be solved by an industry-wide effort. Permanent damages would themselves be a spur to conduct more research. Future owners of this land would not be able to recover additional damages since the award is to the land. Reversed and remanded.

DISSENT: (Jasen, J.) The majority approach is licensing a continuing wrong. Furthermore, permanent damages alleviate the need for more research and decrease incentive.

ANALYSIS

The reasoning advanced here has been carried one step further by other courts. In *Pennsylvania Coal Co. v. Sanderson*, 113 Pa. St. 126, 6 A. 453 (1886), a suit for damages was frowned upon by the Supreme Court of Pennsylvania, which said, "To encourage the development of the great natural resources of a country, trifling inconveniences to particular persons must sometimes give way to the necessities of a great community."

Quicknotes

INJUNCTION A court order requiring a person to do or prohibiting that person from doing a specific act.

NUISANCE An unlawful use of property that interferes with the lawful use of another's property.

TEMPORARY DAMAGES Monetary compensation awarded by the court to a party for injuries sustained as the result of another party's occasional wrongful actions.

CHAPTER 10

Private Land Use Controls: The Law of Servitudes

Quick Reference Rules of Law

PAGE

1. *Willard v. First Church of Christ, Scientist.* Contrary to the ancient common-law rule, modernly, a grantor, in deeding property to one person, may effectively reserve and vest an interest in the same property in a third party. *82*

2. *Mund v. English.* In Oregon, when a licensee makes valuable improvements on the basis of a promise, the licensor will not be permitted to assert that the license is revocable. *83*

3. *Van Sandt v. Royster.* A purchaser may be charged with notice of a prior necessary use, so as to create an implied easement, where the use was not visible, but a reasonable inspection would have made the use apparent. *85*

4. *Othen v. Rosier.* In order to create an easement by necessity, the necessity must have existed at the time that the estate was created. *87*

5. *Brown v. Voss.* If an easement is appurtenant to a particular parcel of land, any extension thereof to other parcels is a misuse of the easement, unless the servient estate does not overburden it. *88*

6. *Preseault v. United States.* A change in use of an easement from a rail line to a recreational path constitutes a taking. *89*

7. *Tulk v. Moxhay.* Privity of estate notwithstanding, a person who acquires real property with notice of a restriction placed upon it will not be allowed, in equity, to violate its terms. *90*

8. *Phillips v. Hatfield.* (1) Developers of a subdivision do not have authority to impose restrictions on lots they have already sold by executing and recording, after the developers' sale of lots, a declaration containing such restrictions that purports to apply to all lots in the subdivision and to bind even purchasers of the lots the developers had sold prior to recording the declaration. (2) The implied negative reciprocal easement doctrine will not be applied to impose a restriction upon subdivision property where the subdivision's developer and original owner of the property no longer owned the property before attempting to impose the restriction, simply because the developer reacquired the property after recording the purported restriction. *91*

9. *River Heights Associates L.P. v. Batten.* A restrictive covenant can be nullified by changed conditions only when the changes are so radical as to destroy the essential objectives and purposes of the covenant. *94*

10. *Shelley v. Kraemer.* State court enforcement of private, discriminatory restrictive covenants constitutes state action under the Fourteenth Amendment. *95*

11. *Nahrstedt v. Lakeside Village Condominium Association, Inc.* A recorded use restriction imposed by a common-interest development in California must be enforced uniformly against all residents of the development unless the restriction is unreasonable. *96*

Willard v. First Church of Christ, Scientist

Subsequent purchaser (P) v. Third-party easement beneficiary (D)

Cal. Sup. Ct., 498 P.2d 987 (1972)

NATURE OF CASE: Appeal in a quiet title action.

FACT SUMMARY: Although when Petersen bought a lot from McGuigan, the deed reserved an easement on the lot for the use of First Church of Christ, Scientist (D), Petersen then sold the lot to the Willards (P) without the easement.

RULE OF LAW

Contrary to the ancient common-law rule, modernly, a grantor, in deeding property to one person, may effectively reserve and vest an interest in the same property in a third party.

FACTS: Having bought lot 19 from McGuigan, Petersen also offered to purchase the abutting lot 20 from her in order to sell both lots to the Willards (P). However, McGuigan, a member of the First Church of Christ, Scientist (the Church) (D), had always allowed the Church (D) to use the lot for parking. Accordingly, McGuigan had a clause included in the deed to Petersen whereby lot 20 was subject to an easement for Church (D) parking to run with the land as long as used for Church (D) purposes. Petersen bought the lot and recorded the deed. However, Petersen did not include the easement in his deed to the Willards (P). When the Willards (P) became aware of it, they brought this quiet title action. At trial, McGuigan testified that she had originally bought lot 20 to provide Church (D) parking and would not have sold it without the easement. The trial court found that, although McGuigan and Petersen intended to convey an easement, the clause was invalidated under the common-law rule that the grantor, in deeding property to one person, cannot reserve an interest in the same property to a third party. The Church (D) appealed.

ISSUE: May a grantor, in deeding property to one person, effectively reserve and vest an interest in the same property in a third party?

HOLDING AND DECISION: (Peters, J.) Yes. Contrary to the ancient common-law rule, modernly, a grantor, in deeding property to one person, may effectively reserve and vest an interest in the same property in a third party. Today, courts primarily try to give effect to the grantor's intent, whereas the common-law rule would defeat that intent. Also, it must be recognized that due to the encumbrance on the property, the grantee paid a reduced price for it. Therefore, it would be inequitable to allow him to remove the third party's interest, thereby greatly increasing the property's value. The determination of whether the common-law rule should still be used involves a balancing of equitable and policy considerations. In this case, despite the Willards' (P) contrary contentions that the grantees and title insurers relied on the common-law rule, we believe the modern position applies. Reversed.

ANALYSIS

Because easements are interests to land, they normally must be in compliance with the Statute of Frauds. However, easements may also exist by implication in those instances where the parties have not expressly reserved or granted them in writing. Since these easements are created by operation of law, no writing under the Statute of Frauds is necessary. However, easements by implication arise only when common title to land is severed.

Quicknotes

EASEMENT The right to utilize a portion of another's real property for a specific use.

EASEMENT BY IMPLICATION An easement that is not expressly stated in a deed, but which is inferred upon conveyance, that a portion of one parcel had been used to benefit the other parcel and that upon sale the buyer of the benefited parcel could reasonably expect such benefits to continue.

ENCUMBRANCE An interest in property that operates as a claim or lien against its title making it potentially unmarketable.

QUIET TITLE Equitable action to resolve conflicting claims to an interest in real property.

STATUTE OF FRAUDS A statute that requires specified types of contracts to be in writing in order to be binding.

Continued on next page.

Mund v. English

Son and daughter-in-law (P) v. Son's mother (D)

Or. Ct. App. 684 P.2d 1248 (1984)

NATURE OF CASE: Appeal from trial court finding that neighboring property did not have permanent and irrevocable interest in a well.

FACT SUMMARY: A husband and wife (D) and their son and daughter-in-law (P) purchased adjacent lots, and a water well was constructed on the husband and wife's (D) lot. There was no written agreement regarding use of the well, and a family quarrel ensued regarding whether the son and daughter-in-law had a permanent and irrevocable interest in the well.

RULE OF LAW

In Oregon, when a licensee makes valuable improvements on the basis of a promise, the licensor will not be permitted to assert that the license is revocable.

FACTS: A husband and wife (the Englishes) (D) and their son and their son's wife (the Munds) (P) bought adjoining one-acre parcels of land. In the same year that each family purchased their respective parcels, a water well was drilled on the Englishes (D) property. There was no written agreement governing the use of the well, and the attorney handling the transaction did not recall the details of the oral agreement. Mrs. English (D) admitted that the Munds (P) were granted the right to use the well and install a pipeline to their property. Evidence demonstrated that Mr. Mund (P) and Mr. English (D) (now deceased) had worked together to install the system, and that the parties shared operating expenses. Additionally, the Munds (P) secured a $40,000 commercial loan and constructed a residence on their property. The residence did not have any water sources beyond the well. Despite the evidence, the trial court found that the Munds (P) did not have a permanent and irrevocable interest in the well and denied the Munds' (P) motion to amend the pleadings to conform to the evidence.

ISSUE: In Oregon, will a licensor be permitted to assert that a license is revocable if the licensee has made valuable improvements on the basis of a promise?

HOLDING AND DECISION: (Rossman, J.) No. In Oregon, when a licensee makes valuable improvements on the basis of a promise, the licensor will not be permitted to assert that the license is revocable. English (D) claimed that the oral agreement dictated that the Munds' (P) rights were not permanent and were subject to certain conditions. The trial court was correct in its finding that the Munds (P) failed to prove that there was an agreement that the Munds (P) were entitled to a one-half interest in the well and a permanent easement over the land for the installation of a water system. However, the Munds (P) are entitled to an irrevocable license, which arises by operation of the law to prevent injustice, because Oregon courts have consistently held that a license cannot be revoked once a licensee has made valuable improvements on the basis of a promise. The Munds (P) clearly made improvements on the basis of the Englishes' (D) promise. Furthermore, because the Munds (P) have no source of water other than the well, Mrs. English (D) is unable to withdraw their license to use the well. Reversed and remanded for entry of a decree granting the Munds (P) a one-half interest in the well and water system; granting the Munds (P) an easement over the property for the purpose of access to the water system; and requiring the Munds (P) and Mrs. English (D) to equally share the cost of maintaining the system.

ANALYSIS

Most courts refer to an irrevocable license as "easement by estoppel." In *Cores v. Laborde*, 2018 WL 3062478 (Tex. Ct. App. - Corpus Christie, 2018), a Texas appellate court ruled that a landowner was entitled to an easement by estoppel for an access road, even though it was not the only way to access the property. The prior owner of the land had used the road, which cut through an adjacent piece of land, without objection for over 30 years. Because the prior owners had continuous access to the road, their access created an easement by estoppel.

Quicknotes

EASEMENT The right to utilize a portion of another's real property for a specific use.

LICENSE A right that is granted to a person allowing them to conduct an activity that without such permission they could not lawfully do, and which is unassignable and revocable at the will of the licensor.

LICENSEE Person known to an owner or occupier of land, who comes onto the premises voluntarily and for a specific purpose although not necessarily with the consent of the owner.

LICENSOR A party that grants another a right allowing them to conduct an activity that without such permission

Continued on next page.

they could not lawfully do, and which is unassignable and revocable at the will of the granting party.

PROMISE The expression of an intention to act, or to forbear from acting, granting a right to the promisee to expect and enforce its performance.

Van Sandt v. Royster

Subsequent purchaser (P) v. Quasi-easement grantees (D)

Kan. Sup. Ct., 83 P.2d 698 (1938)

NATURE OF CASE: Action to enjoin Royster (D) and Gray (D) from using an underground sewer drain across Van Sandt's (P) property.

FACT SUMMARY: Van Sandt (P) found his cellar flooded with sewage and discovered for the first time the existence of a sewer-drain across his property. Royster (D) and Gray (D) refused to stop using the drain.

RULE OF LAW

A purchaser may be charged with notice of a prior necessary use, so as to create an implied easement, where the use was not visible, but a reasonable inspection would have made the use apparent.

FACTS: Bailey owned three adjoining lots numbered 4, 20, and 19. In 1904, a private lateral drain was built running from the house on Lot 4 across Lots 20 and 19. Bailey conveyed Lot 20 to Murphy by a general warranty deed without exceptions or reservations in 1904. Title passed to Royster (D). In 1904, Bailey also conveyed Lot 19 to Jones by a general warranty deed without exceptions or reservations. Jones conveyed part of Lot 19 to Reynolds, who in 1924 conveyed to Van Sandt (P). Gray (D) succeeded title to Lot 4. In 1936, Van Sandt (P) discovered his basement flooded with sewage and filth. Upon investigation, he discovered for the first time the existence of a sewer drain running on, across, and through his property. Royster (D) and Gray (D) refuse to stop using the sewer. Van Sandt (P) argues that no easement has been created on his land, and even assuming there was an easement created, he took the land free from the burden of the easement because he was a bona fide purchaser, without notice. The court decided for the defendants and Van Sandt (P) appealed.

ISSUE: May a purchaser be charged with notice of a prior necessary use, so as to create an implied easement, where the use was not visible, but a reasonable inspection would have made the use apparent?

HOLDING AND DECISION: (Allen, J.) Yes. A purchaser may be charged with notice of a prior necessary use, so as to create an implied easement, where the use was not visible, but a reasonable inspection would have made the use apparent. When one utilizes part of his land for the benefit of another, a quasi-easement exists. The part of the land being benefited is referred to as the quasi-dominant tenement, and the part being utilized is referred to as the quasi-servient tenement. If the owner of land, one part of which is subject to a quasi-easement, conveys the quasi-dominant tenement, an easement corresponding to such quasi-easement is vested in the grantee, provided such quasi-easement is apparent and continuous. An implied easement, in favor of either the grantor or the grantee arises as an inference of the intentions of the parties. This inference is drawn from the circumstances under which the conveyance is made. Factors to consider include whether the claimant is the grantee or grantor, the terms of the conveyance, the consideration given, the extent of necessity of the easement and the extent to which the use, which is the subject of the easement, was or might have been known to the parties. Parties to a conveyance will be assumed to know and to contemplate the continuance of reasonably necessary uses that have so altered the premises as to make them apparent upon reasonably prudent investigation. The degree of necessity required to imply an easement in favor of the grantor is greater than that required in the case of the grantee. But where land may be used without an easement, but cannot be used without disproportionate effort and expense, an easement may be implied in favor of either the grantor or grantee on the basis of necessity alone. In this case, the trial court found that Jones was aware of the sewer at the time he purchased Lot 19. It further found that the easement was necessary to the comfortable enjoyment of the grantor's (Bailey's) land. Van Sandt (P) cannot claim that he purchased without notice. He inspected the property at the time of purchase and knew the house was equipped with modern plumbing that had to drain into a sewer. The majority view is that appearance and visibility of easements is not synonymous, and the fact that the pipe, sewer, or drain is hidden underground does not make it nonapparent. Here the easement was apparent within this meaning, and Van Sandt (P) is charged with notice of its existence. Affirmed.

ANALYSIS

The law does not favor implied easements since they are in derogation of the rule that written instruments speak for themselves. They also retard building and improvements and violate the policy of recording acts. The implication of easements is based on the theory that when one conveys property they include, or intend to include, in the conveyance whatever is necessary for its beneficial use and enjoyment and to retain whatever is necessary for the use and enjoyment of the land retained. In view of the rule that a conveyance is to be construed most strongly against the grantor, an

Continued on next page.

easement in favor of the grantee will be implied more readily than one in favor of the grantor.

Quicknotes

IMPLIED EASEMENT An easement that is not expressly stated in a deed, but which is inferred upon conveyance, that a portion of one parcel had been used to benefit the other parcel and that upon sale the buyer of the benefited parcel could reasonably expect such benefits to continue.

QUASI-DOMINANT TENEMENT Property whose owners benefit from the use of another's property.

QUASI-SERVIENT TENEMENT Property that is burdened in some aspect for the benefit of a dominant estate.

Othen v. Rosier

Road user (P) v. Property owner (D)

Tex. Sup. Ct., 226 S.W.2d 622 (1950)

NATURE OF CASE: Appeal from judgment denying the existence of an easement by either prescription or necessity.

FACT SUMMARY: Othen (P) alleged that he had acquired an easement across the land of Rosier (D), after Rosier (D) erected a levee on the land.

RULE OF LAW

In order to create an easement by necessity, the necessity must have existed at the time that the estate was created.

FACTS: Othen (P) and Rosier (D) own tracts of land that were formerly part of one larger parcel. In order to reach any public highways, Othen (P) must cross over someone else's property. Othen (P) had used a road that ran across Rosier's (D) property, which Rosier (D) kept in repair. As a result of encroaching surface waters, Rosier (D) erected a levee on his property, which made the road so muddy that for weeks at a time it was impassable except by horseback. Othen (P) filed suit for injunctive and declaratory relief, and for damages. The trial court found that Othen (P) had acquired an easement by necessity. However, the appellate court reversed, holding that Othen (P) had acquired neither an easement by necessity nor one by prescription.

ISSUE: In order to create an easement by necessity, must the necessity have existed at the time that the estate was created?

HOLDING AND DECISION: (Brewster, J.) Yes. Before an implied easement by necessity can be held to be created, it must be shown that there was a unity of ownership of the alleged dominant and servient estates; that the roadway is a necessity and not a mere convenience; and that the necessity existed at the time of severance of the two estates. Here, there was unity of ownership of the lands now owned by Othen (P) and Rosier (D). However, no easement may be implied for the road because the original owner did not reserve such an easement when he first sold the property now owned by Rosier (D). The record does not indicate that the roadway was a necessity as of the date of the original grant deed, rather than a mere convenience. Othen (P) has additionally not acquired an easement by prescription, because his use of the road was not under claim of right. Othen's (P) use of the roadway was merely permissive and therefore constituted only a license, which could not and did not ripen into a prescriptive right. Affirmed.

ANALYSIS

Several states have attempted to solve the problems posed by landlocked property through statutory provisions providing for condemnation of private ways. While the statutory provisions vary from state to state, all jurisdictions require payment to be made for the land taken by the owner of the benefited property. The degree of necessity required for condemnation also varies; some states require a showing of strict necessity; while others require only that the necessity be reasonable under all the circumstances.

Quicknotes

CLAIM OF RIGHT Person claiming a right in property is in possession and intends to claim ownership of that property without regard to the record title owner.

CONDEMNATION The taking of private property for public use so long as just compensation is paid therefor.

DOMINANT ESTATE Property whose owners benefit from the use of another's property.

EASEMENT BY NECESSITY An easement that arises by operation of law without which the owner of the benefited property is deprived of the use and enjoyment of their property.

EASEMENT BY PRESCRIPTION A manner of acquiring an easement in another's property by continuous and uninterrupted use in satisfaction of the statutory requirements of adverse possession.

LICENSE A right that is granted to a person allowing them to conduct an activity that without such permission they could not lawfully do, and which is unassignable and revocable at the will of the licensor.

PRESCRIPTIVE RIGHTS Rights to an easement in another's property acquired by continuous and uninterrupted use in satisfaction of the statutory requirements of adverse possession.

SERVIENT ESTATE Property that is burdened in some aspect for the benefit of a dominant estate.

Brown v. Voss

Easement grantee (P) v. Easement grantor (D)

Wash. Sup. Ct., 715 P.2d 514 (1986)

NATURE OF CASE: Appeal from denial of injunctive relief.

FACT SUMMARY: The court of appeals held that an easement granted for the benefit of one dominant estate could be used for two dominant estates where no increased burden to the servient estate is shown.

RULE OF LAW

If an easement is appurtenant to a particular parcel of land, any extension thereof to other parcels is a misuse of the easement, unless the servient estate does not overburden it.

FACTS: In 1952, Voss (D) granted an easement to Brown (P) to allow ingress and egress to Voss's (D) property. Brown (P) subsequently obtained title to a third parcel and attempted to use the easement to gain access thereto. Brown (P) sued to establish the right to so use the easement, yet Voss (D) sought an injunction to forbid such use. The trial court denied the injunction, the court of appeals reversed, and Voss (D) appealed.

ISSUE: If an easement is appurtenant to a particular parcel of land, is any extension thereof to other parcels a misuse of the easement, unless the easement is not overburdened?

HOLDING AND DECISION: (Brachtenbach, J.) Yes. If an easement is appurtenant to a particular parcel of land, any extension thereof to other parcels is a misuse of the easement, unless the use does not overburden the easement. The easement received no greater use as a result of Brown's (P) acquisition of the second parcel. Brown (P) reasonably developed his property, and thus the injunction was correctly denied. Reversed.

DISSENT: (Dore, J.) Any extension of this easement is a misuse. Thus, injunctive relief should have been granted.

ANALYSIS

This case illustrates that while the law of easements can be traced back to common law, it is subject to judicial interpretation. Here, the reasonableness of the development, in the eyes of the court, served as the basis for denying the injunction.

Quicknotes

APPURTENANT A burden attached to real property that either benefits or burdens the owner's right to utilize that property.

DOMINANT ESTATE Property whose owners benefit from the use of another's property.

EASEMENT The right to utilize a portion of another's real property for a specific use.

INJUNCTIVE RELIEF A court order issued as a remedy, requiring a person to do, or prohibiting that person from doing, a specific act.

SERVIENT ESTATE Property that is burdened in some aspect for the benefit of a dominant estate.

Preseault v. United States

Right-of-way owners (P) v. Federal government (D)

100 F.3d 1525 (Fed. Cir. 1996)

NATURE OF CASE: Appeal from judgment rejecting claim for compensation due to exercise of eminent domain.

FACT SUMMARY: The Preseaults (P) contended that the federal Government (D) took their property when it authorized the conversion of a former railroad right-of-way over their property to public trail use.

RULE OF LAW

A change in use of an easement from a rail line to a recreational path constitutes a taking.

FACTS: An agreement executed in 1899 gave the federal government an easement across three parcels of land owned by the Preseaults' (P) predecessor for use as a rail line. The line began operating not long thereafter, but by 1970, rail operations had ceased. In 1975, the switches and tracks were removed. In 1986, under the Federal Rails-to-Trails Act, the land on which the rail line had once run was converted into a recreational trail. The Preseaults (P) filed suit in the Court of Federal Claims, contending that the new use constituted a taking for which they were entitled to compensation. The Court of Federal Claims rejected this contention, and the Preseaults (P) appealed.

ISSUE Does a change in use of an easement from a rail line to a recreational path constitute a taking?

HOLDING AND DECISION: (Plager, J.) Yes. A change in use of an easement from a rail line to a recreational path constitutes a taking. Typically, an easement does not contain a specific termination date, but usually ends by way of abandonment. Abandonment is not effected merely by nonuse, but rather by acts that are inconsistent with the use for which the easement exists. Here, in 1975, the railroad took out the rail hardware, an act inconsistent with use as a rail line. At that point, then, abandonment was effected. At this point, the interest the Government (D) had in the Preseaults' (P) property was extinguished. The creation of the recreational path, therefore, was not a legitimate expansion of the original easement, but, rather, a taking of the Preseaults' (P) property, which, under the Fifth Amendment, required compensation. Reversed and remanded.

ANALYSIS

It is not uncommon for strips of land to be deeded for transport purposes. The drafters of these documents are not always careful in the language utilized, and the question often arises as to whether it was an easement or fee simple that was conveyed. As a rule, courts tend to view "right-of-way" language in such instruments as conveying easements, not fees.

Quicknotes

ABANDONMENT The voluntary relinquishment of a right without the intent of reclaiming it.

EASEMENT The right to utilize a portion of another's real property for a specific use.

EMINENT DOMAIN The governmental power to take private property for public use so long as just compensation is paid therefor.

FEE SIMPLE An estate in land characterized by ownership of the entire property for an unlimited duration and by absolute power over distribution.

RIGHT-OF-WAY The right of a party to pass over the property of another.

TAKING A governmental action that substantially deprives an owner of the use and enjoyment of their property, requiring compensation.

Tulk v. Moxhay

Original covenantor (P) v. Subsequent purchaser (D)

Ct. Ch., 2 Phillips 774, 41 Eng. Rep. 1143 (1848)

NATURE OF CASE: Bill for injunction to enforce covenant in deed.

FACT SUMMARY: Moxhay (D) indicated an intention to build upon a park-like piece of land, even though he was aware of an original, prohibitive covenant passed on by Tulk (P), 40 years earlier, which forbade any construction on the ground.

RULE OF LAW

Privity of estate notwithstanding, a person who acquires real property with notice of a restriction placed upon it will not be allowed, in equity, to violate its terms.

FACTS: Tulk (P), owner in fee of a square garden containing a statue, as well as adjacent houses, sold the property to Elms. A covenant in the deed of conveyance prohibited Elms and his assigns from ever constructing upon the ground. The piece of land eventually came into the hands of Moxhay (D), whose purchase deed contained no similar covenant, yet Moxhay (D) admitted he knew of the original covenant. When Moxhay (D) indicated he wanted to build on the piece of ground, Tulk (P) successfully obtained an injunction.

ISSUE: Can the purchaser of a deed of conveyance containing a restriction violate the restriction if he has notice of the original covenant?

HOLDING AND DECISION: (Cottenham, Lord Chan.) No. To hold otherwise would make it impossible for an owner of land to sell part of it without running the risk of seeing the part he retained rendered worthless. At issue is not whether the covenant "runs" with the land, but whether a party may violate a contract entered by his vendor by using the land in an inconsistent manner. If there was mere agreement and no covenant, a court would enforce it against a party purchasing with notice; so long as equity is attached by an owner, no one purchasing with notice can stand in a different situation than the original purchaser. Injunction refused.

ANALYSIS

Notice is the key element of the principle, commonly referred to as "the doctrine of *Tulk v. Moxhay*," enunciated in this case. Notice of the restriction may be either actual, inquiry, or record. The rights and obligations recognized here are variously named but are generally known as "equitable servitudes." The restriction in the transfer of land need not be embodied in covenant—an informal contract or agreement is sufficient. A party intended to receive the benefit, as well as the original covenantor, can bring the suit in equity. However, proof of notice is essential to the doctrine.

Quicknotes

CONVEYANCE The transfer of property, or title to property, from one party to another party.

COVENANT A written promise to do, or to refrain from doing, a particular activity.

***DIVERS MESNE* CONVEYANCE** A conveyance falling between the original owner and the present owner in the chain of title.

EQUITABLE SERVITUDE Land use restriction enforceable in equity.

EQUITY Fairness; justice; the determination of a matter consistent with principles of fairness and not in strict compliance with rules of law.

INJUNCTION A court order requiring a person to do or prohibiting that person from doing a specific act.

OWNER IN FEE An owner of an absolute and unlimited interest in property.

PRIVITY OF ESTATE Common or successive relation to the same right in property.

Phillips v. Hatfield

Subdivision property owner (P) v. Subdivision property owner (D)

Tenn. Sup. Ct., 624 S.W.3d 464 (2021)

NATURE OF CASE: Appeal from affirmance of declaratory judgment and grant of injunctive relief for plaintiff in action to restrict subdivision property owner's proposed commercial use of property.

FACT SUMMARY: Ritchie and Roma Phillips ("the Phillips") (P), who owned plots in a subdivision, contended that Mark Hatfield's (D) intended use of his property in the subdivision for a retail business was prohibited by an implied negative reciprocal easement that prohibited non-residential use, as set forth in a declaration recorded by the subdivision's developers, notwithstanding that the developers did not own Hatfield's (D) lots when they recorded the declaration. Hatfield (D) contended that his property was not bound by the declaration's restriction because the developers had no authority to subject his property to the restriction after they had sold the lots that subsequently became his property.

RULE OF LAW

(1) Developers of a subdivision do not have authority to impose restrictions on lots they have already sold by executing and recording, after the developers' sale of lots, a declaration containing such restrictions that purports to apply to all lots in the subdivision and to bind even purchasers of the lots the developers had sold prior to recording the declaration.

(2) The implied negative reciprocal easement doctrine will not be applied to impose a restriction upon subdivision property where the subdivision's developer and original owner of the property no longer owned the property before attempting to impose the restriction, simply because the developer reacquired the property after recording the purported restriction.

FACTS: In 1946, Mary and J.C. Chambers ("the Chambers") acquired a 417-acre tract of land, and, on a portion of that land, set out to develop the subdivision known as Sunnybrook Addition. To that end, the Chambers recorded a plat for Sunnybrook Addition in 1953, that contained 79 lots, and that did not restrict the lots to residential use. Over the course of 1953 and 1954, the Chambers sold 67 of the 79 lots. Included in the deeds conveying the vast majority of those lots were several expressly stated restrictive covenants ("the Original Restrictive Covenants") that were to run with the land, one of which restricted the lots to residential use. However, the deeds stated that the covenants were binding for a period of only 20 years. In 1955, the Chambers recorded a general declaration, the 1955 Restrictive Covenants, that purported to bind all the properties in the subdivision, including those that the Chambers had already sold prior to 1955. One of the restrictive covenants contained in the declaration restricted the properties to residential use. Mark Hatfield (D) purchased property in the Sunnybrook Addition in 2016 and 2017, with the intention of developing the property for retail business use. Hatfield's (D) neighbors in the subdivision, Ritchie and Roma Phillips ("the Phillips") (P), brought suit for declaratory and injunctive relief to enjoin Hatfield's (D) retail use of his property, on the grounds that the 1955 Restrictive Covenants prohibited such use. The initial deeds for all of the parties' lots contained the Original Restrictive Covenants, but, because by the terms of the deeds, the covenants were binding for a period of only 20 years, it was uncontested that the express residential-use restriction contained in the deeds for Hatfield's (D) property had terminated by its own terms long before Hatfield (D) purchased the property. Although the Chambers repurchased the lots making up Hatfield's (D) property in 1956, and resold those lots in 1960, none of the deeds that conveyed those lots after 1955 incorporated or referred to the 1955 Restrictive Covenants. Some of the deeds involving Hatfield's (D) predecessors-in-title contained no restrictive language at all, and some of the deeds contained general language that the conveyance was subject to valid restrictive covenants of record, if any. In any event, the 1955 Restrictive Covenants did not appear in the chain of title to Hatfield's (D) property. Based on this evidence, the trial court concluded that Hatfield's (D) property was subject to an implied negative reciprocal easement through the 1955 Restrictive Covenants. In reaching this conclusion, the trial court found that: (1) the Chambers were the original developers of and common grantor for the Sunnybrook Addition subdivision; (2) the Chambers had a general plan of development for the subdivision; (3) the Chambers intended for the 1955 Restrictive Covenants to apply to all of Sunnybrook Addition; and (4) Hatfield (D) acquired his property "subject to valid restrictive covenants . . . appearing of record" and "had, at a minimum, constructive notice of the restrictions owing to their public recording and due to the general nature of the property." Accordingly, the trial court enjoined Hatfield (D) from constructing any retail business or commercial enterprise on his property. The state's intermediate appellate court affirmed, and the state's highest court granted review.

Continued on next page.

ISSUE:

(1) Do developers of a subdivision have authority to impose restrictions on lots they have already sold by executing and recording, after the developers' sale of lots, a declaration containing such restrictions that purports to apply to all lots in the subdivision and to bind even purchasers of the lots the developers had sold prior to recording the declaration?
(2) Will the implied negative reciprocal easement doctrine be applied to impose a restriction upon subdivision property where the subdivision's developer and original owner of the property no longer owned the property before attempting to impose the restriction, simply because the developer reacquired the property after recording the purported restriction?

HOLDING AND DECISION: (Bivins, C.J.)

(1) No. Developers of a subdivision do not have authority to impose restrictions on lots they have already sold by executing and recording, after the developers' sale of lots, a declaration containing such restrictions that purports to apply to all lots in the subdivision and to bind even purchasers of the lots the developers had sold prior to recording the declaration. For a restrictive covenant to qualify as a servitude and run with the land, the covenant not only must have been intended to run with the land, it also must have been created effectively. To effectively create a servitude, the grantor must own the servient estate. Here, the Chambers did not own the lots at issue when they recorded the 1955 Restrictive Covenants; in other words, the Chambers did not own the servient estate. Therefore, the Chambers lacked the authority to subject the property at issue to the 1955 Restrictive Covenants.
(2) No. The implied negative reciprocal easement doctrine will not be applied to impose a restriction upon subdivision property where the subdivision's developer and original owner of the property no longer owned the property before attempting to impose the restriction, simply because the developer reacquired the property after recording the purported restriction. Although some of the deeds by which Hatfield (D) came to acquire his property contained language that the conveyance was subject to valid restrictive covenants, if any, appearing of record, such general language did not reflect sufficient intent on the part of any grantor subsequent to the recording of the 1955 Restrictive Covenants to subject the property to the unnamed restrictions, which did not appear in the property's chain of title, given that courts must resolve any doubt against the existence of such a restriction, and given that courts justifiably are hesitant to find the intent to create servitudes in vague language or informal writings because servitudes create interests running with the land that affect people beyond the immediate parties. Moreover, the implied negative reciprocal easement doctrine cannot be used under the circumstances of this case to imply that the restrictions in the 1955 Restrictive Covenants ran with the land. The doctrine of implied negative reciprocal easements is an extension of the original concept that addresses circumstances in which the creation of a servitude on certain land is not expressly apparent and, therefore, must be implied. Under the doctrine, the creation of a servitude can be implied by virtue of, among other circumstances, the conveyance of land pursuant to a general plan of development. The quintessential example occurs in the context of restrictive covenants applicable to a residential subdivision, and the creation of servitudes by implication normally arises on severance of a single possessory interest into two or more possessory interests. However, the factual scenario presented in this case, at least with respect to the 1955 Restrictive Covenants, is not the typical one recognized under the implied negative reciprocal easement doctrine. By the time the Chambers recorded the 1955 Restrictive Covenants, they had conveyed the vast majority of lots, and they owned none of the parties' lots. The land remaining under ownership of the Chambers at the time they recorded the 1955 Restrictive Covenants consisted of only 12 of 79 lots, spread sporadically through only six of the eight sections of Sunnybrook Addition— and not including the entire section that contained all of the parties' lots. Thus, by the time the Chambers recorded the 1955 Restrictive Covenants, they were no longer acting as the common grantor with respect to the parties' properties, because they did not then own those lots. Under these circumstances, the 1955 Restrictive Covenants cannot burden Hatfield's (D) property by virtue of an implied negative reciprocal easement. To hold otherwise would be to impose the 1955 Restrictive Covenants retroactively, which is not permitted under the doctrine. Further, the Chambers' reacquisition of the lots in 1956 by itself does not permit application of the doctrine, because, at that point, the Chambers stood in the same shoes as any other purchaser, and acquired the lots subject only to the Original Restrictive Covenants, but their reacquisition and later resale of the lots did not trigger the imposition of the 1955 Restrictive Covenants as a servitude upon the property. Reversed.

ANALYSIS

As the court in this case emphasizes, the implied negative reciprocal easement doctrine does not permit reciprocal negative easements that are retroactive. This is because the retroactive effect of applying restrictions

Continued on next page.

to land not owned by the grantor at the time the restrictions were created is at odds with the reciprocal negative easement requirement of common ownership at the time the express restrictions are created. If a negative reciprocal easement attaches at all, it must do so while the property is held by the common grantor. Because the Chambers no longer owned the lots at issue when they recorded the 1955 Restrictive Covenants, the court in this case found that the servitudes could not have attached while the property was held by a common grantor. However, for example, the implied negative reciprocal easement doctrine would have applied for the enforcement of the Original Restrictive Covenants, as in that scenario there would not have been a need to apply the restrictions retroactively. In that case, the Chambers would have owned all of the land comprising Sunnybrook Addition as of 1946, recorded a plat for the subdivision in 1953, and sold 67 of 79 lots over the course of 1953–1954. The deeds for nearly all of these conveyances, including all of those that occurred in 1953, expressly listed in the Original Restrictive Covenants. Therefore, the implied negative reciprocal easement doctrine would operate to subject the lots remaining in the hands of the Chambers to the Original Restrictive Covenants.

Quicknotes

DEED A signed writing transferring title to real property from one person to another.

IMPLIED NEGATIVE RECIPROCAL EASEMENT DOCTRINE Equitable doctrine under which reciprocal servitudes are implied where a developer who owns and subdivides a tract of land, and sells the different lots to separate grantees, and puts in each deed restrictions upon the use of each lot conveyed, in accordance with a general building, improvement, or development plan, so that such restrictions may be enforced by any grantee against any other grantee, but only if injustice can be avoided by implying the reciprocal servitudes.

PLAT A map, or representation on paper, of a piece of land subdivided into lots, showing streets, alleys, easements, and other features, usually drawn to scale.

RESTRICTIVE COVENANT A promise contained in a deed to limit the uses to which the property will be made.

SUBDIVISION Division of improved or unimproved land for the purpose of sale or lease or financing, whether immediate or future.

River Heights Associates L.P. v. Batten

Owner of undeveloped lots (P) v. Residential property owner (D)

Va. Sup. Ct., 591 S.E.2d 683 (2004)

NATURE OF CASE: Appeal from lower court decision finding that subdivision's restrictive covenant prohibiting commercial use was enforceable.

FACT SUMMARY: Alice Batten (P), a residential property owner in a subdivision, sought to prevent commercial development of four undeveloped lots within the subdivision. The subdivision was created in 1959 with a restrictive covenant that all lots would be used only for residential homes.

RULE OF LAW

A restrictive covenant can be nullified by changed conditions only when the changes are so radical as to destroy the essential objectives and purposes of the covenant.

FACTS: Alice Batten (P), a residential property owner in the Carrsbrook Subdivision in Virginia, sought to prevent commercial development of four undeveloped lots within the subdivision. Wendell Wood (D) had an ownership interest in the four different entities that owned the four undeveloped lots. The subdivision was created in 1959 with a restrictive covenant that all lots would be used only for residential homes. The four lots in question had frontage on Route 29. When the subdivision was created, Route 29 was a two-lane road. Both residential homes and small businesses existed along the road. Currently, Route 29 is a bustling eight-lane thoroughfare lined with hotels, shopping centers, and restaurants. No residential properties have been built on Route 29 near the subdivision in over 30 years. The trial court found that the subdivision itself had not undergone any radical changes and found the restrictive covenant to be enforceable. Wood (D) and the four entities appealed.

ISSUE: Can a restrictive covenant be nullified by changed conditions only when the changes are so radical as to destroy the essential objectives and purposes of the covenant?

HOLDING AND DECISION: (Carrico, J.) Yes. A restrictive covenant can be nullified by changed conditions only when the changes are so radical as to destroy the essential objectives and purposes of the covenant. The initial inquiry is a determination of the area that must be examined to determine whether changed conditions exist. Wells (D) argues the trial court improperly examined only the subdivision itself and not the surrounding areas. In particular Wells (D) argues that Route 29 has changed from a small road to a major commercial district. Wells (D) is incorrect. He seeks a rule that would ignore the changes, or lack thereof, within the subdivision itself. The subdivision at issue remains an entirely residential area. To ignore the subdivision would deny the lot owners the protection of the covenant to which they are entitled. The court agrees the analysis to determine if the covenant still serves its intended purposes should include a review of the subdivision as well as the surrounding areas. Based on this court's review, particularly the fact that the subdivision itself has not changed at all in 30 years, the changes are not so radical as to defeat the original purposes of the covenant. Affirmed.

ANALYSIS

The changed condition doctrine varies from jurisdiction to jurisdiction. This case provides the common-law interpretation as it applies to restrictive covenants. The doctrine can also be used to attack easements or other types of servitudes, although not in all jurisdictions.

Quicknotes

RESTRICTIVE COVENANT A promise contained in a deed to limit the uses to which the property will be made.

Shelley v. Kraemer

Home buyer (D) v. Neighbors (P)

334 U.S. 1 (1948)

NATURE OF CASE: Appeal from state high court decision in favor of defendants.

FACT SUMMARY: Shelley (D), an African-American, sought to purchase a home. A group of neighbors sought to uphold a restrictive covenant that prohibited the sale of any neighborhood homes to any person "not of the Caucasian race."

RULE OF LAW

State court enforcement of private, discriminatory restrictive covenants constitutes state action under the Fourteenth Amendment.

FACTS: On February 16, 1911, 30 of 39 owners of property in a neighborhood of St. Louis executed an agreement prohibiting the sale of any of the homes to any person "not of the Caucasian race." In 1945, Shelley (D), an African-American, sought to buy one of the homes covered by the agreement. Other homeowners, led by Kraemer (P), brought suit to uphold the restrictive covenant and to prevent the sale. The Missouri Supreme court upheld the validity of the restrictive covenant. Shelley (D) appealed to the United States Supreme Court.

ISSUE: Does state court enforcement of private, discriminatory restrictive covenants constitute state action under the Fourteenth Amendment?

HOLDING AND DECISION: (Vinson, C.J.) Yes. State court enforcement of private, discriminatory restrictive covenants constitutes state action under the Fourteenth Amendment. First, the Fourteenth Amendment requires equality in the enjoyment of property rights. Moreover, if the prohibition in the private agreement was contained in a state statute or local ordinance, the Fourteenth Amendment would bar such prohibition because state action would be present. Here, the restrictive covenant is contained in an agreement between private individuals. We therefore conclude that without any state court intervention, private, restrictive covenants, even if discriminatory, do not run afoul of the Fourteenth Amendment because no state action is present. However, in the instant case, state courts have entered the fray and upheld the validity of the clearly discriminatory, private agreement. We have long held that "state action" includes action of the state courts and judicial officials. Therefore, the state court's intervention to uphold the covenants constitutes state action. That action is a violation of Shelley's (D) right to equal protection under the laws. Reversed.

ANALYSIS

Shelley was the first case to strike down private, race-based restrictive covenants. The Civil Rights Act, plus a host of other state and local ordinances now outlaw discrimination in the private, residential housing market.

Quicknotes

FOURTEENTH AMENDMENT Declares that no state shall make or enforce any law that shall abridge the privileges and immunities of citizens of the United States. No state shall deny to any person within its jurisdiction the equal protection of the laws.

RESTRICTIVE COVENANT A promise contained in a deed to limit the uses to which the property will be made.

Nahrstedt v. Lakeside Village Condominium Association, Inc.

Cat lover (P) v. Homeowners association (D)

Cal. Sup. Ct., 878 P.2d 1275 (1994)

NATURE OF CASE: Suit challenging the validity of a provision in a common-interest development's Covenants, Conditions and Restrictions that prohibited the keeping of pets in the development.

FACT SUMMARY: A resident of a common-interest development in California kept three cats in her condominium in violation of the development's governing Covenants, Conditions and Restrictions. The condominium's homeowners' association therefore assessed continuing penalties against her for the violations.

RULE OF LAW

A recorded use restriction imposed by a common-interest development in California must be enforced uniformly against all residents of the development unless the restriction is unreasonable.

FACTS: Nahrstedt (P) owned and lived in a condominium in Lakeside Village, a 530-unit common-interest development in Los Angeles County overseen by the Lakeside Village Condominium Association ("the homeowners' association") (D). Nahrstedt's (P) ownership of her condominium gave her membership in the homeowners' association (D). One of the homeowners' association's (D) duties was to enforce Lakeside Village's governing, duly recorded Covenants, Conditions and Restrictions (CC&Rs). One clause of the CC&Rs provided that "[n]o animals (which shall include dogs and cats) . . . shall be kept in any unit." Nahrstedt (P), who alleged that she did not know of the pet restriction when she bought her condominium, lived in her unit with her three cats, but she did not let her cats have free run of Lakeside Village's common areas. When the homeowners' association (D) learned that Nahrstedt (P) was keeping the cats in her home, it started assessing monthly fines against her for violating the CC&Rs. Nahrstedt (P) sued the homeowners' association (D), asking the trial court to invalidate the assessments already imposed against her, to enjoin the homeowners' association (D) from making such assessments against her in the future, and to declare the pet restriction in the CC&Rs "unreasonable" as applied to situations involving non-disturbing, essentially entirely in-home pet ownership like hers. The homeowners' association (D) filed a demurrer to Nahrstedt's (P) complaint [i.e., the homeowners' association (D) moved to dismiss her complaint for failing to state a claim upon which relief could be granted]. The trial court agreed with the homeowners' association (D) and dismissed Nahrstedt's (P) complaint. On Nahrstedt's (P) appeal, the intermediate appellate court reversed the trial court's judgment, agreeing with Nahrstedt (P) that the reasonableness of a recorded use restriction in a common-interest development must be determined on a case-by-case basis. The homeowners' association (D) petitioned the California Supreme Court for further review.

ISSUE: Must a recorded use restriction imposed by a common-interest development in California be enforced uniformly against all residents of the development unless the restriction is unreasonable?

HOLDING AND DECISION: (Kennard, J.) Yes. A recorded use restriction imposed by a common-interest development in California must be enforced uniformly against all residents of the development unless the restriction is unreasonable. Homeowners, in a common-interest development, sacrifice certain freedoms in exchange for, among other things—their ability to enforce restrictive covenants against other homeowners in the development. These restrictions are enforceable, though, only if they qualify as equitable servitudes or as covenants running with the land. In Section 1354(a) of the California Civil Code, California's legislature has established the test for determining whether a common-interest development's use restrictions are enforceable: under Section 1354(a), a recorded declaration's use restrictions are "enforceable . . . unless unreasonable." Some states have reached similar conclusions through the courts. For example, in *Hidden Harbour Estates v. Basso*, 393 So. 2d 637 (Fla. Ct. App. 1981), a Florida appellate court held that a recorded declaration's stated use restrictions are entitled to a heavy presumption of validity, so much so that even somewhat unreasonable restrictions should nevertheless be enforced. The *Hidden Harbour Estates* court concluded further arbitrary restrictions or those that violate public policy or a fundamental constitutional right should not be enforced. In a case involving a pet restriction, *Noble v. Murphy*, 612 N.E.2d 266 (Mass. App. Ct. 1993), the court agreed with the *Hidden Harbour Estates* rationale that otherwise-valid use restrictions should be enforced unless they violate constitutional rights or public policy. This court concludes, then, that recorded restrictive covenants should not be enforced when they violate public policy, as in *Shelley v. Kraemer*, 334 U.S. 1 (1948) (racial restriction), or when they are arbitrary and bear no rational relation to a purpose involving the land. In such cases, the harm resulting from enforcement of arbitrary use restrictions or restrictions that violate fundamental public

Continued on next page.

policy always outweighs any benefit that such restrictions might confer. Such principles also inform Section 1354(a) of the California Civil Code, which this court interprets as requiring enforcement of use restrictions unless they are arbitrary, violate public policy, or impose burdens outweighing any benefit. This presumption of validity for recorded restrictive covenants means that homeowners' associations can enforce their covenants without fear of instigating litigation. The presumption also relieves the judicial system from making case-by-case determinations of whether covenants are reasonable as applied to a particular homeowner. The presumption thus in turn means that homeowners in common-interest developments will have the assurance that their covenants will be enforced uniformly and predictably. In this particular case, the appellate court failed to apply the pertinent rules governing equitable servitudes and erroneously relied on two opinions, *Portola Hills Community Assn. v. James*, 5 Cal. Rptr. 2d 580 (Cal. Ct. App. 1993), and *Bernardo Villas Management Corp. v. Black*, 235 Cal. Rptr. 509 (Cal. Ct. App. 1987), both of which are hereby disapproved because those courts did not use appropriately deferential review of the covenants at issue in those cases. Whether a use restriction is reasonable or unreasonable must be determined by referring to the entire common-interest development, not by referring to the particular facts of a specific complaining homeowner. More specifically, the court holds that the Lakeside Village pet restriction is not arbitrary because it rationally promotes the other owners' legitimate concerns about health, sanitation, and noise; Nahrstedt (P) has failed to allege that the restriction's burden is so disproportionate to the legitimate benefits that the pet restriction is unreasonable. Moreover, no fundamental public policy requires that pets be kept in a condominium development, and no constitutional provision or California statute grants the right to keep pets in such a situation, either. Reversed and remanded.

DISSENT: (Arabian, J.) The majority's reasoning has technical merit, but the application of that analysis to these facts reveals a narrow understanding of the relationship between the law and the human spirit. The pet restriction at issue here violates Section 1354(a). It is arbitrary and unreasonable, within the meaning of Section 1354(a), because it imposes an undue burden on owners who keep their pets within their units and do not permit their pets to disturb the use of other homeowners' properties. The restriction's burden on such homeowners outweighs those homeowners' quality of life in the common-interest development, and indeed the restriction only worsens the breakdown of our social fabric. All that the majority has done today is to accept, uncritically, the homeowners' association's (D) assurances that uniform enforcement will promote all owners' "health and happiness." The first question in an appropriately probing inquiry should be to recognize that the burden on the particular use at issue here goes well beyond the impersonal and mundane issues normally covered by restrictive covenants. The majority instead asks only whether the use restriction at issue was stated in the original recorded declaration. If it was, it now shall be presumed valid unless it violates public policy. Such a standard means that almost all recorded use restrictions are valid, a status that only the commandments issued by Moses have enjoyed before today. Further, the proscribed activity here, pet ownership that is wholly confined to one's own home, deprives homeowners of the American dream, a notion that has always included the ownership and full enjoyment of one's home. Courts should rule with more humanity and strive to create harmony, not division, within the populace.

ANALYSIS

Despite the emotionalism of Justice Arabian's dissent, and despite the intermediate appellate court's contrary ruling (relying on two now-invalidated opinions), today this case seems relatively easy for all the reasons cited by the majority. Public policy argues heavily against Nahrstedt's (P) position because that position would create great instability within homeowners' associations, and because the burden of deciding enforceability of use restrictions on a case-by-case basis would substantially increase the caseloads of a judicial system that is already overburdened. Under the rationale of *Nahrstedt* and cases like it, homeowners now can know that, when they sign a development's recorded covenants and use restrictions, those covenants and restrictions will almost certainly be enforced.

Quicknotes

CC&RS Covenants, conditions, and restrictions that residents of a condominium development agree to abide by when they take ownership of a unit in that development.

DECLARATORY RELIEF A judgment of the court establishing the rights of the parties.

CHAPTER 11

Legislative Land Use Controls: The Law of Zoning

Quick Reference Rules of Law

Village of Euclid v. Ambler Realty Co.

Municipal corporation (D) v. Tract owner (P)

272 U.S. 365 (1926)

NATURE OF CASE: Action to enjoin enforcement of a zoning ordinance.

FACT SUMMARY: Euclid (D) zoned property of Ambler Realty (P) in a manner that materially reduced its potential value.

RULE OF LAW

A zoning ordinance, as a valid exercise of the police power, will only be declared unconstitutional where its provisions are clearly arbitrary and unreasonable, having no substantial relation to the public health, safety, morals, or general welfare.

FACTS: Ambler Realty (P) was the owner of 68 acres in the village of Euclid (D). Though surrounded primarily by residential neighborhoods, the 68 acres is also bounded by a major thoroughfare to the south and a railroad to the north. Euclid (D) instituted zoning ordinances placing use, height, and area restrictions. Restrictions were placed on Ambler Realty's (P) property prohibiting (1) apartment houses, hotels, churches, schools, or any other public or semi-public buildings for the first 620 feet from Euclid Avenue, the above-described major thoroughfare, and (2) industry, theatres, banks, shops, etc., for the next 130 feet after that. As a result of this zoning, the value of Ambler Realty's (P) property has declined from $10,000 per acre to $2,500 per acre. Ambler Realty (P) brought an action to enjoin Euclid (D) from enforcing the ordinance on the ground that it constitutes a violation of Fourteenth Amendment due process. From a decree in favor of Amber Realty (P), Euclid (D) appeals, contending that the ordinance was a valid exercise of the police power of the state.

ISSUE: Is a zoning ordinance unconstitutional as a deprivation of property without due process because it results in a diminution of value in the property zoned?

HOLDING AND DECISION: (Sutherland, J.) No. A zoning ordinance, as a valid exercise of the police power, will only be declared unconstitutional where its provisions are clearly arbitrary and unreasonable, having no substantial relation to the public health, safety, morals, or general welfare. Zoning ordinances, and all similar laws and regulations, must find their justification in some aspect of the police power, asserted for the public welfare. Until recent years, urban life was comparatively simple; but with the great increase and concentration of population, problems have developed which require new restrictions on the use and occupation of private lands in urban communities. There is no serious difference of opinion on the state power to avoid the nuisances which industry may cause in a residential area. As for residential regulation, many considerations point toward their validity. Segregation of residential business and industrial buildings makes it easier to provide appropriate fire apparatus, for example. Further, it is often observed that the construction of one type of building destroys an area for other types. In light of these considerations, the court is not prepared to say that the end of public welfare here is not sufficient to justify the imposition of this ordinance. It clearly cannot be said that it "... passes the bounds of reason and assumes the character of a merely arbitrary fiat." The decree must be reversed.

ANALYSIS

Village of Euclid v. Ambler Realty is the landmark United States Supreme Court decision on zoning ordinances as valid exercises of the police power. Essentially, any zoning ordinance that is tied to public health, safety, morals, or welfare will be upheld unless clearly arbitrary and unreasonable. So-called *Euclidian* Zoning, which resulted from this decision, usually consists in the division of areas into zones, in which building use, height, and area are regulated in a manner designed to guarantee homogeneity of building patterns. All too often, however, zoning operates not so much to protect the public interest as to protect the vested interests in a community. Building restrictions may all too easily be used as an economic sanction by which social segregation is perpetuated. (Barring low-cost housing keeps out an economically deprived segment of the population.) Note, however, that *Euclid* did not foreclose the possibility that government land-use regulations may constitute a "taking" which requires compensation. In *Pennsylvania Coal Co. v. Mahon*, 260 U.S. 393 (1922), the United States Supreme Court held that an anti-mining restriction, which totally destroyed the interest of the party who owned only the mineral rights, constituted a taking as to that person for which compensation had to be paid. In the *Mahon* case, the diminution in value of the party's property was total and was thus clearly a "taking."

Continued on next page.

Quicknotes

INJUNCTION A court order requiring a person to do or prohibiting that person from doing a specific act.

POLICE POWER The power of a government to impose restrictions on the rights of private persons, as long as those restrictions are reasonably related to the promotion and protection of public health, safety, morals, and the general welfare.

PUBLIC WELFARE The well-being of the general community.

TAKING A governmental action that substantially deprives an owner of the use and enjoyment of their property, requiring compensation.

ZONING ORDINANCE A statute that divides land into defined areas and that regulates the form and use of buildings and structures within those areas.

Jones v. Lutken

RV park owner (P) v. Nearby homeowners (D)

Miss. Ct. App., 62 So. 3d 455 (2011)

NATURE OF CASE: Appeal from denial of a permit for a permissible non-conforming use of property.

FACT SUMMARY: A county passed a zoning ordinance that changed property around a lake to be largely residential but allowed a vacation-focused RV park to continue its non-conforming use, as long as it did not expand. The RV park owner began selling portable cabins, which he displayed on the property for sale and sold to two individuals who placed them on RV lots.

RULE OF LAW

The placement of portable cabins on RV lots is a permissible continuation of a non-conforming use.

FACTS: Jones (P) operated an RV campground, convenience store, and cabin-rental business on leased land near a lake in Washington County, Mississippi. The County passed a zoning ordinance that changed most of the property around the lake, including the property leased by Jones (P), to residential. The ordinance expressly permitted non-conforming uses that were in existence at the time of the zoning change but prohibited expansion of non-conforming properties. Jones (P) was permitted to continue operating as a permissible non-conforming entity until he expanded his business to include the sale of portable cabins (small manufactured buildings that could be loaded on trucks and transported), which he displayed on the property. Jones (P) applied for a permit and the Washington County Planning Commission (Commission) determined that while it was an impermissible expansion for Jones (P) to display the cabins for sale, it was a permissible continuation of Jones's (P) existing non-conforming use to allow two portable cabin owners to keep their cabins on Jones's (P) RV lots. A group of nearby homeowners (D) appealed the Commission's decision to the Washington County Board of Supervisors (Board), where it was affirmed. The group of homeowners (D) then appealed the Board's decision to the circuit court, where it was reversed.

ISSUE: Is the placement of portable cabins on RV lots a permissible continuation of a non-conforming use?

HOLDING AND DECISION: (Griffis, J.) Yes. The placement of portable cabins on RV lots is a permissible continuation of a non-conforming use. Because the Board of Supervisors (Board) determined that the portable cabins qualify as RVs under an ordinance that defines RVsas "portable or mobile living unit[s] for temporary human occupancy away from the place of residence of the occupants," the placement of the cabins on RV lots in a permissible continuation of a non-conforming use When determining how to construe a zoning ordinance, Mississippi courts are required to affirm local authorities' decisions that are "fairly debatable." The Board was tasked with determining first, whether placing the portable cabins on the RV lot was an expansion of Jones's non-conforming use, and second, whether the portable cabins qualified as RVs under the County's ordinance. In making its affirmative finding, the Board interpreted the zoning-ordinance language, in which the words "expansion" and "continuation" were not clearly defined and applied it to the specific facts of this case. The Board's determination that the definition of an RV could include portable cabins was "fairly debatable" and not manifestly unreasonable. Therefore, the Board's determination that the portable cabins qualified as RVs and could be used for recreation on Jones's (P) property was not improper. Reversed.

ANALYSIS

Another area of legal conflict in zoning is intensity of use. In *Trip Associates, Inc. v. Mayor and City Council of Baltimore*, 898 A.2d 449 (Md. App. 2006), the Baltimore Municipal and Zoning Appeals Board permitted an adult entertainment venue to continue a non-conforming use but restricted the venue to two days a week of adult entertainment with non-adult entertainment on the other nights. The Maryland Court of Appeals ruled that adult entertainment would be permitted five days a week, because it was an intensification of the continued use instead of a prohibited expansion of use.

Quicknotes

NON-CONFORMING USE The use of a structure that is rendered unlawful by the promulgation or revision of a zoning ordinance.

ZONING ORDINANCE A statute that divides land into defined areas and that regulates the form and use of buildings and structures within those areas.

PA Northwestern Distributors, Inc. v. Zoning Hearing Board

Adult bookstore owner (P) v. Zoning board (D)

Pa. Sup. Ct., 584 A.2d 1372 (1991)

NATURE OF CASE: Appeal from dismissal of action challenging constitutionality of amortization ordinance.

FACT SUMMARY: Three weeks after PA Northwestern Distributors, Inc. (P) opened an adult bookstore in Moon Township, Pennsylvania, the Board of Supervisors adopted an ordinance restricting permissible locations for bookstores and allowing only 90 days for non-conforming uses to either comply or shut down.

RULE OF LAW

A zoning ordinance that requires the amortization and discontinuance of a lawful preexisting non-conforming use is confiscatory and violative of the state constitution as a taking of property without just compensation.

FACTS: After obtaining the necessary permits, PA Northwestern Distributors, Inc. (PA Northwestern) (P) opened an adult bookstore in Moon Township. Three weeks later, following a public meeting, the Moon Township Board of Supervisors amended the zoning ordinances to impose extensive restrictions on the location and operation of "adult commercial enterprises." Any preexisting use in conflict with the new amendments was given 90-days' grace period, designed as a period of amortization, to either come into compliance with the ordinance or discontinue business. PA Northwestern (P) could not meet the place restrictions set forth in the ordinance because it was not located in an area designated for adult commercial enterprises. It filed an appeal with the Zoning Hearing Board (D), challenging the validity of the amortization provision, but the Hearing Board (D) validated the provision. PA Northwestern (P) appealed to the Court of Common Pleas, which dismissed the appeal. The Commonwealth Court affirmed applying the criteria set forth in *Sullivan v. Zoning Bd.*, 83 Pa. Commw. 228, 478 A.2d 912 (1984), comparing the impact of the provision on the property to the beneficial effects that would accrue to the community as a result of a discontinuance of the use. PA Northwestern (P) appealed.

ISSUE: Is a zoning ordinance that requires the amortization and discontinuance of a lawful preexisting non-conforming use confiscatory and violative of the state constitution as a taking of property without just compensation?

HOLDING AND DECISION: (Larsen, J.) Yes. A zoning ordinance that requires the amortization and discontinuance of a lawful preexisting non-conforming use is confiscatory and violative of the state constitution as a taking of property without just compensation. Contrary to the appellate court's interpretation, *Sullivan* is not a correct statement of Pennsylvania law regarding amortization provisions. The usual presumption of a zoning ordinance's validity must be tempered by the fact that zoning involves governmental restrictions on a property owner's constitutionally guaranteed right to use his property, except where the use violates a law or creates a nuisance. Municipalities lack the power to compel a change in the nature of an existing lawful use of property. A lawful non-conforming use establishes in the property owner a vested property right that cannot be abrogated or destroyed. A "taking" under the Pennsylvania Constitution is not limited to actual physical possession or seizure of property. If the effect of the zoning law is to deprive an owner of the lawful use of his property, it amounts to a taking for which he must be compensated. In this case, the amortization ordinance deprived PA Northwestern (P) of the lawful use of its property because it forced it to cease using its property as an adult book store within 90 days. Therefore, the amortization provision was unconstitutional on its face because it effected a taking of PA Northwestern's (P) property without just compensation. Reversed.

CONCURRENCE AND DISSENT: (Nix, C.J.) Although the amortization provision in this case is unreasonable and must be struck down because it failed to provide adequate time for elimination of the non-conforming use, the per se prohibition against amortization provisions advanced by the majority is too restrictive. Amortization provisions that provide adequate notice to the property owner so that he is not deprived of the property or its use are an effective way to reconcile community interests with business needs.

ANALYSIS

Pennsylvania is part of a small minority of states that forbid amortization ordinances altogether. In most states, a requirement that a non-conforming use cease within a certain time period does not constitute a taking, so long as the time period is reasonable. If the time period gives the owner adequate time to make new plans, any loss they suffer may be offset by the monopoly position they occupy for as long as the non-conforming business remains in place.

Continued on next page.

Quicknotes

AMORTIZATION The satisfaction of a debt by the tendering of regular, equal payments over a period of time.

TAKING A governmental action that substantially deprives an owner of the use and enjoyment of their property, requiring compensation.

State ex rel. Stoyanoff v. Berkeley

Landowner (P) v. Architectural board (D)

Mo. Sup. Ct., 458 S.W.2d 305 (1970)

NATURE OF CASE: Appeal from finding of property deprivation without due process.

FACT SUMMARY: Stoyanoff (P) desired to build a house of unusual shape in a St. Louis, Missouri, suburb.

RULE OF LAW

The protection of property values is a legitimate objective of zoning ordinances.

FACTS: Stoyanoff (P) desired to build a home in the City of Ladue, which is one of the finer suburbs in the St. Louis area. The plans called for the home to be of pyramid shape, with a flat top, and with triangular-shaped windows or doors at one or more corners. A city ordinance established an architectural board to ensure that new residences "conform to certain minimum architectural standards of appearance and conformity with surrounding structures, and that unsightly, grotesque and unsuitable structures detrimental to the . . . welfare of surrounding property . . . be avoided." The homes surrounding Stoyanoff's (P) lot were virtually all two-story houses of conventional architectural design. After the architectural board (D) denied Stoyanoff's (P) application for a building permit, a trial court issued a peremptory writ of mandamus to compel the City of Ladue to issue Stoyanoff (P) a residential building permit.

ISSUE: Is the protection of property values a legitimate objective of zoning ordinances?

HOLDING AND DECISION: (Pritchard, Commr.) Yes. The stabilizing of property values and giving some assurance to the public that, if property is purchased in a residential district, its value will be preserved, is a legitimate objective for zoning ordinances. Property use that offends sensibilities and decreases property values affects not only the adjoining property owners in that vicinity, but the general public as well. When property values are destroyed or seriously impaired, the tax base of the community is affected, and the public suffers economically as a result. Here, the denial of a building permit for Stoyanoff's (P) highly modernistic residence in an area where traditional Colonial, French Provencial, and English Tudor styles of architecture are erected does not appear to be arbitrary and unreasonable when the basic purpose to be served is that of the general welfare of persons in the entire community. Reversed.

ANALYSIS

The court in this case rested its decision on the objective of protecting property values. This is because many early cases held that aesthetic concerns were insufficient to support restrictive zoning regulations. The modern trend, though, shows that many courts are inclined to accept the legitimacy of zoning based exclusively on aesthetic considerations.

Quicknotes

WRIT OF MANDAMUS A court order issued commanding a public or private entity, or an official thereof, to perform a duty required by law.

ZONING ORDINANCE A statute that divides land into defined areas and that regulates the form and use of buildings and structures within those areas.

Moore v. City of East Cleveland

Extended family (D) v. City (P)

431 U.S. 494 (1977)

NATURE OF CASE: Appeal from affirmance of judgment upholding a criminal violation and the constitutionality of a housing ordinance regulating.

FACT SUMMARY: Moore (D), who lived with her own son and two grandsons, first cousins to each other, was directed to remove one of her grandsons from her home in compliance with a housing ordinance of the City of East Cleveland (East Cleveland) (P), which defined which family members could live with each other. Moore (D) challenged the ordinance as an unconstitutional, facial violation of the Due Process Clause.

RULE OF LAW

Freedom of personal choice in matters of marriage and family life is one of the liberties protected by the Due Process Clause of the Fourteenth Amendment and any zoning ordinance infringing on these freedoms is subject to strict scrutiny.

FACTS: Moore (D) lived in her City of East Cleveland (East Cleveland) (P) home together with her son and her two grandsons. The two boys were first cousins. Moore (D) received a notice of violation of a housing ordinance from the City of Cleveland (P) stating that John, her grandson, was an illegal occupant and directing her to comply with the ordinance. East Cleveland's (P) housing ordinance limited occupancy of a dwelling unit to members of a single family, but it contained an unusual and complicated definitional section that recognized as a family only a few categories of related individuals. Moore's (D) family did not fit into any of these categories. When Moore (D) failed to remove her grandson from her home, East Cleveland (P) filed a criminal charge against her. Moore (D) moved to dismiss, claiming that the ordinance was constitutionally invalid on its face. The motion was overruled, and, upon conviction, Moore (D) was sentenced to five days in jail and a fine. The state's intermediate appellate court affirmed, and the state's highest court denied review. The United States Supreme Court granted certiorari.

ISSUE: Does a housing ordinance that infringes on a person's freedom of choice in matters of family life violate the Due Process Clause where the ordinance marginally serves the governmental purposes that purportedly justify the ordinance?

HOLDING AND DECISION: (Powell, J.) Yes. A housing ordinance that infringes on a person's freedom of choice in matters of family life violates the Due Process Clause where the ordinance marginally serves the governmental purposes that purportedly justify the ordinance. This Court has long recognized that freedom of personal choice in matters of marriage and family life is one of the liberties protected by the Due Process Clause of the Fourteenth Amendment. When government intrudes on choices concerning family living arrangements, this Court must scrutinize carefully the importance of the governmental interests advanced and the extent to which they are served by the challenged regulation. When thus examined, the East Cleveland ordinance cannot survive. East Cleveland (P) sought to justify it as a means of preventing overcrowding, minimizing traffic and parking congestion, and avoiding an undue financial burden on the school system. Although these are legitimate goals, the ordinance serves them marginally at best. For example, the ordinance permits any family consisting only of husband, wife, and unmarried children to live together, even if the family contains a half-dozen licensed drivers, each with his own car. At the same time, it forbids an adult brother and sister to share a household, even if both faithfully use public transportation. The ordinance would permit a grandmother to live with a single dependent son and children, even if his school-age children number a dozen, yet it forces Moore (D) to find another dwelling for her grandson, simply because of the presence of his uncle and cousin in the same household. Given the Constitution's protection of the family, and the nation's long history of protecting the sanctity of the family, the East Cleveland (P) ordinance cannot stand. Reversed.

ANALYSIS

The United States Supreme Court relied on *Pierce v. Society of Sisters*, 268 U.S. 510, 268 U.S. 534-535 (1925), to support its decision in *Moore*. *Pierce* struck down an Oregon law requiring all children to attend the state's public schools, holding that the Constitution excludes any general power of the state to standardize its children by forcing them to accept instruction from public teachers only. In *Moore*, the Court reasoned that by the same token the Constitution prevents East Cleveland (P) from standardizing its children and its adults by forcing all to live in certain narrowly defined family patterns.

Continued on next page.

Quicknotes

FREEDOM OF ASSOCIATION The right to peaceably assemble.

TAKING A governmental action that substantially deprives an owner of the use and enjoyment of their property, requiring compensation.

City of Edmonds v. Oxford House, Inc.

Municipality (P) v. Halfway house (D)

514 U.S. 725 (1995)

NATURE OF CASE: Review of order striking down municipal land-use regulation.

FACT SUMMARY: The City of Edmonds (the City) (P) contended that its limitation of residences to single-family use was exempt from the ambit of the Fair Housing Act.

RULE OF LAW

A family-composition zoning rule is not exempt from Fair Housing Act scrutiny.

FACTS: The City of Edmonds (the City) (P) had enacted a zoning ordinance that, among other things, limited occupancy of certain areas of resident property to "single family" use. "Single family" was defined as a group of people related by blood, marriage, or adoption, or any group of five or fewer unrelated persons living in the same household. Oxford House, Inc. (Oxford) (D), instituted at a dwelling covered by the ordinance a halfway house for recovering alcoholics and drug addicts. The City (P) cited Oxford (D) for violating the regulation. It then sued in federal court, seeking a declaration that the Fair Housing Act did not constrain its family definition rule. Oxford (D) counterclaimed, contending that the City (P) had not made a reasonable accommodation for its group home as required by the Fair Housing Act. The district court ruled that the ordinance was a reasonable restriction on the maximum number of occupants, which was exempt from the Fair Housing Act per § 3607(b)(1) of the Act. The Ninth Circuit Court of Appeals reversed and held the ordinance to violate the Fair Housing Act. The United States Supreme Court granted review.

ISSUE: Is a family-composition zoning rule exempt from the Fair Housing Act?

HOLDING AND DECISION: (Ginsburg, J.) No. A family-composition zoning rule is not exempt from the Fair Housing Act. Section 3607(b)(1) of the Fair Housing Act exempts from its ambit laws or ordinances that limit the number of persons living in a household. This exemption was inserted into the Act as recognition that localities have an interest in preventing overcrowding. Here, the district court, apparently looking at the portion of the ordinance defining a "family" as, among other things, "five or fewer individuals," concluded that the ordinance fell within the exemption. This was an incorrect analysis. "Family" is also defined in the ordinance as persons related by blood, marriage, or adoption, without regard to number of persons. Consequently, the rule at issue here is not in any real sense a limitation on the number of persons living in a dwelling. The district court therefore erred in so holding. Affirmed.

ANALYSIS

The United States Supreme Court's decision here was a rather narrow one. It did not decide whether or not the City's (P) ordinance actually violated the Fair Housing Act; rather, it simply decided that § 3607's exemption did not apply. The present decision will most likely be of little import in future Fair Housing Act cases.

Quicknotes

FAIR HOUSING ACT 42 U.S.C. § 3601 Prohibits housing discrimination on the basis of familial status.

LAND-USE REGULATION Regulation governing the development and/or zoning of real estate.

SINGLE-FAMILY USE With respect to zoning refers to area restricted to single-family housing.

ZONING ORDINANCE A statute that divides land into defined areas and which regulates the form and use of buildings and structures within those areas.

Southern Burlington County NAACP v. Township of Mount Laurel

Civil rights organization (P) v. Municipality (D)

N.J. Sup. Ct., 336 A.2d 713, *appeal dismissed and cert. denied*, 423 U.S. 808 (1975)

NATURE OF CASE: Appeal from invalidation of zoning ordinance.

FACT SUMMARY: The trial court held that a bona fide attempt by a municipality to provide zoned land for low-cost housing fulfilled its constitutional obligations.

RULE OF LAW

Municipal land-use regulations must provide a realistic opportunity for low- and moderate-income housing.

FACTS: The National Association for the Advancement of Colored People (NAACP) (P) sued Mount Laurel (D), contending the municipality's zoning scheme violated the New Jersey constitution by failing to provide for low-income housing outside of depressed areas. The New Jersey Supreme Court invalidated the ordinances and remanded for further proceedings. The trial court held that it was sufficient that Mount Laurel (D) had made a bona fide attempt to comply with the Supreme Court decision and upheld the new ordinance enacted in response. The NAACP (P) appealed, contending a mere attempt to provide such zoning did not discharge Mt. Laurel's (D) constitutional obligations.

ISSUE: Must municipal land-use regulations provide a realistic opportunity for low- and moderate-income housing?

HOLDING AND DECISION: (Hall, J.) Yes. Municipal land-use regulations must provide a realistic opportunity for low- and moderate-income housing. Such obligation extends beyond attempting to provide for such housing. The housing must be in direct proportion to the percentage of lower income residents in the city. To reach this goal, affirmative governmental action may be required. The elimination of some obstacles and the creation of a new zoning scheme may be frustrated by other restrictions that effectively deprive the poor of adequate housing. Therefore, the zoning scheme, which merely manifested intent to abide by the original Supreme Court, holding was insufficient to discharge Mount Laurel's (D) constitutional obligations. Reversed and judgment of the Law Division modified.

ANALYSIS

The rationale behind the *Mount Laurel* case is that the use of all land is controlled by the state. The state has constitutional obligations to all its residents whether rich or poor. Municipalities, as state subjects, must set aside a fair share of its land for lower income housing. They cannot allocate only dilapidated land for the poor and retain valuable land for the rich exclusively. While this rationale appears clear in theory, in execution it has proven very difficult. The main difficulty is in developing an equitable formula for determining "fair share." Until a definitive formula is developed, this will prevent widespread application of this rule.

Quicknotes

AFFIRMATIVE ACTION A form of benign discrimination designed to remedy existing discrimination by favoring one group over another.

LAND-USE REGULATION Regulation governing the development and/or zoning of real estate.

ZONING ORDINANCE A statute that divides land into defined areas and which regulates the form and use of buildings and structures within those areas.

CHAPTER 12

Eminent Domain and the Problem of Implicit Takings

Quick Reference Rules of Law

Kelo v. City of New London

Landowners (P) v. Municipality (D)

545 U.S. 469 (2005)

NATURE OF CASE: Suit for orders enjoining a city from taking private properties to promote the city's planned economic revitalization.

FACT SUMMARY: A city adopted a development plan designed to revitalize the local economy. To implement its plan, the city sought to condemn 15 properties owned by nine private landowners who refused to sell their properties to the city.

RULE OF LAW

A city's proposed taking of private property for general economic development qualifies as a public use consistent with the Takings Clause of the Fifth Amendment to the United States Constitution.

FACTS: In 1990, a Connecticut state agency officially designated the City of New London ("the City" or "New London") (D) as a "distressed municipality." New London's (D) economy worsened in 1996 when the federal government closed a facility that employed 1,500 people. The City's (D) unemployment rate almost doubled that for the rest of the state, and its population had dwindled to its lowest level in almost 80 years. State and local officials therefore targeted the City (D) for economic revitalization. Eventually a development plan focused on a 90-acre area known as Fort Trumbull as the center of the City's (D) revitalization efforts. The drafters designed the development plan to coincide with the expected arrival of a major company, Pfizer Inc., and to rejuvenate the local economy with jobs, tax revenue, and a generalized momentum for future growth and recreational activities. Most landowners in the Fort Trumbull area agreed to sell their properties to the City (D). Nine owners, however, refused to sell their 15 properties, and the City (D) initiated condemnation proceedings for the 15 properties. The City (D) condemned the properties purely because they were within the area designated for development; the City (D) never alleged that the properties were in any degree of substandard condition. Susette Kelo (P) and the other eight resisting owners sued the City (D) in state court, where the trial judge permanently enjoined the City (D) from taking 11 of the contested properties but permitted the taking of the other four properties. Both sides appealed to the Connecticut Supreme Court, which held that all 15 properties could properly be taken by New London (D). Applying state statute, that court held that the proposed taking was for a public use that satisfied both state and federal constitutional requirements. Kelo (P) and her fellow landowners petitioned the United States Supreme Court for further review.

ISSUE: Does a city's proposed taking of private property for general economic development qualify as a public use consistent with the Takings Clause of the Fifth Amendment to the United States Constitution?

HOLDING AND DECISION: (Stevens, J.) Yes. A city's proposed taking of private property for general economic development qualifies as a public use consistent with the Takings Clause of the Fifth Amendment to the United States Constitution. A government may not take private property merely to transfer it to another private owner; conversely, private property may be taken, if the taking is legitimately for "use by the public." Neither of these general propositions controls this case, though, because the question here narrows to whether a proposed taking for general economic development serves a "public purpose," which is the broader reading of "public use" that this Court has consistently used for more than a century. The Court upheld the redevelopment plan at issue in *Berman v. Parker*, 348 U.S. 26 (1954), because creating a "better balanced, more attractive community" was a valid public purpose. Similarly, in *Hawaii Housing Authority v. Midkiff*, 467 U.S. 229 (1984), the Court upheld a state statute that took fee title from lessors and vested title in lessees to eliminate the "social and economic evils of land oligopoly." These cases show that the determinative question is the proposed taking's purpose, not the specific means by which the government proposes to achieve its purpose. Under this appropriately deferential standard of review, New London's (D) proposed takings here do meet the public-use requirement imposed by the Takings Clause. Kelo's (P) request that the Court reject economic development as an acceptable public use contradicts not only precedent but also logic because no principled distinction exists between economic development and other accepted public uses. Further, her objection that economic development confuses the distinction between public and private use also contradicts precedent; public use often benefits specific private owners, too. Finally, Kelo's (P) objection that nothing would stop a city from transferring land from one private owner to another specific private owner for a public purpose presents issues that are not before the Court in this case. Accordingly, this Court's takings jurisprudence provides no basis for enjoining the City of New London (D) from taking the 15 properties in the Fort Trumbull area. Affirmed.

CONCURRENCE: (Kennedy, J.) Deferential review should not become so deferential that it ignores

Continued on next page.

a taking designed primarily to favor another private party. Furthermore, a more stringent standard of review might apply in cases where economic development is the asserted public use.

DISSENT: (O'Connor, J.) Past cases have recognized three kinds of takings that meet the public-use requirement: transferring private property to public ownership, to private ownership for common public use, and to private ownership within a program serving a public purpose. The third category, represented by *Midkiff* and *Berman*, raises the most questions. The takings in those two cases addressed identifiable public harms (oligopoly and blight, respectively), but this case goes beyond curing a public harm—and it goes too far.

ANALYSIS

Despite the firestorm of criticism that greeted the *Kelo* decision, the majority opinion fits only the most naive definitions of judicial activism. Indeed, at least in the casebook excerpts, it is Justice O'Connor's reasoning in dissent that seems the more ill-considered: If New London's (D) chronic and deepening economic demise does not qualify as a public harm, what does?

Quicknotes

EMINENT DOMAIN The governmental power to take private property for public use so long as just compensation is paid therefor.

FIFTH AMENDMENT Provides that no person shall be compelled to serve as a witness against himself, or be subject to trial for the same offense twice, or be deprived of life, liberty, or property without due process of law.

PUBLIC USE Basis for governmental taking of property pursuant to its power of eminent domain so that property taken may be utilized for the benefit of the public at large.

TAKING A governmental action that substantially deprives an owner of the use and enjoyment of their property, requiring compensation.

TAKINGS CLAUSE Provision of the Fifth Amendment to the United States Constitution prohibiting the government from taking private property for public use without providing just compensation therefor.

Pennsylvania Coal Co. v. Mahon

Surface rights owner (P) v. Coal company (D)

260 U.S. 393 (1922)

NATURE OF CASE: Appeal from the granting of an injunction.

FACT SUMMARY: Mahon (P) desired to prevent the exercise of the mineral rights that the Pennsylvania Coal Co. (D) reserved in a deed transferring certain surface property to Mahon (P).

RULE OF LAW

Private property may be regulated pursuant to the police power of the state to protect public health, safety, or morals; but if such regulation goes so far as to destroy or appropriate a property right, it becomes a "taking" under the Fifth and Fourteenth Amendments, requiring just compensation therefor.

FACTS: In 1878, Pennsylvania Coal Co. (Coal Co.) (D) transferred certain real property to Mahon (P) by a deed in which Coal Co. (D) reserved the mineral rights on the property and Mahon (P) waived all rights to object to or receive damages for the removal of such minerals. In 1921, the Pennsylvania legislature enacted the "Kohler Act," which forbade the mining of coal in such a way as to cause the subsidence of any human habitation. When Coal Co. (D) decided to exercise its mineral rights pursuant to the deed, Mahon (P) instituted an action for an injunction on the grounds that the mining would violate the Kohler Act by causing the subsidence of his home. From a decree granting the injunction, Coal Co. (D) appealed, contending that such an application of the statute would constitute a taking without compensation contrary to due process.

ISSUE: Will an exercise of the police power be upheld if it, in effect, provides for the destruction or appropriation of a private property right?

HOLDING AND DECISION: (Holmes, J.) No. Private property may be regulated pursuant to the police power of the state to protect public health, safety, or morals; but if such regulation goes so far as to destroy or appropriate a property right, it becomes a "taking" under the Fifth and Fourteenth Amendments, requiring just compensation therefor. It is well established, of course, that some property rights must yield to the public interest and the police power. Here, however, the limited public interest in protecting Mahon's (P) surface rights does not justify the total destruction of the mineral rights that Coal Co. (D) reserved in its deed to Mahon (P). As such, the Kohler Act is unconstitutional insofar as it fails to provide for compensation for the taking of Coal Co.'s (D) property rights. The decree that was based upon it is accordingly reversed.

DISSENT: (Brandeis, J.) No taking occurred here. Rather, the state merely exercised the police power to prevent a noxious use of property. The property remains in the possession of the owners.

ANALYSIS

This case illustrates the minority rule. Generally, when a landowner conveys to someone else a right to take minerals underneath the surface of their land, the grantee owes the grantor-landowner the duty to support the surface in its natural state (i.e., without any buildings). Furthermore, generally, ownership of land carries with it the right to have the land supported in its natural state by adjoining land (i.e., the right to have the support of the land undisturbed by excavation on adjoining land). Under this general rule, if an adjoining landowner excavates in such a manner as to cause subsidence on one's own land, they are "absolutely liable" for such subsidence. If, however, there is a structure on the land that subsides "and the land would not have subsided but for such structure," the adjoining landowner is not liable as a matter of law (i.e., they are not "absolutely liable"), but they may be liable for negligent excavation.

Quicknotes

FIFTH AMENDMENT Provides that no person shall be compelled to serve as a witness against himself, or be subject to trial for the same offense twice, or be deprived of life, liberty, or property without due process of law.

FOURTEENTH AMENDMENT 42 U.S.C. § 1983 Defamation by state officials in connection with a discharge implies a violation of a liberty interest protected by the due process requirements of the United States Constitution.

INJUNCTION A court order requiring a person to do or prohibiting that person from doing a specific act.

KOHLER ACT Legislation passed in 1921 that prohibited the mining of coal that would cause the caving in, collapse, or subsidence of a number of specific structures or public facilities.

POLICE POWER The power of a government to impose restrictions on the rights of private persons, as long as those restrictions are reasonably related to the promotion and protection of public health, safety, morals, and the general welfare.

Penn Central Transportation Company v. City of New York

Railroad (P) v. City (D)

438 U.S. 104 (1978)

NATURE OF CASE: Appeal from denial of compensatory relief.

FACT SUMMARY: Penn Central Transportation Company (P) contended that New York City (D) had taken its property without just compensation when it declared its station a historical landmark.

RULE OF LAW

A city may place restrictions on the development of individual historic landmarks without effecting a taking requiring just compensation.

FACTS: In 1965, New York City (D) adopted the Landmarks Preservation Law, which was enacted to identify and preserve historic and scenic landmarks. Under the law, the Landmarks Preservation Commission would identify properties and areas to be designated as landmarks. The owner of the property in question had the right to appeal the decision at several levels, including judicial review. The law also allowed such property owners to transfer development rights to other parcels of land. On January 22, 1968, Penn Central Transportation Company (Penn Central) (P) entered a contract with UGP Properties, Inc. to construct a multistory office building above the Grand Central Terminal, which had previously been designated a landmark. After the Commission rejected its application, Penn Central (P) filed suit, alleging that the application of the law had taken its property without just compensation in violation of the Fifth and Fourteenth Amendments. The New York Court of Appeals found no denial of due process, and Penn Central (P) appealed.

ISSUE: May a city place restrictions on the development of individual historic landmarks without effecting a taking requiring just compensation?

HOLDING AND DECISION: (Brennan, J.) Yes. In deciding whether a particular governmental action has effected a taking, the focus is both on the character of the action and on the nature and extent of the interference with rights in the parcel as a whole. It is true the Landmarks Law has a more severe impact on some landowners than on others, but that in itself does not mean that the law affects a taking. Legislation designed to promote the general welfare commonly burdens some more than others. The Landmarks Law's effect is simply to prohibit Penn Central (P) or anyone else from occupying portions of the air space above the Terminal, while permitting Penn Central (P) to use the remainder of the parcel in a gainful fashion. The New York City (D) law is not rendered invalid by its failure to provide just compensation whenever a landmark owner is restricted in the exploitation of property interests, such as air rights, to a greater extent than provided for under applicable zoning laws. The restrictions imposed are substantially related to the promotion of the general welfare and not only permit reasonable beneficial use of the landmark site but also affords Penn Central (P) opportunities further to enhance not only the Terminal site, but also other properties. Affirmed.

DISSENT: (Rehnquist, J.) The City of New York (D) has imposed a substantial cost on less than one one-tenth of one percent of the buildings in New York City for the general benefit of all its people. It is exactly this imposition of general costs on a few individuals at which the taking protection is directed.

ANALYSIS

One commentary on this case, states: "The majority implied that esthetics is no less a compelling governmental interest than public health and that the relative sizes of the groups benefited and burdened are, at best, of minor importance. With the tests upon which many courts have come to rely no longer controlling, the protection of private property from governmental interference will depend more than ever on each court's subjective interpretation of 'fairness and justice.'" "The Supreme Court, 1977 Term," 92 *Harv. L. Rev.* 57, 228-232 (1978).

Quicknotes

DUE PROCESS The constitutional mandate requiring the courts to protect and enforce individuals' rights and liberties consistent with prevailing principles of fairness and justice and prohibiting the federal and state governments from such activities that deprive its citizens of life, liberty, or property interest.

TAKINGS CLAUSE Provision of the Fifth Amendment to the United States Constitution prohibiting the government from taking private property for public use without providing just compensation therefor.

Loretto v. Teleprompter Manhattan CATV Corp.

Fee owners (P) v. State (D)

458 U.S. 419 (1982)

NATURE OF CASE: Appeal from enforcement of state statute.

FACT SUMMARY: Loretto (P) contended that a New York law requiring apartment house owners to allow for the installation of cable television equipment allowed a taking of property without just compensation.

RULE OF LAW

Any permanent physical occupation of an owner's property that is governmentally authorized constitutes a taking of property for which just compensation must be paid.

FACTS: New York enacted a statute that required apartment house owners to provide tenants with access to cable television reception. Loretto (P) brought a class action against Teleprompter Manhattan CATV Corp. (Teleprompter) (D), contending its placement of its cable television installation equipment constituted trespass and that the statute allowed for a taking of her property without just compensation. The trial court granted summary judgment for Teleprompter (D), upholding the constitutionality of the statute. The appellate court affirmed, and Loretto (P) appealed to the United States Supreme Court.

ISSUE: Is any permanent physical occupation of an owner's property that is authorized by the government a taking of property that requires the payment of just compensation?

HOLDING AND DECISION (Marshall, J.) Yes. Any permanent physical occupation of an owner's property that is authorized by the government constitutes a taking of property that requires a payment of just compensation. Any occupation, no matter how slight, impacts on the owner's right to exclusive possession of his property. In this case, the equipment occupied a very small area of the property. Yet its presence constituted a physical occupation and thus necessarily must be classified as a taking of property within the meaning of the Fifth Amendment. Therefore, just compensation must be paid. Reversed and remanded.

DISSENT: (Blackmun, J.) The Court goes against established precedent by recognizing a per se "taking" rule. It has previously been held on many occasions that each taking case must be considered on its peculiar facts. A rigid per se rule finding a taking in every physical encroachment will require compensation in situations not justified under previous interpretations of the taking clause.

ANALYSIS

The United States Supreme Court recognizes the fundamental inconsistency with the elements of private ownership presented by any physical invasion of the property by a stranger. When such an invasion is authorized by the government, a compensable taking occurs. The amount of money necessary to constitute just compensation will vary with the case. The Court declined to rule on whether the $1 per unit payment was sufficient in this case.

Quicknotes

CLASS ACTION A suit commenced by a representative on behalf of an ascertainable group that is too large to appear in court, who shares a commonality of interests, and who will benefit from a successful result.

JUST COMPENSATION The right guaranteed by the Fifth Amendment to the U.S. Constitution that when private property is taken for public use by the government, the owner is to receive adequate compensation to restore them to the position they enjoyed prior to the taking/appropriation.

SUMMARY JUDGMENT Judgment rendered by a court in response to a motion by one of the parties, claiming that the lack of a question of material fact in respect to an issue warrants disposition of the issue without consideration by the jury.

TAKING A governmental action that substantially deprives an owner of the use and enjoyment of their property, requiring compensation.

TRESPASS Unlawful interference with, or damage to, the real or personal property of another.

Lucas v. South Carolina Coastal Council

Beachfront property owner (P) v. State (D)

505 U.S. 1003 (1992)

NATURE OF CASE: Appeal from reversal of award of damages in action for compensation under the Takings Clause.

FACT SUMMARY: After Lucas (P) invested $975,000 in two beachfront lots, South Carolina (D) enacted a statute prohibiting construction on the barrier islands where the lots were located, entitling him, he contended, to compensation under the Takings Clause.

RULE OF LAW

The state must compensate a landowner when a regulatory action denies an owner economically viable use of his land, unless the prohibited use of the land constitutes a nuisance under state common law.

FACTS: Lucas (P) purchased two residential lots for $975,000 on the Isle of Palms, a barrier island off the coast of South Carolina, on which he planned to build single-family homes. The Isle of Palms development, of which Lucas (P) was a co-owner, was located on highly unstable ground, prone to flooding and erosion. At the time of purchase, the state, county, and town had not imposed any restrictions on residential use of the property. However, two years after Lucas's (P) purchase, but before he began construction, South Carolina (D) enacted the Beachfront Management Act (the Act), in an attempt to counteract the critical erosion of South Carolina beaches. The Act prohibited, without exception, the construction of any habitable improvements seaward of a baseline connecting historical points of erosion on the Isle of Palms. Lucas's (P) lots were located within the restricted area. He filed suit against South Carolina (D), contending that the Act's ban on construction amounted to a taking of his property without just compensation. He conceded that the Act was a lawful exercise of South Carolina's (D) police power but claimed that the Act rendered his property valueless, entitling him to compensation. The trial court agreed and ordered South Carolina (D) to pay $1,232,387. The Supreme Court of South Carolina reversed, ruling that when an otherwise valid regulation respecting the use of property is designed to prevent public harm, as this Act was, no compensation was owed. Lucas (P) appealed, and the United States Supreme Court granted certiorari.

ISSUE: Must the state compensate a landowner when a regulatory action denies an owner economically viable use of his land?

HOLDING AND DECISION: (Scalia, J.) Yes. The state must compensate a landowner when a regulatory action denies an owner economically valuable use of his land, unless the prohibited use of the land constitutes a nuisance under state common law. Traditionally, compensation has been required for two separate categories of regulatory actions: (1) those that cause a physical invasion of private property and (2) those that deprive a landowner of all economically beneficial or productive use of land. However, there is also a long line of cases denying compensation to owners whose property is regulated to prevent a public harm, the seminal case being *Mugler v. Kansas*, 123 U.S. 623 (1887), in which a law prohibiting the manufacture of alcoholic beverages was sustained against a taking claim brought by a brewery owner. Under this line of cases, regulation of "harmful or noxious uses" of property was allowed to affect property values without obligating the government to pay compensation. This early focus on noxious uses later evolved into the Court's contemporary analysis that finds no taking if a land-use regulation substantially advances a legitimate state interest. Whether the regulation prevents a harmful use can no longer be the basis for an exception from the rule that total regulatory taking must be compensated; if it were, no compensation would ever be necessary, since most regulations may be described as mitigating some harm, depending on the observer's point of view. Instead, a better test is that confiscatory regulations, i.e., those that prohibit all economically beneficial use of land, may not be enacted without compensation, unless the regulation serves to prohibit a purpose that was already unlawful under existing nuisance and property law. In this case, the Act rendered Lucas's (P) lots valueless by requiring that they remain in their natural state. Therefore, South Carolina (D) must either identify the relevant common-law principles of nuisance and property that would prohibit construction on Lucas's (P) beachfront property or compensate him for the value of his property. Reversed and remanded.

CONCURRENCE: (Kennedy, J.) The majority provided the lower courts with guidance regarding the analysis on remand but did not reach the ultimate question of whether a taking had occurred. The factual record is not complete. It is an open question whether the owner of the property actually intended to build homes on the property. The majority improperly concludes that the beach front property loses all value based on the new regulations. However, the determination of value must be considered by referring to the owner's reasonable

Continued on next page.

expectations. Those reasonable expectations are shaped by what the judicial branch says about how far legislatures can go when regulating property. Where a regulatory taking allegedly deprives the property of all value, the test is whether the deprivation is inconsistent with reasonable, investment-backed expectations of the property owner.

CONCURRENCE: (Souter, J.) This Court improperly granted a writ of certiorari to this appeal. The state trial court concluded that the state regulation deprived the owner of his entire economic interest in the property. That no longer appears to be the case, based on our prior decisions. The issue of whether a total deprivation occurred is not reviewable and was not briefed by the parties. Because the factual record is not complete, the Court should not have accepted this case for further review.

DISSENT: (Blackmun, J.) This Court has consistently upheld regulations that prohibit an owner from using his property in a way that is harmful to the public. Lucas (P) never challenged the legislature's findings that a building ban was necessary to protect property and life and, therefore, the lower court correctly found no taking. Now, with this case, the majority has created a new rule and an exception, based on the trial court's finding that the property had lost all economic value. Furthermore, the majority alters the traditional rule that the plaintiff challenges the constitutionality of an ordinance, by requiring the state to convince the courts that its legislative judgments are correct. Finally, the majority decides that it will permit a state to regulate all economic value only if the state prohibits uses that would not be permitted under state common law, notwithstanding that the Court has previously and explicitly rejected any consideration of a nuisance when evaluating a taking. There is no reason to believe the majority's claim that new interpretation of old common-law nuisance doctrine will be any more objective or value-free than reliance on legislative judgments of what constitutes harm.

DISSENT: (Stevens, J.) The majority's categorical rule that total regulatory takings must be compensated is an unsound and unwise addition to the law, unsupported by prior decisions, and its exception to that rule is too rigid and too narrow. Because the majority's new rule only applies to total regulatory takings, it arbitrarily awards compensation to a landowner whose property is diminished by 100 percent, while denying compensation to one who suffers a 95 percent diminishment. Furthermore, the Court's holding effectively freezes a state's traditional common law, making it immune to legislative revision.

ANALYSIS

Note the central debate in *Lucas* is actually over who should have the authority to allocate loss. *Lucas* allocates the authority to decide which regulations will require compensation to the state judiciary, rather than to the state legislature. *Lucas* implies that the state's ability to completely extinguish the value of a parcel of land gives it too much power and potential for excessive legislative regulation, necessitating an independent judicial determination of what constitutes a nuisance. Although *Lucas* was the most closely watched land-use case of 1991 (over 50 amicus briefs were filed), its impact may turn out to be relatively slight since its fact pattern is relatively rare.

Quicknotes

CERTIORARI A discretionary writ issued by a superior court to an inferior court in order to review the lower court's decisions; the United States Supreme Court's writ ordering such review.

JUST COMPENSATION The right guaranteed by the Fifth Amendment to the U.S. Constitution that when private property is taken for public use by the government, the owner is to receive adequate compensation to restore them to the position they enjoyed prior to the taking/appropriation.

NUISANCE An unlawful use of property that interferes with the lawful use of another's property.

REGULATORY TAKING A governmental action that substantially deprives an owner of the use and enjoyment of their property, whereby the application of a law or regulation deprives the owner of economically viable use of their property, requiring compensation.

TAKINGS CLAUSE Provision of the Fifth Amendment to the United States Constitution prohibiting the government from taking private property for public use without providing just compensation therefor.

Cedar Point Nursery v. Hassid

Agricultural employer (P) v. State official (D)

141 S. Ct. 2063 (2021)

NATURE OF CASE: Appeal from affirmance of denial of declaratory and injunctive relief in action challenging as an unconstitutional, per se uncompensated taking, a state regulation permitting union organizers to enter onto the property of agricultural employers for the purpose of organizing workers under limited circumstances.

FACT SUMMARY: Two agricultural employers (P), Cedar Point Nursery (P) and Fowler Packing Co. (P), contended that a regulation promulgated by the California Agricultural Labor Relations Board (D) permitting union organizers onto their properties under limited circumstances effected an unconstitutional per se physical taking, and sought declaratory and injunctive relief prohibiting the enforcement of the regulation against them.

RULE OF LAW

A state regulation that grants labor organizations a right to access an agricultural employer's property to solicit support for unionization under specified, limited conditions constitutes a per se uncompensated taking under the Fifth and Fourteenth Amendments.

FACTS: A California regulation promulgated by the California Agricultural Labor Relations Board granted labor organizations a "right to take access" to an agricultural employer's property to solicit support for unionization. The regulation mandated that agricultural employers had to allow union organizers onto their property for up to three hours per day, 120 days per year. Organizers from the United Farm Workers sought to take access to property owned by two agricultural employers (P), Cedar Point Nursery (P) and Fowler Packing Co. (P). The agricultural employers (P) filed suit in federal district court seeking to enjoin enforcement of the access regulation on the grounds that it appropriated without compensation an easement for union organizers to enter their property and therefore constituted an unconstitutional per se physical taking under the Fifth and Fourteenth Amendments. The Federal District Court denied the agricultural employers' (P) motion for a preliminary injunction and dismissed the complaint, holding that the access regulation did not constitute a per se physical taking because it did not allow the public to access the agricultural employers' (P) property in a permanent and continuous manner. The United States Court of Appeals for the Ninth Circuit affirmed, and the United States Supreme Court granted certiorari.

ISSUE: Does a state regulation that grants labor organizations a right to access an agricultural employer's property to solicit support for unionization under specified, limited conditions constitute a per se uncompensated taking under the Fifth and Fourteenth Amendments?

HOLDING AND DECISION: (Roberts, C.J.) Yes. A state regulation that grants labor organizations a right to access an agricultural employer's property to solicit support for unionization under specified, limited conditions constitutes a per se uncompensated taking under the Fifth and Fourteenth Amendments. The Takings Clause of the Fifth Amendment, applicable to the states through the Fourteenth Amendment, provides: "[N]or shall private property be taken for public use, without just compensation." When the government physically acquires private property for a public use, the Takings Clause obligates the government to provide the owner with just compensation. The Court assesses such physical takings using a per se rule: The government must pay for what it takes. See *Tahoe-Sierra Preservation Council, Inc. v. Tahoe Regional Planning Agency*, 535 U.S. 302, 322 (2002). A different standard applies when the government rather than appropriating private property for itself or a third party instead imposes regulations restricting an owner's ability to use his own property. To determine whether such a use restriction amounts to a taking, the Court has generally applied the flexible approach set forth in *Penn Central Transportation Co. v. New York City*, 438 U.S. 104 (1978), considering factors such as the economic impact of the regulation, its interference with reasonable investment-backed expectations, and the character of the government action. However, when the government physically appropriates property, *Penn Central* has no place in the analysis—regardless whether the government action takes the form of a regulation, statute, ordinance, or decree. Here, the access regulation appropriates a right to invade the agricultural employers' (P) property and therefore constitutes a per se physical taking. Rather than restraining the agricultural employers' (P) use of their own property, the regulation appropriates for the enjoyment of third parties (here union organizers) the owners' right to exclude. The right to exclude is a fundamental element of the property right, and the Court's precedents have accordingly treated government-authorized physical invasions as takings requiring just compensation regardless whether

Continued on next page.

they cause only trivial economic loss. The Court has often described the property interest taken as a servitude or easement. As in those previous cases, the government here has appropriated a right of access to private property. Because the regulation appropriates a right to physically invade the agricultural employers' (P) property—to literally "take access"—it constitutes a per se physical taking under the Court's precedents. The view that the access regulation cannot qualify as a per se taking because it does not allow for permanent and continuous access 24 hours a day, 365 days a year is insupportable. The Court has held that a physical appropriation is a taking whether it is permanent or temporary; the duration of the appropriation bears only on the amount of compensation due. The regulation here is not transformed from a physical taking into a use restriction just because the access granted is restricted to union organizers, for a narrow purpose, and for a limited time, as it is undisputed that absent the regulation, the agricultural employers (P) would have the right to exclude the union organizers from their property. The Court has recognized that the government can commit a physical taking either by appropriating property through a condemnation proceeding or by simply entering into physical possession of property without authority of a court order. Any other result would allow the government to appropriate private property without just compensation so long as it avoids formal condemnation, a result that has never been tolerated. The Court's decision in *PruneYard Shopping Center v. Robins,* 447 U.S. 74 (1980), does not cut against the conclusion that the access regulation here constitutes a per se taking. In *PruneYard* the California Supreme Court recognized a right to engage in leafleting at the *PruneYard,* a privately owned shopping center, and the Court applied the *Penn Central* factors to hold that no compensable taking had occurred. *PruneYard* does not establish that limited rights of access to private property should be evaluated as regulatory rather than per se takings. Restrictions on how a business generally open to the public such as the *PruneYard* may treat individuals on the premises are readily distinguishable from regulations granting a right to invade property closed to the public. The California Agricultural Labor Relations Board's (D) fear that treating the access regulation as a per se physical taking will endanger a host of state and federal government activities involving entry onto private property is unfounded. First, the Court's holding does nothing to efface the distinction between trespass and takings. The Court's precedents make clear that isolated physical invasions, not undertaken pursuant to a granted right of access, are properly assessed as individual torts rather than appropriations of a property right. Second, many government-authorized physical invasions will not amount to takings because they are consistent with longstanding background restrictions on property rights, including traditional common-law privileges to access private property. Third, the government may require property owners to cede a right of access as a condition of receiving certain benefits, without causing a taking. Under this framework, government health and safety inspection regimes will generally not constitute takings. In this case, however, none of these considerations undermine the Court's determination that the access regulation gives rise to a per se physical taking. Reversed and remanded.

DISSENT: (Breyer, J.) If the regulation at issue appropriates employers' property, the case is straightforward: the government must pay just compensation. However, if the regulation merely regulates the employers' property rights, it must be determined if the regulation "goes too far" under established precedent, such as *Pennsylvania Coal Co. v. Mahon,* 260 U.S. 393 (1922), and *Penn Central Transportation Co. v. New York City,* 438 U.S. 104 (1978). The majority holds that the regulation at issue amounts to a physical appropriation of property, and that nearly every government-authorized invasion is such an appropriation. It does so by concluding that the regulation "appropriates" a right to invade, or a right to exclude. However, the regulation appropriates nothing, but instead, regulates an employer's right to exclude others. It is a temporary invasion, which precedent holds is not a taking unless it "goes too far." Such precedent holds that temporary takings are not per se takings and are not takings if they do not unreasonably impair the value or use of the property as it is currently used. Per se takings previously were held to occur only when the government directly appropriates private property for its own use or when the government causes a permanent physical occupation of private property. The regulation here does neither. Precedent explains the distinction between permanent physical occupations and temporary limitations on the right to exclude, saying that when the government permanently occupies property, it "does not simply take a single 'strand' from the 'bundle' of property rights: it chops through the bundle, taking a slice of every strand," "effectively destroy[ing]" "the rights to possess, use and dispose of it." *Loretto v. Teleprompter Manhattan CATV Corp.,* 458 U.S. 419, 435 (1982). In such a case, the property owner has no right to possess the occupied space and also has no power to exclude the occupier from possession and use of the space. The regulation that effects a permanent physical occupation forever denies the owner any power to control the use of the property or make any nonpossessory use of it. From the agricultural employers' (P) perspective, it restricts when and where they can exclude others from their property. The regulation grants a small group of people the right to enter private property for a limited time to speak about a specific subject—a much lesser invasion than similar, less circumscribed invasions that the Court previously held were not per se

Continued on next page.

takings. Nothing in the Court's precedents ever suggested, however, as the majority rules here, that compensation is automatically required for a temporary right of access. Likewise, nothing in those precedents supports the distinction the majority makes between "trespass" and "takings." Accordingly, the majority is wrong to characterize the regulation at bar, or similar regulations, as a per se taking. Disregarding the permanent/temporary distinction of numerous cases, which permits government to regulate and not have to pay every property owner for any brief use of their land, and recognizing that the categorical, per se rule it announces likely will lead to adverse results, given the large numbers of ordinary regulations in a host of different fields that, for a variety of purposes, permit temporary entry onto a property owner's land, e.g., inspections of all sorts, the majority attempts to create exceptions to this per se rule. It says: (1) "Isolated physical invasions, not undertaken pursuant to a granted right of access, are properly assessed as individual torts rather than appropriations of a property right." It also would except from its per se rule (2) government access that is "consistent with longstanding background restrictions on property rights," including "traditional common law privileges to access private property." It also adds that (3) "the government may require property owners to cede a right of access as a condition of receiving certain benefits, without causing a taking." These exceptions raise numerous questions. As to the first exception, what will count as "isolated"? How is an "isolated physical invasion" different from a "temporary" invasion, and where should one draw the line between trespass and takings? As to the second exception, a court must focus on "traditional common law privileges to access private property." Just what are they? Do only those exceptions that existed in, say, 1789 count? Should courts apply those privileges as they existed at that time, when there were no union organizers? Or do we bring some exceptions (but not others) up to date, e.g., a necessity exception for preserving animal habitats? And, as to the third, what is the scope of the phrase "certain benefits"? Does it include, for example, the benefit of being able to sell meat labeled "inspected" in interstate commerce? What about the benefit of having electricity? Of sewage collection? Of internet accessibility? Myriad regulatory schemes based on just these sorts of benefits depend upon intermittent, temporary government entry onto private property. In the instant case, labor peace brought about through union organizing is one such benefit, at least in the view of elected representatives, who may well have believed that union organizing brings with it "benefits," including community health and educational benefits, higher standards of living, and labor peace. A landowner, of course, may deny the existence of these benefits, but a landowner might do the same were a regulatory statute to permit brief access to verify proper preservation of wetlands or the habitat enjoyed by an endangered species or, for that matter, the safety of inspected meat. So, if a regulation authorizing temporary access for purposes of organizing agricultural workers falls outside of the Court's exceptions and is a per se taking, then to what other forms of regulation does the Court's per se conclusion also apply? A right of access that is nonpermanent is not automatically a "taking," but instead is a regulation that falls within *Penn Central's* scope, and this case, therefore, should have been decided according to the precepts of that case.

ANALYSIS

In terms of property rights, the access regulation at issue does not amount to the taking of any traditional property interest in land. It does not, for example, take from the agricultural employers (P), or provide to the labor organizers, any freehold estate (e.g., a fee simple, fee tail, or life estate); any concurrent estate (e.g., a joint tenancy, tenancy in common, or tenancy by the entirety); or any leasehold estate (e.g., a term of years, periodic tenancy, or tenancy at will). Nor does it provide the organizers with a formal easement or access resembling an easement, since it does not burden any particular parcel of property—the burden of an easement in gross is appurtenant to the real property of another, and the burden of an easement or profit is always appurtenant. The Court concludes nevertheless that the regulation amounts to a physical taking of property because it is like cases in which the Court held that appropriation of property rights amounts to a physical per se taking. The dissent, however, argues that the regulation appropriates nothing, and merely regulates (but does not appropriate) the landowners' right to exclude. Thus, for the dissent, the issue is whether a regulation that temporarily limits an owner's right to exclude others from property automatically amounts to a Fifth Amendment taking, and the dissent concludes it does not. The majority responds by saying that the right to exclude is not an empty formality subject to modification at the government's pleasure, but, on the contrary, is a fundamental element of the property right that cannot be balanced away.

Quicknotes

CONCURRENT ESTATE Possession of or ownership in property by two or more persons at the same time.

DECLARATORY RELIEF Request to a court for determination of legal status, rights, or ownership of a thing.

EASEMENT The right to utilize a portion of another's real property for a specific use.

Continued on next page.

EASEMENT IN GROSS A right to use the land of another that is specific to a particular individual and that expires upon the death of that person.

FEE TAIL A limitation in either a deed or will limiting succession of property to a grantee and the heirs of their body.

FEE SIMPLE An estate in land characterized by ownership of the entire property for an unlimited duration and by absolute power over distribution.

FREEHOLD ESTATE An estate in land or real property that had title of interest, even if the title is limited in time to a present possessory estate.

INJUNCTIVE RELIEF A court order issued as a remedy, requiring a person to do, or prohibiting that person from doing, a specific act.

LIFE ESTATE An interest in land measured by the life of the tenant or a third party.

PER SE By itself; without more; taken alone; not requiring additional evidence for proof; as a matter of law.

SERVITUDE Land use restriction enforceable in equity.

TAKING A governmental action that substantially deprives an owner of the use and enjoyment of their property, requiring compensation.

USE RESTRICTION A restriction on the right to utilize one's personal or real property.

Glossary

Common Latin Words and Phrases Encountered in the Law

A FORTIORI: Because one fact exists or has been proven, therefore a second fact that is related to the first fact must also exist.

A PRIORI: From the cause to the effect. A term of logic used to denote that when one generally accepted truth is shown to be a cause, another particular effect must necessarily follow.

AB INITIO: From the beginning; a condition that has existed throughout, as in a marriage that was void ab initio.

ACTUS REUS: The wrongful act; in criminal law, such action sufficient to trigger criminal liability.

AD VALOREM: According to value; an ad valorem tax is imposed upon an item located within the taxing jurisdiction calculated by the value of such item.

AMICUS CURIAE: Friend of the court. Its most common usage takes the form of an amicus curiae brief, filed by a person who is not a party to an action but is nonetheless allowed to offer an argument supporting their legal interests.

ARGUENDO: In arguing. A statement, possibly hypothetical, made for the purpose of argument is one made arguendo.

BILL QUIA TIMET: A bill to quiet title (establish ownership) to real property.

BONA FIDE: True, honest, or genuine. May refer to a person's legal position based on good faith or lacking notice of fraud (such as a bona fide purchaser for value) or to the authenticity of a particular document (such as a bona fide last will and testament).

CAUSA MORTIS: With approaching death in mind. A gift causa mortis is a gift given by a party who feels certain that death is imminent.

CAVEAT EMPTOR: Let the buyer beware. This maxim is reflected in the rule of law that a buyer purchases at their own risk because it is their responsibility to examine, judge, test, and otherwise inspect what they are buying.

CERTIORARI: A writ of review. Petitions for review of a case by the United States Supreme Court are most often done by means of a writ of certiorari.

CONTRA: On the other hand. Opposite. Contrary to.

CORAM NOBIS: Before us; writs of error directed to the court that originally rendered the judgment.

CORAM VOBIS: Before you; writs of error directed by an appellate court to a lower court to correct a factual error.

CORPUS DELICTI: The body of the crime; the requisite elements of a crime amounting to objective proof that a crime has been committed.

CUM TESTAMENTO ANNEXO, ADMINISTRATOR (ADMINISTRATOR C.T.A.): With will annexed; an administrator c.t.a. settles an estate pursuant to a will in which they are not appointed.

DEBONISNON,ADMINISTRATOR(ADMINISTRATOR D.B.N.): Of goods not administered; an administrator d.b.n. settles a partially settled estate.

DE FACTO: In fact; in reality; actually. Existing in fact but not officially approved or engendered.

DE JURE: By right; lawful. Describes a condition that is legitimate "as a matter of law," in contrast to the term "de facto," which connotes something existing in fact but not legally sanctioned or authorized. For example, de facto segregation refers to segregation brought about by housing patterns, etc., whereas de jure segregation refers to segregation created by law.

DE MINIMUS: Of minimal importance; insignificant; a trifle; not worth bothering about.

DE NOVO: Anew; a second time; afresh. A trial de novo is a new trial held at the appellate level as if the case originated there and the trial at a lower level had not taken place.

DICTA: Generally used as an abbreviated form of obiter dicta, a term describing those portions of a judicial opinion incidental or not necessary to resolution of the specific question before the court. Such nonessential statements and remarks are not considered to be binding precedent.

DUCES TECUM: Refers to a particular type of writ or subpoena requesting a party or organization to produce certain documents in their possession.

EN BANC: Full bench. Where a court sits with all justices present rather than the usual quorum.

EX PARTE: For one side or one party only. An ex parte proceeding is one undertaken for the benefit of only oneparty, without notice to, or an appearance by, an adverse party.

EX POST FACTO: After the fact. An ex post facto law is alaw that retroactively changes the consequences of a prior act.

EX REL.: Abbreviated form of the term "ex relatione," meaning upon relation or information. When the state brings an action in which it has no interest against an individual at the instigation of one who has a private interest in the matter.

FORUM NON CONVENIENS: Inconvenient forum. Althougha court may have jurisdiction over the case, the action should be tried in a more conveniently located court, one to which parties and witnesses may more easily travel, for example.

GUARDIAN AD LITEM: A guardian appointed by the court to represent a minor or incompetent person in a legal action.

HABEAS CORPUS: You have the body. The modern writ of habeas corpus is a writ directing that a person (body) being detained (such as a prisoner) be brought before the court so that the legality of their detention can be judicially ascertained.

IN CAMERA: In private, in chambers. When a hearing is held before a judge in their chambers or when all spectators are excluded from the courtroom.

IN FORMA PAUPERIS: In the manner of a pauper. A party who proceeds in forma pauperis because of their poverty is one who is allowed to bring suit without liability for costs.

INFRA: Below, under. A word referring the reader to a later part of a book. (The opposite of supra.)

IN LOCO PARENTIS: In the place of a parent.

IN PARI DELICTO: Equally wrong; a court of equity will not grant requested relief to an applicant who is in pari delicto, or as much at fault in the transactions giving rise to the controversy as is the opponent of the applicant.

IN PARI MATERIA: On like subject matter or upon the same matter. Statutes relating to the same person or things are said to be in pari materia. It is a general rule of statutory construction that such statutes should be construed together, i.e., looked at as if they together constituted one law.

IN PERSONAM: Against the person. Jurisdiction over the person of an individual.

IN RE: In the matter of. Used to designate a proceeding involving an estate or other property.

IN REM: A term that signifies an action against the res, or thing. An action in rem is basically one that is taken directly against property, as distinguished from an action in personam, i.e., against the person.

INTER ALIA: Among other things. Used to show that the whole of a statement, pleading, list, statute, etc., has not been set forth in its entirety.

INTER PARTES: Between the parties. May refer to contracts, conveyances, or other transactions having legal significance.

INTER VIVOS: Between the living. An inter vivos gift is a gift made by a living grantor, as distinguished from bequests contained in a will, which pass upon the death of the testator.

IPSO FACTO: By the mere fact itself.

JUS: Law or the entire body of law.

LEX LOCI: The law of the place; the notion that the rights of parties to a legal proceeding are governed by the law of the place where those rights arose.

MALUM IN SE: Evil or wrong in and of itself; inherently wrong. This term describes an act that is wrong by its very nature, as opposed to one which would not be wrong but for the fact that there is a specific legal prohibition against it (malum prohibitum).

MALUM PROHIBITUM: Wrong because prohibited, butnot inherently evil. Used to describe something that is wrong because it is expressly forbidden by law but thatis not in and of itself evil, e.g., speeding.

MANDAMUS: We command. A writ directing an official to take a certain action.

MENS REA: A guilty mind; a criminal intent. A term used to signify the mental state that accompanies a crime or other prohibited act. Some crimes require only a general mens rea (general intent to do the prohibited act), but others, like assault with intent to murder, require the existence of a specific mens rea.

MODUS OPERANDI: Method of operating; generally refers to the manner or style of a criminal in committing crimes, admissible in appropriate cases as evidence of the identity of a defendant.

NEXUS: A connection to.

NISI PRIUS: A court of first impression. A nisi prius court is one where issues of fact are tried before a judge or jury.

N.O.V. (NON OBSTANTE VEREDICTO): Notwithstanding the verdict. A judgment n.o.v. is a judgment given in favor of one party despite the fact that a verdict was returned in favor of the other party, the justification being that the verdict either had no reasonable support in fact or was contrary to law.

NUNC PRO TUNC: Now for then. This phrase refers to actions that may be taken and will then have full retroactive effect.

PENDENTE LITE: Pending the suit; pending litigation underway.

PER CAPITA: By head; beneficiaries of an estate, if they take in equal shares, take per capita.

PER CURIAM: By the court; signifies an opinion ostensibly written "by the whole court" and with no identified author.

PER SE: By itself, in itself; inherently.

PER STIRPES: By representation. Used primarily in thelaw of wills to describe the method of distribution where a person, generally because of death, is unable to take that which is left to them by the will of another, and therefore their heirs divide such property between them rather than take under the will individually.

PRIMA FACIE: On its face, at first sight. A prima facie case is one that is sufficient on its face, meaning that the evidence supporting it is adequate to establish the case until contradicted or overcome by other evidence.

PRO TANTO: For so much; as far as it goes. Often used in eminent domain cases when a property owner receives partial payment for their land without prejudice to their right to bring suit for the full amount they claim their land to be worth.

QUANTUM MERUIT: As much as they deserve. Refers to recovery based on the doctrine of unjust enrichment in those cases in which a party has rendered valuable services or furnished materials that were accepted and enjoyed by another under circumstances that would reasonably notify the recipient that the rendering party expected to be paid. In essence, the law implies a contract to pay the reasonable value of the services or materials furnished.

QUASI: Almost like; as if; nearly. This term is essentially used to signify that one subject or thing is almost analogous to another but that material differences between them do exist. For example, a quasi-criminal proceeding is one that is not strictly criminal but shares enough of the same characteristics to require some of the same safeguards (e.g., procedural due process must be followed in a parole hearing).

QUID PRO QUO: Something for something. In contract law, the consideration, something of value, passed between the parties to render the contract binding.

RES GESTAE: Things done. In evidence law, this principle justifies the admission of a statement that would otherwise be hearsay when it is made so closely to the event in question as to be said to be a part of it, or with such spontaneity as not to have the possibility of falsehood.

RES IPSA LOQUITUR: The thing speaks for itself. This doctrine gives rise to a rebuttable presumption of negligence when the instrumentality causing the injury was within the exclusive control of the defendant, and the injury was one that does not normally occur unless a person has been negligent.

RES JUDICATA: A matter adjudged. Doctrine which provides that once a court of competent jurisdiction has rendered a final judgment or decree on the merits, that judgment or decree is conclusive upon the parties to the case and prevents them from engaging in any other litigation on the points and issues determined therein.

RESPONDEAT SUPERIOR: Let the master reply. This doctrine holds the master liable for the wrongful acts of their servant (or the principal for their agent) in those cases in which the servant (or agent) was acting within the scope of their authority at the time of the injury.

STARE DECISIS: To stand by or adhere to that which has been decided. The common law doctrine of stare decisis attempts to give security and certainty to the law by following the policy that once a principle of law as applicable to a certain set of facts has been set forth in a decision, it forms a precedent that will subsequently be followed, even though a different decision might be made were it the first time the question had arisen. Of course, stare decisis is not an inviolable principle and is departed from in instances where there is good cause (e.g., considerations of public policy led the Supreme Court to disregard prior decisions sanctioning segregation).

SUPRA: Above. A word referring a reader to an earlier part of a book. (The opposite of infra.)

ULTRA VIRES: Beyond the power. This phrase is most commonly used to refer to actions taken by a corporation that are beyond the power or legal authority of the corporation.

Addendum of French Derivatives

CHATTEL: Tangible personal property.

CY PRES: Doctrine permitting courts to apply trust funds to purposes not expressed in the trust but necessary to carry out the settlor's intent.

IN PAIS: Not pursuant to legal proceedings.

PER AUTRE VIE: For another's life; during another's life. In property law, an estate may be granted that will terminate upon the death of someone other than the grantee.

PROFIT A PRENDRE: A license to remove minerals or other produce from land.

VOIR DIRE: Process of questioning jurors as to their predispositions about the case or parties to a proceeding in order to identify those jurors displaying bias or prejudice.

QUICK COURSE OUTLINE

PROPERTY

CONCURRENT ESTATES

RIGHTS OF CO-TENANTS BETWEEN THEMSELVES

1. **Possession:** Co-tenants are equally entitled to possession of the property and cannot exclude other co-tenants.
2. **Contribution for expenses:** Co-tenants in rightful possession of property bear the cost of maintenance and upkeep such as taxes, insurance, and ordinary repairs. *Barrow v. Barrow*, 527 So. 2d 1373 (Fla. 1988).
3. **Right to lease property:** A co-tenant may lease the property without the consent of the other co-tenants, but lessee takes subject to the rights of the nonconsenting co-tenants. *Carr v. Deking*, 52 Wash. App. 880, 765 P.2d 40 (1988).
4. **Accounting:** Co-tenant in possession is responsible for accounting of all rents and profits from third party lessees. *Georgen v. Maar*, 2 A.D.2d 276 [3d Dept. 1956], 153 N.Y.S.2d 826 (1956).
5. **Ouster/Partition:** Co-tenant takes affirmative actions to take sole possession and exclusive use of the property; co-tenant may file action for partition in court to divide property into individual tenancies, unless all co-tenants voluntarily agree to divide. *Penfield v. Jarvis*, 175 Conn. 463, 399 A.2d 1280 (1978).
6. **Effect of will:** Since a co-tenant's interest ceases at death, the co-tenant has no interest that can pass by will. *Huff v. Metz*, 676 So. 2d 264 (Miss. 1996).

DOCTRINE OF WASTE (TENANT'S DUTY TO REPAIR)

A tenant who is not the owner of land, or possesses the same interest in property at the same time as one or more co-tenants, is responsible to her co-tenants for any decrease in the value of the property through waste. *Kimbrough v. Reed*, 943 P.2d 1232 (Idaho 1997).

1. **Permissive Waste:** Tenant allows land to fall into disrepair; must preserve land and structures to a reasonable degree.
2. **Voluntary (Affirmative) Waste:** Tenant cannot use natural resources on land; use is permissible only for repair and maintenance, where permission is expressly given, or where land is only suitable for such use.
3. **Ameliorative Waste:** Tenant's use substantially changes the value of property, but the use increases the value of the land; may do it where the market value of future interests is not impaired, and change in character of neighborhood deprives the property of value in its current form.

COMMUNITY PROPERTY

1. ***Example:*** A husband and wife form a community, which is a separate entity that owns property for the benefit of the husband and wife; all property acquired during marriage is generally characterized as community property.

   Separate Property: Property acquired by gift, bequest, or devise during the marriage is characterized as separate property, belonging to the individual spouse who receives it.
2. **Division of the Community:**
   - **a.** **At Death:** Community dissolves at death of one spouse; each spouse owns half an interest in each community asset.
   - **b.** **At Divorce:** Community dissolves upon divorce and all community assets are owned by each spouse as tenants in common and may be divided according to settlement.

LICENSES & PROFITS

LICENSE

1. Bare revocable interest to use property for limited purpose and duration.
2. **Irrevocable License:** Cannot be revoked if consideration is given.

PROFITS

Right to come onto land solely to remove minerals or other value.

TYPES OF PROPERTY INTERESTS

INTERESTS IN THINGS

1. **Wild Animals:**
   - **a.** **Right to possess:** Deprive them of natural liberty [*Pierson v. Post*, 3 Cai. R. 175 (N.Y. Sup. 1805).]:
     - **i.** Actual physical possession.
     - **ii.** Mortally wounding/continued pursuit.
     - **iii.** Capture/netting.
2. **Natural Gas and Oil:**
   - **a.** **Right to possess:** Whoever extracts first regardless of where.
3. **Lost Property:**
   - **a.** ***Definition:***
     - **i.** **Lost:** Possessor can no longer find it.
     - **ii.** **Mislaid:** Possessor voluntarily leaves it, but forgets where.
     - **iii.** **Abandoned:** Possessor voluntarily relinquishes possession; ordinarily belongs to finder.
     - **iv.** **Treasure trove:** Property hidden and found, owner unknown.
   - **b.** **General Rule:** Prior possessor has superior rights to finder. *Armory v. Delamirie*, 1 Strange 525, 93 Eng. Rep. 664 (1722).
   - **c.** **Owner of Land *(Locus in Quo)*:** Owner of land where lost property is found has superior rights to finder who is trespasser. *Favorite v. Miller*, 407 A.2d 974 (Conn. 1978).
4. **Bailments/Borrowed Property:**
   - **a.** ***Definition of Bailment*:** Owner (bailor) transfers possession (but not title) to another (bailee), who is in lawful possession of the transferred property and has title against wrongdoers.
   - **b.** **Legal Relationship:** Bailee is liable to bailor for negligent damage to property, or conversion.

OTHER INTERESTS IN LAND

1. **Easements:** A nonpossessory interest entitling holder to some type of use or enjoyment of another person's land.
2. **Covenants/Equitable Servitudes:** A covenant is a type of servitude created by deed or contract and whose benefits or burdens "run with the land" to bind successors in interest. When the rules regarding real covenants are not met, the agreement may be enforced in equity as an equitable servitude.
3. **Licenses:** Owner grants permission to another to use the land.
4. **Profits:** An easement entitling holder to come onto the land in order to take something off it.

MISCELLANEOUS PROPERTY INTERESTS

1. **Bona Fide Purchaser (BFP):**
   - **a.** ***Definition*:** One who takes possession:
     - **i.** In good faith,
     - **ii.** For valuable consideration, and
     - **iii.** Without notice of any wrongful possession.

Types of Property Interests continues on page 2

LEGAL CONSIDERATIONS ARISING FROM LEASE

	SUBLET		ASSIGNMENT	
	Tenant (T1) transfers less than the entire remaining estate to transferee (T2)			
	Privity of Estate	Privity of Contract	Privity of Estate	Privity of Contract
T2 to Landlord (L)	NO	NO	YES	NO
Unless	1. T2 agrees with T1 to assume all lease provisions 2. T2 enters into separate agreement with L			
T1 to L	YES	YES	NO	YES
T2 to T1	T1 can be reimbursed by T2 for any rent paid to L under sublease		T1 can be reimbursed by T2 for any rent paid to L under assignment	

Estate in perpetuity, lasts forever		
Estate in perpetuity, lasts forever	Terminates automatically on occurrence of an event; otherwise lasts forever	Occurrence or nonoccurrence of condition sometime in future, as set out in governing instrument
Estate in perpetuity, lasts forever	Doesn't terminate automatically; unless condition occurs, lasts forever	Grantor elects to terminate due to occurrence of condition
Estate for duration of owner's life	Assures that lands stay within a family from generation to generation by passing to owner's heirs	Owner's death
Estate with duration measured by life of another	Measuring life can be either land holder or another party	Measuring life ends
resent and future interests can be concurrent.		
Equal right of possession of the whole by each co-tenant, regardless of the actual share owned; nay be freely conveyed	Modern Law: Any conveyance to two or more people creates a presumption of a tenancy in common	Partitioned through mutual agreement of co-tenants or judicial decree
Equal right of possession of the whole by each o-tenant, regardless of the actual share owned; iowever, cannot be freely conveyed (Right of urvivorship: once a co-tenant dies, remain-ng co-tenants take property free and clear of eceased co-tenant's interest)	**1.** Common Law: Any conveyance to two or more people creates a presumption of a joint tenancy **2.** Conveyance: If any co-tenant conveys interest, transferee takes as a tenant-in-common, while remaining co-tenants continue to hold in joint tenancy	Partitioned through mutual agreement of co-tenants or judicial decree
qual right of possession of the whole by each o-tenant, regardless of the actual share owned; nay be freely conveyed	Any conveyance to two or more people creates a presumption of a tenancy in common	Partitioned through mutual agreement of co-tenants or judicial decree
ne form of duties owed between a landlord and the renter of the land.		
Right to occupy tenancy for fixed period (year, month, week, or day)		
Right to occupy tenancy beginning on a fixed date and ending on a fixed date	Can also last for a period measured by the happening of an event or condition	Fixed end date arrives, or ending event takes place; no notice required
Right to occupy tenancy "at will" as long as both he landlord and tenant so desire	Law disfavors; some states have statutes requiring notice to terminate	May be terminated by either party without notice; death of either party can also terminate
Holdover tenant is treated as trespasser and evicted, or new periodic tenancy is imposed	Landlord has the right to elect either eviction or creation of new tenancy	If landlord chooses to evict, tenancy ends
[illegible]		
Balance of estate left after grantor transfers less than she has	May or may not become possessory in future; freely alienable, devisable, and descendible	Interest does not become possessory if prior estate given by grantor does not end
Balance of estate in fee simple absolute, left after grantor originally transfers less than she has	Landlord has the right to elect either eviction or creation of new tenancy	If landlord chooses to evict, prior tenancy ends
Balance of estate in fee simple absolute, left after grantor originally transfers less than she has	Does not go to grantor automatically; grantor must elect to enforce interest	If condition occurs and landlord chooses to enforce interest, prior tenancy ends
Balance of estate in fee simple absolute, left after grantor originally transfers less than she has		
An interest limited by the existence of a currently possessory estate created at the same time		

b. Interest in Property: A BFP has superior rights to others claiming an interest in the same property, including the actual owner, where the BFP takes possession in good faith and pays value.

2. Adverse Possessor (AP):
   a. *Definition*: One who takes possession contrary to the possessory rights of another. Requires that possession by the AP throughout the entire statutory period required be:
      i. Actual; open and notorious; exclusive; continuous; and hostile under Claim of Right.
   b. Interest in Property: Adverse possessor acquires superior title good against all the world.

LANDLORD AND TENANT

THE LEASE

The interest in property between a landlord and tenant is controlled by the lease.

1. For a proper lease:
   a. Formal lease requirements:
      i. Identification of landlord and tenant;
      ii. Adequate description of the premises;
      iii. Amount of rent/dates to pay rent (if no rent amount, reasonable value); and
      iv. Duration of lease.
   b. Statute of Frauds (if lease > 1 year):
      i. Must be in writing; and
      ii. Signed by the party to be charged.
2. The lease terms create the type of estate ("leasehold").
   a. Periodic Tenancy: Right to occupy tenancy for fixed period (year, month, week, or day).
   b. Tenancy for Years: Right to occupy tenancy beginning on a fixed date and ending on a fixed date.
   c. Tenancy at Will: Right to occupy tenancy "at will" as long as both landlord and tenant so desire.
   d. Tenancy at Sufferance: Holdover tenant is treated as trespasser and evicted, or new periodic tenancy is imposed.
3. The lease defines rights and duties between Landlord and Tenant.
   a. *Example*: All L's duties are done in exchange for T's payment of rent, if landlord breaches duties, tenant can withhold rent, if T breaches duties (e.g., fails to pay rent), L can evict.
   b. Lease terms/duties are independent:
      i. Failure to perform by one party does not excuse other party from performing.
      ii. Exception: if warranty of habitability is breached.
4. Other legal considerations arising from lease:
   a. Assignments/Subleases (see chart on p.1)
   b. Fixtures: Personal property or chattels that have been permanently attached to land:
      i. Common Law: Becomes property of landlord.
      ii. American courts: Look to objective intent of tenant, determined by: manner of attachment, damage from removal, fixture in context of property. *Sigrol Realty Corp. v. Valcich*, 11 N.Y.2d 668, 180 N.E.2d 904, 225 N.Y.S.2d 748 (1962).
      iii. Trade fixtures: Used to carry on a trade or business; tenant can remove but is responsible for any damage. Restatement of Property: all fixtures installed by T are trade fixtures.

LANDLORD'S RIGHTS / REMEDIES

1. Security deposit: L retains amount of posted deposit for T's costs and damages.
2. Rent acceleration clause: If T defaults on rent, all future rents become immediately due and payable.
3. Sue for unpaid rent: In the absence of an acceleration clause, L may only sue for the rental amount owed for the current lease period.
4. Eviction: If T materially breaches any lease term, including failure to pay rent timely; may evict by: ejectment, self-help (physical ouster), or summary proceedings.

DUTIES OF LANDLORD

1. Duty to Deliver Possession:
   a. Right to Possess: Breach if someone has superior right to possess at time of commencement of lease; T not required to move in
   b. Actual Possession: Under English Rule, L must deliver actual possession. *Dieffenbach v. McIntyre*, 208 Okla. 163, 254 P.2d 346 (1952); under American Rule (minority), L's not required to deliver. *Hannan v. Dusch*, 154 Va. 356, 153 S.E. 824 (1930).
2. Covenant of Quiet Enjoyment (implied): L promises that neither L nor third party will interfere with T's use and enjoyment of premises.
   a. Actual Eviction: Physical expulsion or exclusion from possession.
   b. Partial Eviction: Denial of possession for only part of the premises.
      i. Common Law: T's obligation to pay entire rent is suspended until possession of entire premises restored.
      ii. Restatement: T can abate rent or terminate lease and seek damages; cannot remain in possession and pay no rent.
   c. Constructive Eviction: L wrongfully performs or fails to perform some duty that substantially deprives T of use and enjoyment of premises.
      i. Common Law: L has no duty to repair premises unless L & T so agree; Statute/Case Law: L makes reasonable repairs. *Chambers v. N. River Line*, 179 N.C. 199, 102 S.E. 198 (1920).
3. Warranty of Fitness for Particular Purpose (implied):
   a. Common Law: In the absence of express lease provision, no warranty by L that premises would be fit for any purpose. *Anderson Drive-In Theatre Inc. v. Kirkpatrick*, 123 Ind. App. 388, 110 N.E.2d 506 (1953).
   b. Exceptions: Short-term lease of furnished residence and building under construction when rented. *Ingalls v. Hobbs*, 156 Mass. 348, 31 N.E. 286 (1892).
4. Warranty of Habitability (implied): L required to take all reasonable action to maintain premises in habitable condition, including duty to repair residential leases only; for commercial leases, implied warranty of suitability for intended commercial purpose. *Davidow v. Inwood North Professional Group*, 747 S.W.2d 373 (Tex. 1988).
5. Retaliatory eviction: L may not evict T, refuse to renew lease, terminate a periodic tenancy, or increase T's rent in retaliation for T's prior actions. *Edwards v. Habib*, 397 F.2d 687 (D.C. Cir. 1968).
   a. Not applicable to commercial leases.
   b. Tenant bears burden of demonstrating retaliatory motive of landlord.

LANDLORD'S TORT LIABILITIES

Generally, L not liable to T or third parties for injuries sustained on the premises.

1. Exceptions:
   a. Common Areas. *Johnson v. O'Brien*, 258 Minn. 502, 105 N.W.2d 244 (1960).
   b. Latent Defects: L fails to disclose.
   c. Negligent Repairs: Only if L voluntarily undertakes to make repair.

DUTIES OF TENANT

1. Duty to Pay Rent: T's obligation to pay rent is independent of L's duties; therefore T must continue to pay rent even if L fails to fulfill duties, unless warranty of habitability is breached.
2. Duty to Take Possession: No duty unless express or implied in lease.
3. Restrictions on use of leased premises:
   a. Cannot use property for illegal purpose
   b. Cannot commit waste (see "Doctrine of Waste" section under "Concurrent Estates").
4. Duty to Repair: No duty unless T expressly agrees; if premises completely destroyed, T might be obligated to rebuild.
5. Duty to Deliver Premises at End of Lease:
   a. T must give premises over timely or be treated as a holdover.
   b. Wrongful Abandonment: If T fails to pay rent and abandons the premises, L may:
      i. Accept the abandonment as a surrender and end the lease,
      ii. Leave premises vacant and sue for rent owed, or
      iii. Re-let premises to minimize T's damages.

TENANT'S RIGHTS / REMEDIES

1. Remain in possession, and
   a. Abate rent, or
   b. Suspend rent
2. Terminate lease, and
   a. Sue for damages, or
   b. Quit premises.

REAL COVENANTS & EQUITABLE SERVITUDES

EQUITABLE SERVITUDES

1. Generally, same as real covenants except that no privity is required;
2. Therefore, must be enforced in equity.
3. Creation: *Tulk v. Moxhay*, 2 Phillips 774, 41 Eng. Rep. 1143 (Ch. 1848).
   a. Express agreement.
   b. Implied:
      i. Implied Reciprocal Agreement.
      ii. Common Scheme.
      iii. Subdivision Plat.
      iv. California rule: will not be enforced unless in deed. *Werner v. Graham*, 181 Cal. 174, 183 P. 945 (Cal. 1919).

Real Covenants & Equitable Servitudes continues on page 3

ii. Tract index: Every document affecting the relevant tract is filed under its own parcel identification number.
iii. Marketable title acts: Limits the title examiner's search by providing that chain of title need only be established within a certain range of years.

OTHER OWNERSHIP RIGHTS

WATER RIGHTS

1. Riparian Doctrine: Water belongs to the owners of land bordering the watercourse.
   a. Natural Flow: Riparian owner is entitled to water without diminution in its quantity.
   b. Reasonable Use: Riparian owner must share with other riparian owners and is entitled only to reasonable use.
2. Prior Appropriation Doctrine: An individual may divert and use water whether or not she borders the watercourse; individual rights are established by actual use.

RIGHT TO LATERAL AND SUBJACENT SUPPORT

Strict liability for owner of land whose excavations cause a neighboring parcel to subside, or which damage buildings on adjacent land.

GIFTS

IN GENERAL

1. *Definition:* A gratuitous voluntary lifetime transfer of property from a donor to donee.
2. Requirements:
   a. Present intent to make a gift;
   b. Delivery by donor; and
   c. Acceptance by donee
3. Classification:
   a. *inter vivos:* Made during donor's lifetime; irrevocable unless donor retains right to revoke.
   b. *gifts causa mortis:* Lifetime gift by donor in contemplation of impending death.
      i. Contemplation of impending death;
      ii. Automatic revocation if donor survives peril;
      iii. Ambiguity of donor's intent; and
      iv. Death from different peril.

INTEREST IN LAND: ESTATES

TYPE	HOW CREATED
***PRESENT POSSESSORY ESTATES** – Property interest in land that is currently in a person's physical possession*	
FEE SIMPLE ABSOLUTE:	Right given by previous owner
FEE SIMPLE DETERMINABLE:	Right given by a grantor
FEE SIMPLE ON CONDITION SUBSEQUENT:	Right given by a grantor
FEE TAIL (FEE SIMPLE CONDITIONAL):	Right given by a grantor
LIFE ESTATE:	Right given by a grantor
***CONCURRENT ESTATES** – Property interest in land currently possessed by several individuals at the same time,*	
TENANCY IN COMMON:	Deed, will, or law of intestate succession
JOINT TENANCY:	Deed and will, but not by intestate succession; requires the following Four Unities: **1.** Time: Co-tenants acquire at same time **2.** Title: Interests acquired under same instrument **3.** Interest: Co-tenants have exactly same interest **4.** Possession: Co-tenants each have possession of entire estate
TENANCY BY ENTIRETY:	Deed, will, or law of intestate succession
***LEASEHOLDS (LANDLORD AND TENANT)** – Interest in land according to the terms of a lease agreement, in*	
PERIODIC TENANCY:	Created by lease; contractual agreement
TENANCY FOR YEARS:	Created by lease; contractual agreement
TENANCY AT WILL:	Created by lease; contractual agreement
TENANCY AT SUFFERANCE:	Created by operation of law when tenant wrongfully remains in possession after end of lawful lease term
***FUTURE INTERESTS** – An interest in property that is not presently possessory, but will come into possession*	
REVERSION (IN GRANTOR):	Automatically at end of transferred estate or by express reservation by grantor after transferring title
POSSIBILITY OF REVERTER (IN GRANTOR):	Occurrence of event terminating a fee simple determinable
RIGHT OF ENTRY (IN GRANTOR):	Occurrence of condition terminating a fee simple on condition subsequent
EXECUTORY INTEREST (IN GRANTEE):	Occurrence of condition as specified by grantor
REMAINDERS (IN GRANTEE):	Occurrence of limitation (not a condition) terminating a prior possessory estate simultaneously created

LAWS AFFECTING INTERESTS

DESCRIPTION OF PROPERTY

1. Metes and bounds.
2. Government survey.
3. Reference to plat/map.
4. Resolving inconsistencies:
   a. Natural monuments.
   b. Artificial monuments.
   c. References to adjacent tracts.
   d. Courses/directions.
   e. Distances.
   f. Area or quantity.
   g. Place names.

TYPES OF DEEDS

1. General Warranty Deed (contains six covenants of title):
   a. Covenant of Seisin: Promise by grantor who owns property to be conveyed.
   b. Covenant of Right to Convey: Promise grantor has power and legal ability to convey property.
   c. Covenant of Against Encumbrances: Promise property is free from encumbrances.
   d. Covenant of Quiet Enjoyment: Promise no third party with legal claim of superior title against grantee and that grantor will compensate grantee for losses incurred as a result.
   e. Covenant of Warranty: Promise grantor will defend against superior claims and will compensate grantee for losses incurred as a result.
   f. Covenant of Further Assurances: Promise grantor will do whatever is reasonably necessary to perfect title if title is defective.
2. Special Warranty Deed: Same covenants as general warranty, but only for the period of time that the grantor owned the property.
3. Quitclaim Deed: Contains no warranties and gives whatever interest in property grantor may have.

ZONING

1. Enacted pursuant to state police power for health, welfare, and safety of community.
2. Prevents certain use of property in favor of public good.
3. May be challenged on constitutional grounds or where benefit is primarily for private, and not public, interests.

NUISANCE

Owner of land may sue for interference with the use and enjoyment of her property. At common law, applied to noise, aesthetic harms, environmental changes, etc.

1. Private nuisance: substantial and unreasonable interference with the private use and enjoyment of another's land. *Hendricks v. Stalnaker*, 181 W.Va. 31, 380 S.E.2d 198 (1989).
   a. Interference must be substantial.
   b. Defendant's conduct must be intentional and unreasonable:
      i. Gravity of the harm outweighs utility, or
      ii. Utility outweighs harm, but harm is serious. *Boomer v. Atlantic Cement Co.*, 26 N.Y. 2d 219, 309 N.Y.S.2d 312, 257 N.E. 2d 870 (N.Y. 1970).
2. Public nuisance: harm to the community's use or enjoyment of public land.
3. Defense to a Nuisance Claim:
   a. Coming to the nuisance.
   b. Contributory negligence.
   c. Assumption of the risk.
   d. Undue hardship.
4. Remedies for Nuisance:
   a. Enjoin D from acting, and
   b. Require D to pay.

THE REAL ESTATE CONTRACT

The sale of land is accompanied by a contract binding the buyer and seller to perform. Requires (must comply with Statute of Frauds):

1. Names of buyer and seller,
2. Description of realty to be sold,
3. Essential terms of the sale, and
4. Signature of party against whom enforcement is sought.

MORTGAGES

The purchase price is usually secured by the buyer from a third-party lender, which results in a lien on the property in favor of the lender.

1. Foreclosure: If the buyer defaults in repaying the lender, the property may be foreclosed upon and sold to repay the buyer's debts; the lender or one with a senior lien on the property will then be paid first out of the proceeds of the sale.
2. Equity of Redemption: Upon default, the buyer has the right to remedy the default and gain clear title to the land; some states limit the time in which the buyer may redeem after foreclosure.
3. Purchase Money Mortgage: When loan funds are used in part to purchase property, the mortgage securing the loan is a purchase money mortgage.

THE REAL ESTATE CLOSING

At closing, seller conveys marketable title in exchange for the buyer's providing the purchase price, and the rights of the parties shift from sale contract to deed.

1. Marketable Title: All defects and encumbrances must be removed by the time of closing; any defect, including those that do not appear in the chain of title, may make the title unmarketable.
2. Equitable Conversion:
   a. Once buyer and seller have signed an enforceable contract (prior to closing, they enter into the contract for the sale of land) equity converts:
      i. Buyer's interest into interest in realty
      ii. Seller's interest into interest in personalty (the purchase price)
   b. Death of party: If buyer or seller dies before closing, converted rights pass to estate of either.
   c. Risk of loss: If property is destroyed, under the general rule buyer is now the owner of the property and will bear the loss.
3. Breach:
   a. Buyer's Remedies: Upon seller's failure to provide marketable title, buyer can demand specific performance, receive damages, or rescind contract.
   b. Seller's Remedies: Upon buyer's failure to pay the purchase price, seller can demand specific performance, receive damages, or rescind contract.

THE DEED

After closing, the duties of the buyer and seller are contained ("merged") in the deed.

1. Formalities:
   a. Statute of Frauds:
      i. Must be in writing and signed by the grantor, and
      ii. Must describe property.
   b. Delivery of the Deed:
      i. Delivery is presumed where deed is in possession of grantee at time the issue arises; deed is recorded by grantor.
      ii. If grantor retains deed in his possession and dies, no legal delivery.
      iii. Deposit with third party: Delivery effective if grantor intended to vest title in grantee and surrendered control to third party; delivery with conditions (no delivery unless); condition is certain to occur and is within control of the grantee.

EMINENT DOMAIN / TAKINGS

1. *Definitions:* A taking of private property (real or personal) for public use without just compensation, can be either physical or regulatory, direct or indirect (property is merely burdened); if government pays just compensation, taking is constitutional and therefore permissible.
2. "Public Use": Must be rationally related to accomplishing a public purpose or use results in a public benefit. *Hawaii Housing Authority v. Midkiff*, 467 U.S. 229 (1984).
3. "Just Compensation": Fair market value, valued at highest and best use, special value to owner is not relevant. *United States v. Fuller*, 409 U.S. 488 (1973).
4. Sovereign may not use its eminent domain power to take property of one private party for sole purpose of transferring it to another private party, even if first party is paid just compensation [*Kelo v. City of New London, Conn.*, 545 U.S. 469 (2005)]. However, state may use its eminent domain power to transfer property from one private party to another if purpose of taking is future use by public, hence a city's exercise of eminent domain power in furtherance of economic development plan satisfied constitutional "public use" requirement [*Kelo v. City of New London, Conn.*, 545 U.S. 469 (2005)]. Many states responded to *Kelo* by limiting the power to take property for economic development purposes.

RECORDATION

Grantee who can show that she received her interest in a deed executed earlier than a competing claimant will be recognized as the true owner. Exception: if subsequent purchase is a bona fide purchase (BFP).

1. Types of Recording Statutes:
   a. Pure Race: Whoever records first.
   b. Notice: Unrecorded conveyance is invalid against a BFP who has no notice, regardless of who records first.
   c. Race-Notice: Whoever records first, unless that person has notice of a prior grant.
2. Chain of Title: A title search can give notice of prior interests in the property at issue.
   a. Title Examination:
      i. Grantor/grantee index: Title is traced back through the seller in grantor's indices, and forward to each buyer through grantee indices.

Laws Affecting Interests continues on page 5

REAL COVENANTS

1. Types of Real Covenants: Restrictive Covenants and Affirmative Covenants
2. Creation of Real Covenants:
   a. Intent: Promisors intend to bind their successors in interest, or covenant will only be enforced against original parties. *Moseley v. Bishop*, 470 N.E.2d 773 (Ind. App. 1984).
   b. Touch and Concern: Successor to burden will only be bound where the covenant has a connection to her use and enjoyment of the land. *Neponsit Property Owners' Assn. v. Emigrant Industrial Savings Bank*, 278 N.Y. 248, 15 N.E.2d 793 (1938).
   c. Privity of Estate:
      i. Horizontal (for burden to run): between original promisor and promisee.
      ii. Vertical (for benefit to run): between original parties and their assigns or successors.
   d. Must also comply with Statute of Frauds.
3. Scope of Real Covenants: Benefit to dominant estate and burden to servient estate.
4. Termination of Real Covenants: Not really termination, but burden or benefit will not run once horizontal/vertical privity is gone.

EASEMENTS

SCOPE OF EASEMENTS

1. Any change in use beyond the intent of the parties that created the easement is beyond the scope of the easement and not allowed.
2. Intent of parties is guiding principle.
3. Increases in frequency or intensity of use are generally permissible.
4. Scope may be determined from duration of easement, location of easement, or reasonable expectation of parties.

TRANSFER OF EASEMENTS

1. In Gross:
   a. Burden: Always transfers with land.
   b. Benefit: Generally transferable unless use as transferred creates unreasonable burden on servient estate.
2. Appurtenant:
   Note: No separate document is required to effectuate transfer, nor is notice of either required.
   a. Burden: Always transfers with land.
   b. Benefit: Always transfers with land.

TERMINATION OF EASEMENTS

Termination of easements can be made by:

- By Terms.
- Merger of Dominant and Servient Estates.
- Prescription.
- Forfeiture.
- Changed Conditions.
- Frustration of Purpose.
- Abandonment—requires intent and clear act.

CREATION OF EASEMENTS

1. Express Grant: Usually contained in a deed.
2. Deed: Owner of land may convey entire estate and reserve an easement for her own use, or to the benefit of a third party.
3. Donative Transfer: Created by gift deed or will; consideration not necessary unless intent is not clear.
4. Contract: Reciprocal easements are adequate consideration.
5. Estoppel: Easement is asserted in equity when land owner who permits certain use attempts to revoke that use at a later time. Requires foreseeable and reasonable reliance, and claimant's changed position, based on prior permission.
6. Implication: In the absence of express agreement, intent of parties to create an easement can be implied from:
   a. Prior use requires that
      i. Dominant/servient estates were originally a single estate;
      ii. Prior use is permanent or long term, and not temporary;
      iii. Prior use is apparent and not concealed [*Romanchuk v. Plotkin*, 215 Minn. 156, 9 N.W.2d 421 (1943)]; and
      iv. Prior use is reasonably necessary to enjoy the property.
   b. Necessity requires either of the following:
      i. Unity of title followed by a severance;
      ii. Strict necessity, e.g., parcel is landlocked.
7. Prescription: Like adverse possession, use must be:
   a. Adverse—inconsistent with owner's use;
   b. Open/notorious—sufficient to put owner on notice;
   c. Continuous; and
   d. Uninterrupted for duration of statutory period.

TYPES OF EASEMENTS

1. Easement in Gross: Not attached to the land, will not transfer unless the owner of the land so intends.
2. Easement Appurtenant: Attached to the land, rights transfer to any new purchaser of the land.
   a. Dominant estate: Estate benefited, appurtenant easement transfers automatically when dominant estate is transferred.
   b. Servient estate: Estate burdened, need not be adjoining to dominant estate.
3. Negative Easements: Owner of easement has right to demand that the owner of the servient estate refrain from using land in a certain way.

FUTURE INTERESTS

TYPES OF FUTURE INTERESTS

1. In Grantor:
   a. Reversion.
   b. Possibility of reverter.
   c. Right of entry.
2. In Grantee:
   a. Executory Interest:
      i. Springing interest; shifting interest.
   b. Remainders:
      i. Vested:
         1. Indefeasibly,
         2. Subject to Open/Partial Divestment—class gifts.
      ii. Contingent:
         1. Subject to Condition Precedent,
         2. Unborn or Unascertained person.

RULE IN SHELLEY'S CASE

Example: Life estate in A, and remainder in "A's heirs" or the "heirs of A's body"

Effect: If the two estates are either both legal or both equitable, remainder is deemed to be in A, not A's heirs or the heirs of A's body

Doctrine of Merger: Where A has life estate and next vested estate, they merge to form a fee simple.

DOCTRINE OF WORTHIER TITLE

Example: O gives life estate in A, remainder in O's heirs; (future interest must be limited to heirs of grantor, and not issue or devise).

Effect: A will get a life estate and O has a reversion; O's heirs get nothing unless O dies within A's lifetime, at which point they get O's reversion.

RULE AGAINST PERPETUTITIES (RAP)

No interest is good unless it must vest, if at all, no later than 21 years (plus a period of gestation) after some life in being at interest creation.

1. Affected Interests: Contingent remainders, executory interests, vested remainders limited in favor of class of persons.
2. "Life in Being": Any life in existence at the time of the creation of the interest that is in any way connected to the interest.

Examples: Parent of class members, person named in instrument of conveyance, life tenant whose death creates interest.

3. "Within 21 Years": Satisfied if it can be shown that the interest vests during the measuring "life in being" plus 21 years (plus any period of gestation for the measuring life); time of death of measuring life is therefore relevant. *Lucas v. Hamm*, 56 Cal.2d 583, 364 P.2d 685 (1961).
4. Special RAP Cases:
   a. Unborn widow:
      i. Gift to issue is invalid.

Examples: O conveys property to son for life, then to son's widow for life, then to issue. Son could remarry a woman not yet born, and pre-decease her before she gives birth to other members of the class.

   b. Fertile octogenarian: *Jee v. Audley*, 29 Eng. Rep. 1186 (Ch. 1787).
      i. Gift to children is invalid

Example: T gives property to A for life, then to A's children "who attain the age of 25."

Example: A could have a child when he is 80 years old, and then die; the youngest child will not reach age 25 within 21 years of the death of A and the gift cannot vest to the entire class of children.

   c. Charitable transfers: RAP is wholly inapplicable to charitable transfers.

Casenote® Legal Briefs

Property, Keyed to Courses Using Dukeminier, Krier, Alexander, Strahilevitz, and Schleicher's Property, Concise Fourth Edition

The clearest, most current and popular case brief series for decades

Casenote® Legal Briefs break down the major cases from your book into a succinct, readable, and uncluttered format that shows you:

- The Nature of the Case
- A Summary of the Facts
- The Rule of Law
- The Facts
- The Issue
- The Holding and Decision
- Dissents and Concurrences
- Analysis

Understand the language of the law.

- **Quicknotes** following each case define the legal terms used in the brief.
- A **Glossary** in the back of your ***Casenote® Legal Briefs*** book lists and defines Latin words and phrases commonly found in the language of the law.

Be prepared for classes and exams.

- **Quick Reference Rules of Law** pages open every chapter and list the rules of law that apply in each case in that chapter.

Use your time efficiently.

- **How to Brief a Case** provides step-by-step instructions on how to format, organize, and write your own case brief with the greatest efficiency.

Cover all your bases.

- A fold-out **Quick Course Outline** highlights the main topics of the course.

For a complete list of titles in the *Casenote® Legal Briefs* series, visit www.AspenPublishing.com.

ISBN 979-8-8941-0433-1

90000

9 798894 104331